Eddy Merckx

RIK VANWALLEGHEM

Eddy Merckx

THE GREATEST CYCLIST OF THE 20TH CENTURY

VeloPress • Boulder • Colorado

Translation copyright

Steve Hawkins

Het Nieuwsblad
DE GOEIE KRANT VAN 'T LEVEN

PINGUIN
PRODUCTIONS

ASLK

VeloPress

1830 North 55th Street

Boulder, CO, USA 80301-2700

An imprint of Inside Communications

ISBN 1-884737-22-6

First English Edition 1996

1 2 3 4 5 6 7 8 9 10

Printed in Canada

Contents

Foreword

I got to know Eddy Merckx on the evening of November 2, 1979, a year and a half prior to that he had ridden his last official race, the Circuit of the Waasland.

That was early in 1978 when I was taking my first steps as a cycling commentator with Belgian television. I am telling you this so that you will appreciate that during Merckx's cycling career I never knew him well. As a cycling fan, I had enjoyed his terrific performances, of course, but up to that point, there had never been any personal contact between the two of us. I had interviewed Merckx as a radio reporter on a handful of occasions, and he had always been something of a closed book: an introverted, suspicious man, who was wrapped up in his profession to a fanatical degree. If truth be told, I found him rather weird, if not exactly creepy.

Neither his motivation nor obsessiveness fit in with the spirit of the times, where the urge to perform was no longer a central value. A new attitude towards life was taking hold, one in which the world was put into perspective. In the old days, we would almost have held an athlete in higher esteem for what he could tell us about the Nobel Prize for Literature rather than what he had to say about his own performances.

Okay ... back to November 2, 1979, a Friday evening. It must have been around 10:30 p.m when I walked into the locker room at the Olympia Sterrebeek soccer stadium. We had just finished a benefit soccer match, which I had organized. By then, all of the players, with one exception, had made their way to the hospitality room for the postgame reception and cold buffet. Only Eddy Merckx was still in the locker room, sitting with a towel over his head. I asked him if he had hurt himself. "No, of course not," he snapped back. There was a short silence before he continued, "Fancy that, eh.... I never miss penalties. I did tonight, though, and that's why we lost. I'm not going to the reception. I'm going home...."

That evening, I got to know Eddy Merckx. After that, we played soccer together on many other occasions. Honesty compels me to say that thanks to having Eddy on the team, we won a lot more matches than we lost. Like the time in Maastricht when we played our colleagues from Dutch television and he scored two of our three goals. I think he enjoyed that victory just as much as his greatest cycling triumphs.

The more I got to know Eddy, the more my admiration grew. More than that, my respect grew, too. Since then I have learned a great deal from him, and also received much human warmth. Hell, not only was my original image of him incomplete, it was flat wrong! And I fear it is an image that lives on for far too many people. I hope this book will finally change that image. That is the very least Eddy Merckx deserves.

– Mark Vanlombeek

CHAPTER ONE

The Sphinx

"Every great man is a puzzle
only future generations can solve."
(Isolde Kurz)

"No one really knows me."
(Eddy Merckx)

△ *To the general public Merckx was a somewhat*
unemotional man, with the facial expression
of a sphinx. (Merckx during the
Tour of Belgium in 1970)

Who is Eddy Merckx? In his native country, Belgium, if 100 ordinary people were asked this question, 99 of them would answer: "Who doesn't know who Eddy Merckx is?" The often seemingly impossible feats performed by Merckx gave him a reputation unmatched by any other cyclist. Millions followed every move of his career, he was stopped by thousands who asked him for his autograph, yet very few even got a chance to speak to him. One thing, however, remained the same: few people ever got very close to the introvert champion. He seemed to live his life without showing emotion and said only what was absolutely necessary. Neither the glow of victory nor the disappointment of defeat left their mark on his face. His expression was that of a sphinx. Everyone recognized Merckx, but no one really knew him. Merckx, the mystery.

◁ *The whole world recognizes Eddy Merckx, but*
who really knows him?

△ 'He was never alone but always solitary'.
(Merckx as the cool victor of the Tour of Flanders
in 1969, his wife Claudine – on the left of the
photo – joins in the celebrations)

"Merckx is never alone, but he's always solitary," wrote journalist Willem Van Wijnendaele some years ago. At one point during his career, the beleaguered star let it slip that he would like to go to live on his own at the top of a mountain. "When I could feel the full force of interest bearing down on me, I would often clam up," he says now. "It was only when I was on my bike that I could be myself."

Neither teammates nor opponents had a clue about what made Merckx tick. "I've known him for something like a quarter of a century now, and yet I'm still not really sure what sort of man he is," says Roger Swerts, for years a teammate and rival. "During all that time Merckx has remained inscrutable."

Jos Huysmans, for years a great support to Merckx, was also left guessing. "Eddy never allowed much to show," says his former lieutenant. "He never said a lot. You needed to have known him for some time before you could tell from his expression or his actions whether he was happy or not."

THE MEDIA STEAMROLLER

Merckx's reticence did not come about by accident. His naturally suspicious nature was reinforced by his experiences as he was developing into a star. In 1964, he won the world amateur road race championship at Sallanches, France. That meant he was only 19 when the media steamroller came along and flattened him. Eloquence and

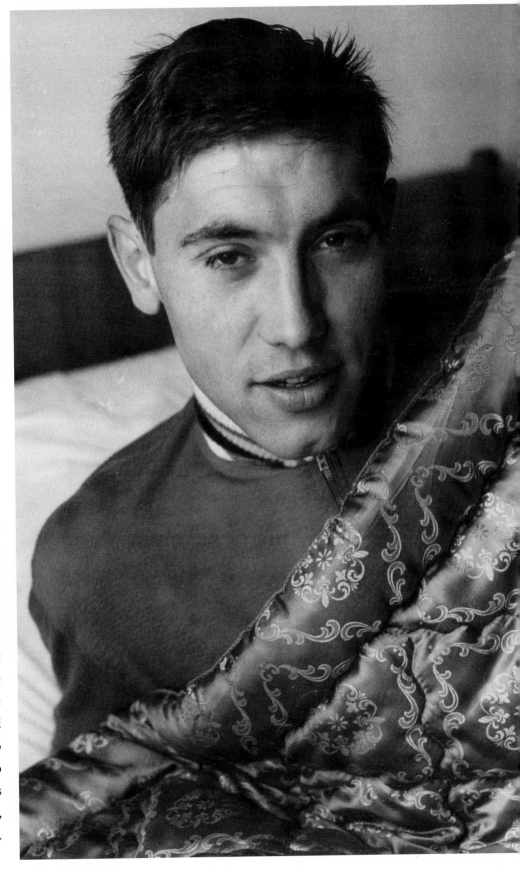

▽ *Merckx retained his childhood innocence for a long time, but with his introduction to the tough sport of cycling, it was not long before he was confronted with the 'wicked' world of adults.*

fluency in company were never among his strong points. There always seemed to be some sort of constraint, as though he thought he ought to be saying something important but feeling as though he never could. Until that time, life had been fairly straightforward for Eddy Merckx: he loved racing and he loved winning. That was all there was to it. No more than that. What else was there to say on the subject? Merckx was still bearing the guilty feelings of his childhood years.

This did not last forever, though. The innocent youngster with the unrestrained ambition found out all about the big "bad" world the hard way: on many occasions, people took advantage of his naïvété. When he was not racing, the man with the voracious appetite for winning on the bike seemed to be a vulnerable, easily influenced figure lacking the shrewdness, guts and maturity to keep the wolves at bay. The press took him for a ride; rivals plotted among themselves how to stop him; supporters became increasingly more demanding; and smooth-talking race organizers would ask ever more of him. Merckx had to put up with all the jokes made at his expense, the envy, conniving, plotting and thieving. At first, it seemed as though the young star's innocence prevented it getting to him. His bike made him relatively immune to it all and provided him with the protective shield he needed to fend off everything the outside world had to throw at him. He could also rely on his formidable manager, Jean Van Buggenhout, to take his mind off all the minor irritations.

■ Savona: A Blow to the Spirit

The 1969 Tour of Italy produced his first breaking point. On Sunday, June 1, after the stage from Parma to Savona, Merckx — wearing the race leader's pink jersey — was positive at the dope control and thrown out of the race. Back home in Belgium, there was widespread uproar: the man in the street, usually so mild-mannered, was outraged; questions were asked in parliament, and there was even a risk of a diplomatic row breaking out between Belgium and Italy. The Swiss tabloid newspaper, Blick, revealed its scoop: "Belgian paratroopers are preparing to free Merckx in Italy." The worst aspect of the affair was that something of Merckx's spirit was broken. His brush with the injustice of Savona caused him to seriously question his sense of trust in the world.

▷ *Who exactly is the man we watched for hours on end and about whom thousands of pages of newspapers were filled? (A tired Merckx after a stage in the Tour of Belgium in 1970)*

"He could see no way of carrying on," remembers his mother. "He wanted to pack it in, there and then. For good. Cycling was his life, but it was this sudden realization of how ugly the sport could be. That came as a great shock."

Merckx was given a rude awakening from the childhood dreams he had cherished. He became aware of the tricks society could play, and he discovered the depths to which some of those around him could sink. This heightened his sense of mistrust, and his inborn cautiousness led him to communicate less and less. It was with even greater determination that he now pushed the pedals around, as the bike was the only weapon he could use to get back at others.

BLOIS: HIS BACK TAKES A HAMMERING

Mental blows were not the only ones he had to suffer, however. In that same year, 1969, on September 9, Merckx's body received such a pounding that the invigorating, almost playful experience of cycling he had enjoyed in his earlier days steadily deteriorated from that day … until it eventually became a great physical burden. On that September day, Merckx crashed during a derny-paced race on the track in the French town of Blois. His pacemaker, Fernand Wambst, was killed in the crash. Merckx received a head injury. It was the hammering his back took, however, which was to cause it to become such a cross for him to bear for the rest of his career.

"From that moment on it was never the same," says Merckx. "After Blois, the pain was with me every time I raced. Sometimes I wept in my saddle with the pain. Had it not been for that crash, my career would have certainly been more pleasant. I may not have won more races than I did, but I would have done it with more panache, more gloss."

That was how Merckx was to embark on the 1970 season, with the same target of winning races he would always set himself, but with deep mental and physical scars. As a result of this, the circumspect, reserved young man withdrew even further into his shell. His pronouncement that we heard earlier – "no one really knows me" – was appropriate now more than ever. Merckx was tense, highly focused and very inaccessible. From February to October he constructed a wall around himself that was virtually impenetrable. Sports journalist Joris Jacobs wrote at the time: "He is always so non-committal. Although he is friendly and prepared to answer any questions, he is always a master of the cautious and evasive reply."

THE STRANGER IN THE PELOTON

"Merckx was also the biggest stranger in the peloton," says his one-time teammate Johan De Muynck. "He would never let his personality show, probably out of a fear

---

THE CONNECTION WITH PAUL VAN HIMST

Paul Van Himst, a pro soccer star in Belgium, is one of the few people who knows what makes Eddy Merckx tick. "It was when I was 16 years old and playing for Anderlecht," says Van Himst. "One day Frans Roelants, a director at Anderlecht and a cycling fan, invited me to go with him to a debutants race.

"'I know a good young rider, his name's Eddy Merckx,' he said. 'I follow him a bit.' I went with him a few times, but I had no contact with Eddy at the time.

"The first time I really met him was after we had played against Beerschot. By then Eddy had won a race in Anderlecht and his parents and mine were sitting in the same cafe, waiting for him. It was there that we spoke to each other for the first time. Over the next few years, though, there was little further contact. I once took him along to the recording of a television program in Namur, and we sometimes met at receptions or award ceremonies. But he had his career and I had mine.

"It was only after he had retired, when he fell into that well-publicized black hole of his that I got to really know him. To the general public, he always seemed to be a rather unemotional man who did not want to divulge too much about himself. What is so contradictory is that once you have penetrated through to him, he seems to be a really pleasant, warm fellow who likes a joke and a good laugh. When he is feeling completely at ease, he opens up, and in a small group of people he can even be the life and soul of the party.

"He will then reveal himself to be a good impressionist and singer. 'Brussels, you have stolen my heart, with your streets up and down' is one of his favorite tunes. People are quick to forget, though, that Merckx was a world star and he was hounded from all sides and always in demand. In the meantime, he just wanted to get on with his challenging job with all the concentration it required. In such circumstances, you find you become wrapped up in yourself, anyway, especially if you have a reserved character like Eddy does."

that it would mean he may reveal his weak points. He simply could not allow anyone to know if something was wrong with him."

Luis Ocaña, the racer who during the 1971 Tour first reminded us that Merckx really was made of flesh and blood after all, spoke in all seriousness of a split personality when talking about his former rival. "At that time, there were actually two Eddy Merckxes, neither one of whom had a great deal to do with the other," said the Franco-Spaniard. "The human, 'normal' Merckx was always pushed into the background by the athlete. And this latter personality was involved with his sport to the point of obsession, always wanting to win and having little or no contact with the outside world. It was as if the part of his brain that controlled his racing career

▽ *Merckx, obsessively engaged in his sport,*
thought about winning at all times.

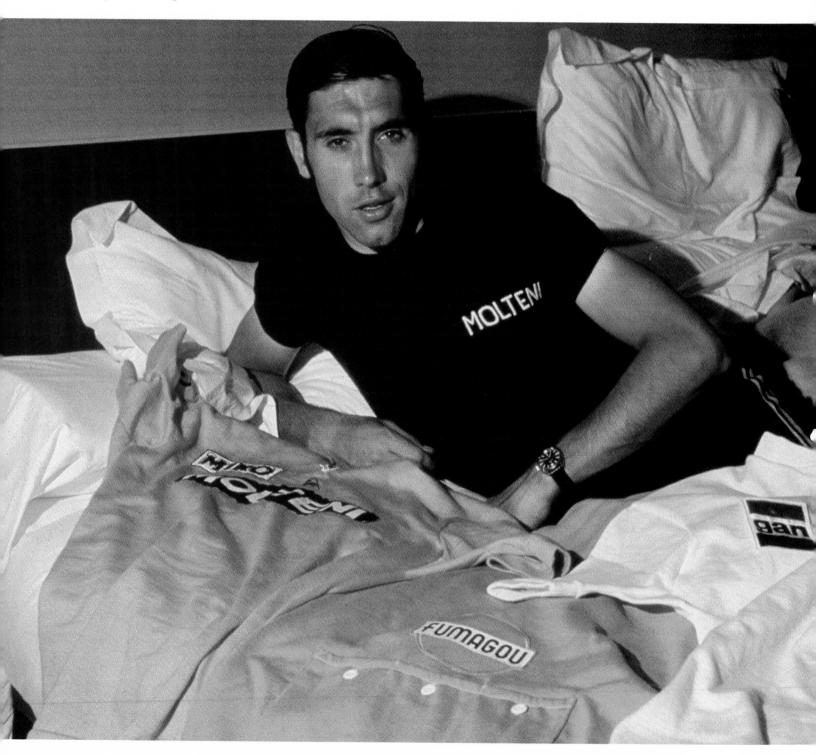

rendered the rest of his gray matter inactive. The bike almost turned him into a different person. Although partly fueled by the cold war that was raging between us, I used to think at the time that Merckx was absolutely heartless. There was something inhuman in the way he put his sport before all else: walking all over people and mercilessly fighting to reach his goal, regardless of whom or what stood in his way. The competitive animal dominated his life. Everything else had to play second fiddle to it. It was only after he retired from racing that I got to know him better, and that was when I realized what a fantastic man he is. But because of his sport, because of the weight on his shoulders, and particularly because of his unbridled ambition, he kept a lid on his other self the entire time."

Neither did it escape the notice of the journalists that during the winter it was a different Merckx they encountered to the one they had to deal with during the hot summer months of the cycling season. In its edition of February 8, 1973, the newspaper *Het Nieuwsblad* summed it up as follows: "All the reserve, the vagueness and the torment that made him so 'unapproachable' before and after a race melted away when he lowered his protective competitive shield. Away from the world of racing, the lifeless athlete is a man of flesh and blood."

A MAN OF FLESH AND BLOOD WHO EATS PEOPLE

Merckx's impenetrability was all the more remarkable in view of how much relentless searching was always going on to try to discover what his true self was. His amazing feats on the bike were now making him the subject of enormous interest. One might ask why a top star's character, lifestyle, opinions and personality need to be opened up in such a way for all the world to see. Merckx probably asked himself this question on any number of occasions while he was having the most unlikely questions fired at him. Part and parcel of stardom is having one's life laid bare for the public – with its insatiable appetite for what are often the most trivial details about their idols

In this book, these trivial details are of no concern to us. Neither is this the place to find out Eddy Merckx's favorite color, toothpaste or film actress. Nor have we asked him about astrology or if the fact that he is a Gemini has had any effect on his career.

What we are looking for in this book is the answer to the question the general public was asking when he retired in rather doleful circumstances in May 1978: 'Just who is this man who we have spent so many hours watching and about whom thousands of newspaper pages have been written? From where did this cycling phenomenon draw his inspiration? Where did he get his strength and his self-belief? What kept that unbelievable fire burning, that unbridled ambition which separated him from his rivals, even more than his athletic prowess? What made this man tick? Of what is he a product? What were his motivations and his emotions as well as his shortcomings and qualities?

THE NICKNAME

Where does the Homeric epithet "The Cannibal" come from? It is often difficult to trace the origin of a nickname, but in Merckx's case it is fairly straightforward. "It was Christian Raymond who called me it for the first time in 1968," Merckx remembers with great certainty. "The year before, Raymond had been a teammate of mine at Peugeot. But I didn't win that much that season. During the following season, however, my honors list started to grow nicely and Raymond would always address me as 'Canni.' What he meant, of course, was Cannibal, and the press took over use of it later."

Is Merckx happy with his nickname? "Well, it's a bit of a barbaric name, but it probably reflected how my rivals truly felt about me."

It is the ambitious aim of this book to show you the real Eddy Merckx. The journey that has been taken in order to do this has been an exciting one. Without the help of many guides along the way – people who know Merckx from up close – it would in fact have been impossible to complete this fascinating journey of discovery. Teammates, rivals, journalists, supporters, family, soigneurs, directeurs sportifs and race organizers put the pieces into place that finally completed the puzzle. We would like to make one thing clear, even at this early stage, so that the record can be put straight on an image that has been constructed: Merckx was not a godlike figure for whom everything ran like clockwork, and he was not an invincible machine placed on a pedestal high above everyone and everything else. Neither was he some sort of gifted being who was spared all misery, great or small. No, the Cannibal was just a man, made of flesh and blood: a quality that only serves to make the greatest cyclist of all time even greater.

▽ *The Cannibal, confronted by himself.*
  He really was made of flesh and blood.

1965

Learning the ropes among the pros

△ *Eddy Merckx in good company from the start. Here on the track in Brussels with Ward Sels and World Champion Tom Simpson on September 24, 1965.*

Team	Solo-Superia
Directeur sportif	Hugo Mariën
Teammates	Roger Baguet, Noël De Pauw, Willy Derboven, Armand Desmet, Henri Dewolf, Mathieu Maes, Joseph Mathy, Joseph Planckaert, Willy Schroeders, Edouard Sels, Patrick Sercu, Edgard Sorgeloos, Julien Stevens, Michel Van Aerde, Bernard Van de Kerckhove, Rik Van Looy, Rik Van Steenbergen.
Number of Races	69
Number of Victories	9

Major Stage Races		
Tour de France		-
Tour of Italy		-

Major One-Day Races		
World Championship		29th
Belgian Championship		2nd
Milan-San Remo		
Tour of Flanders		-
Paris-Roubaix		-
Liège-Bastogne-Liège		-
Amstel Gold Race		-
Tour of Lombardy		-
Het Volk		-
Ghent-Wevelgem		-
Flèche-Wallonne		abandoned
Paris-Tours		-
Paris-Brussels		-

"The Flèche Wallonne on April 24, 1965 was my first race as a professional. It was a real let-down. Earlier on during that season, when I was still racing in the amateur category, I had won four of the five races I had taken part in. My first taste of life with the pros, however, was one I regretted. In that edition of the Walloon classic I had nothing left in me after I tried to get back up to the front of the race after puncturing. It wasn't long after that before I was done for. My plans to race Liège-Bastogne-Liège, which was on my schedule, were immediately scrapped. It's just as well, too. That day, I took part in a warm-up meeting at the Rocourt track and later watched the riders coming in to finish the race. They looked terrible. I thought: is that what it's going to be like with the pros?

"Gradually, though, there was an improvement in my performances. On May 11, I won my first race as a professional at Vilvoorde by beating Emiel Daems in the sprint. 'Miel' was not very happy about that. When I was a youngster, I used to train regularly with him, and he had given me a lot of good advice. But I wanted to win, no matter what.

"My biggest disappointment that year was the national championship at Vilvoorde, where I was well and truly stitched up by the teammates Godefroot and De Cabooter. Godefroot won and I came second. Later that season I did well in the Paris-Luxembourg stage race, in which I had a second place and a third, in spite of the lack of support I was getting from the Solo team. By that time, I had long decided that I was going to look for another team.

"During the winter of 1965-66, I rode my first six-day race with Patrick Sercu in Berlin. I really suffered at first there too. But in our second six-day event, in Brussels, we finished second. And not long after that we came up trumps at the race in Ghent."

CHAPTER TWO

The Oyster

"Solitude is the fatherland of great minds."
(Etienne Rey)

"In my eyes, a real friend means something.
He is someone who possesses a little bit
of your heart. In my position, it's
impossible to make friends like that in the
peloton, among the journalists
or from my entourage."
(Eddy Merckx)

It is not an easy job trying to fathom someone who is renowned for their reserve. Merckx was certainly not the most expansive rider in the peloton, and he always kept his cards close to his chest. If someone tried to knock at the door to see into his personality he would be quite willing and pleasant enough about opening it, but it would usually be left only slightly ajar. The few who were allowed to enter had to concede that it was a very bare room in which there were several doors from which he could soon be let out. Merckx protected his soul in the same way an oyster protects its pearl.

In order to get to know this somewhat uncommunicative figure better, it is a good idea to take a round-about route and sound out the people who were closest to him: the ones who inspired confidence in him and on whom he could count. In Merckx's case this might have been his teammates and racing companions. A great deal can also be learned, however, by listening to what his enemies have to say: those who have challenged him, who have been with him not only in times of glory but also in times of trouble and who tried to seek out his weak spots, from their sense of rivalry.

△ *An oyster shielding its pearl, his soul.*
(Merckx on the podium during
Tirreno-Adriatico in 1976)

◁ *Known by millions, never alone, often solitary.*
Always surrounded, even during his many solo exploits.
(Merckx on his successful escape during the Tour of Flanders in 1969)

TEAMMATES, RIVALS, JOURNALISTS AND SUPPORTER

Jan Janssen became the world professional road-race champion at Sallanches in 1964, the day after Eddy Merckx had taken the amateurs' rainbow jersey. "The next day we were both honoured before the start of the G.P. of Brasschaat," says Janssen. "I remember a shy young man, not in the slightest bit pushy and certainly no conversationalist. That was just his nature, but journalists often had trouble with it. To them, he was a 'disaster.' It has always been difficult for us, his rivals, to figure him out. He always kept his cards close to his chest. He limited himself to the clichés. 'How are your wife? And your children?' That sort of thing. What did strike me about him was his closeness to his father and mother. We once stayed several nights at the same hotel in France, and each night he spoke to them on the telephone."

The relationship between the extrovert Janssen and the clam-like Merckx remained a distant one. "Yet from the beginning there was a feeling of respect," says Janssen, clarifying this. "I had a feeling right from the start that this young man had an unusually large amount of talent. I felt that he held me in high regard, too, something along the lines of: 'I'll have to keep an eye out for that crafty Dutchman.' Generally speaking, he had an enormous amount of respect for his opponents. He never challenged them openly, he never made a big show of his victories, and he remained fearful of everyone. He did sometimes have tricks up his sleeve, though. During the Tour of Belgium in 1970 the weather was absolutely dreadful, it was bitterly cold and snowing. I can remember as if it were yesterday that after a little moaning and groaning, Merckx, who was riding alongside me, gave the impression he was about to abandon. This happened by the roundabout in Aalter, next to the motorway. I thought: 'If he packs it in I think I will, too'. And I actually did get off and climb into the broom wagon. Merckx, though, hesitantly kept going and eventually continued on his way. Soon after that the sun broke through. And if my memory serves me well, I think he even went on to win that particular Tour!"

Another way of shedding light on Merckx is by asking the opinions of one particular group of people who spent so much time picking at him: journalists. These often desperate scribes who had to find ways of padding out their copy because that maddeningly successful Merckx kept on winning, tried to get every possible angle on him. They chased after him until they were chilled to the bone; they credited him with heroic feats on the strength of one minor quote; they frantically grubbed around into his private life; they tried to elicit the ultimate statement from his lips and then stood perplexed at the man's ability to say things that had no meaning whatsoever. In spite of this, however, some journalists – albeit only a few – became confidants of Merckx: people to whom he dared to open his heart occasionally.

And what about the thousands upon thousands of Merckx supporters? Most of them were happy just to get a glimpse of their idol or a shake of his hand, or even an autograph. There were also those who literally went and parked themselves on his doorstep, and even then that was not enough to satisfy some. Others, however, became friends of Merckx and are able to tell you stories and anecdotes which characterize him. They, too, are given a chance to have their say.

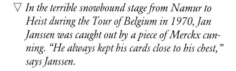

▽ *In the terrible snowbound stage from Namur to Heist during the Tour of Belgium in 1970, Jan Janssen was caught out by a piece of Merckx cunning. "He always kept his cards close to his chest," says Janssen.*

My first Milan-San Remo win

△ *His first win in Milan-San Remo. Durante (out of view) and Vanspringel lose out.*

Team	Peugeot
Directeur sportif	Gaston Plaud (Fra)
Teammates	André Beyssière, Francis Bazire, Raymond Delisle, Henry Duez, Jean Dumont, Charly Grosskost, François Hamont, Pierre Le Mellec, Camille Le Menn, Desire Letort, Michel Nedelec, Hubert Niel, Francis Pamart, Jean-Paul Paris, Roger Pingeon, Christian Raymond, André Zimmermann (all France), Tom Simpson (GB).
Number of Races	95
Number of Victories	20
Major Stage Races	Tour de France - Tour of Italy -
Major One-Day Races	World Championship 12th Belgian Championship 15th Milan-San Remo 1st Tour of Flanders - Paris-Roubaix 15th Liège-Bastogne-Liège 8th Amstel Gold Race - Tour of Lombardy 2nd Het Volk 3rd Ghent-Wevelgem 9th Flèche-Wallonne - Paris-Tours 20th Paris-Brussels 20th
Other victories	G.P. Pino Cerami, Championship of Flanders, Baracchi Trophy (with Ferdinand Bracke)...

"The season began brilliantly with my victory in Milan-San Remo. That was the first real classic I had raced in. Not only that, but it was my very first race on Italian soil. Before the start of the race I didn't rate my chances of winning at all, because of how long the race was. During Paris-Nice, though — where I finished fourth — I had built myself up into a good condition. Just before the Poggio I got up to the leading group. I still wasn't thinking about winning, and just a place on the podium would have been fantastic. I started the sprint from a long way out, and to my utter amazement no one got past me. Although there was a photo finish, all that was to prove was that it was me and not Adriano Durante who had won.

"There was little danger that I would get too big for my boots as a result of this unexpected win. The month of April turned out to be really disappointing in fact. In the Tour of Flanders, just past Kerkhove, I made a real blunder and was left covered in grazes from head to toe. In Paris-Roubaix, I was stopped in my tracks in the finishing stages of the race by a problem with my chain. In other races my inexperience or ignorance was mercilessly exposed. In Liège-Bastogne-Liège I was left with nothing to do but look on exhausted as Anquetil called all the shots. In the Tour of Lombardy, I was at the front with the two Salvarani teammates, Adorni and Gimondi. During the final sprint on the velodrome I dived into the 'gap' alongside Adorni, but he promptly used his elbows to shut it. While this was going on, Gimondi was flying away on the other side of the track. Even though 1966 saw me win Milan-San Remo, it also showed that I was still a little wet behind the ears. There was plenty more learning to be done."

The Recluse

"One is never less solitary than
when one is alone."
(Scipio Africanus)

"You have to put your own
interests ahead of camaraderie."
(Eddy Merckx)

During a professional career lasting from May 1965 to May 1978, Merckx had many teammates. Some of them decided that one season of riding in the service of the champion was enough for them, while others stayed by his side for many years. But for most of them Merckx was an impenetrable, occasionally unknown quantity whose motives and innermost feelings remained shrouded in mystery. Even Jos Huysmans, his right-hand man from 1970 to 1978, had to admit that Merckx very rarely revealed anything of himself. "He never allowed very much to be apparent," says Huysmans. "His pet hate was going over tactics. All we ever had to worry about was what was expected of us. And it was pretty obvious what that was, of course. Everything was done for Eddy's benefit. And since he just kept on winning, it was very rarely questioned."

▷ *Even his teammates were never really sure what
was going on in his head.
(The recluse inspects his troops at the 1970
Tour de France team presentation)*

Noël Foré, who seems to have regularly observed the group around Merckx, puts it like this: "At the dinner table you always had two groups: Eddy Merckx and the others. Eddy's not a bad fellow, but as a person you can never get a lot out of him. He lives completely for himself, within himself." Belgian sprinter Guido Reybrouck, who can by no means be classed as one of Merckx's closest friends, said in 1974: "Merckx is always deadly serious and thinks about nothing else but racing and riding his bike. You never heard him say a word about anything else. He was totally dedicated to his profession." Herman Vanspringel, Merckx's first lieutenant in 1971 and 1972, also found it difficult to feel settled within his teams. "The atmosphere was always businesslike and cool," he says. "It was also hard to get through any deeper to the man himself. Contact with him was always on a superficial level."

■ SELF-INTEREST VERSUS CAMARADARIE

While riding with the Solo team in 1965 and Peugeot in 1966 and 1967, Merckx had not yet become the out-and-out team leader, around whom the team's whole tactics revolved. It was only with his move to the Italian Faema team that he assumed such a major role. The young, and probably still somewhat naïve, Merckx soon discovered, however, that in the sport of professional cycling it is not only the noblest of motives which are at play. After his brilliant 1969 season – in which he won his first Tour de France – quite a few riders left his team. Reybrouck, Martin Van den Bossche, Patrick Sercu, Frans Brands, Bernard Van De Kerckhove, Valère Van Sweevelt and Herman Vrijders all went off to ride in different colors the following season. "It's a shame, but I had to accept that not all of my teammates were friends, and that you had to put self-interest ahead of camaraderie," declared Merckx at the time.

▽ For Merckx, the personal qualities of his teammates were just as important as their cycling ability. (Merckx in the Yellow Jersey offers his hand to Jos Spruyt the stage winner in Orange during the 1974 Tour)

Dutch star Jan Janssen was inspired by the above quote to make the following comment: "In his own circles, Merckx may be a great bloke. I somehow doubt it, though, if half his teammates from 1969 are leaving his team to join another one. I doubt whether they've done so for financial reasons alone. Merckx is incredibly ambitious, so much so that it can no longer be held to be a quality. It is us, his opponents, who have to pay the price for it. At times he can be incredibly surly, but generally he is withdrawn. It is difficult to tell from his expression what sort of mood he is in."

When choosing new teammates, Merckx was primarily interested in their specific capabilities. "I needed a relatively large number of riders who could climb a bit," he says. "And yet I also asked both Godefroot and De Vlaeminck at certain points to come and join my team. During the major stage races, they could have taken some of the weight off my shoulders by winning stages. It was absolutely essential that these stage victories kept coming so that the money continued to flow into the team."

Equally important to Merckx when selecting teammates, though, were the human qualities he wanted them to possess. "I never wanted anyone in my team I knew I couldn't trust, or who was known to 'swallow' pills," says Merckx, studiously avoiding naming names.

ROGER SWERTS' PAY INCREASE

Roger Swerts rode in Merckx's team between 1968 and 1973 and again in 1976 and 1977. He sketches a picture of relationships and customs within the Merckx-dominated team and of the role of its leader.

"When I first started in Merckx's team I was on a monthly wage of BF 25,000 (about $800)," says Swerts. "Paid ten months a year. It wasn't a terrific amount, but when I made my professional debut with Mercier I was only getting BF 8000 ($260) a month. With Faema everyone in the team got as much as each other, Merckx insisted on this principle so that there would not be any jealousy. Thanks to win bonuses and prize money, however, we earned good money. Let's just say that in those days you could buy a house from your cycling earnings, but you certainly couldn't put millions of francs away for a rainy day."

After three years of riding as an out-and-out domestique, Swerts started to become more ambitious. And that created problems right away (see elsewhere in this chapter), because Swerts broke through the clearly defined role pattern that was inevitably in force as a result of Merckx's dominance.

"In 1971, the team rode the Tour of Italy without Merckx," says Swerts. "Although I had to lead out the sprints for Marino Basso, I had a free hand for the rest of the time. I was riding well, and even though I was no climber, I finished 12th overall. That fact had not escaped Felice Gimondi. For three years my wages in Merckx's team had stayed at BF 25,000 per month, and in 1970 Jean Van Buggenhout had refused me a rise. During the Tour of Italy, Gimondi put a proposal to me, offering me BF 50,000 ($1600) a month but only if I signed there and then. I jumped at the chance."

"After the Giro, during a race in Belgium, when I informed Merckx of the contract I had signed with Salvarani he was furious. 'Why didn't you come and talk to me first,' he said, and I couldn't really blame him, but the damage had been done. Over the next few weeks, however, Merckx continued to act in a very proper manner and did not take any sanctions against me. When I was selected for the world championships in Mendrisio, though, he did everything he could to get me

thrown out of the team. He didn't go behind my back to do it, either, he openly told me that he was afraid I would ride for Gimondi. That caused communication between us to break down completely. On the eve of the world title race a meeting was held in the Belgian team hotel, and I was not invited to it. Merckx promised all the other riders BF 25,000 ($800) if he won the title. Now it was my turn to be angry. The following morning we rode by bike to the start and I went to ride alongside Merckx. He was as nervous as hell, which was a good sign as it meant he was feeling sharp. I asked him why I hadn't been invited to the meeting the previous evening and why I wouldn't be getting the BF 25,000. 'If you put in 100-percent effort for me, you'll get your 25,000,' he promised."

During the actual race there was a very early escape including Joop Zoetemelk, Giovanni Cavalcanti, Franco Bitossi and Roger Swerts.

"I never rode a single meter at the front," says Swerts, sounding as proud of the fact as ever. "Nevertheless, we built up a lead of several minutes and Bitossi started to fancy his chances of winning. He approached me with a proposal, and as our chances of success increased it got more and more attractive. At a certain point he promised me BF 300,000 ($10,000). In those days that was a hell of a lot of money. But I refused. We were eventually caught and Merckx went on to become world champion. Because I had refused to help Bitossi, I was almost lynched by the Italian fans after the race. I had fruit of every description thrown at my head, and my arms were black and blue from all the blows I had to take. In the Belgian camp that evening the champagne was really flowing. When everyone was a little 'tiddly', Merckx grabbed hold of me and bellowed: 'Dolf, Don't leave us, stay with our team.' (Swerts was known as 'Dolf' within the team because he loved singing German songs when he had had a glass or two too many). I would have liked to, but I had already signed a contract with Gimondi. Over the following few weeks, fortunately, a deal was worked out in which Marino Basso and Guerrino Tosello — both of whom were still contracted to Merckx's team — were allowed to leave for Gimondi's team if my contract with them was nullified. And in that season, 1972, I earned about as much with Merckx as I had been offered by Gimondi."

■ STRANGERS IN HIS MIDST

It says something that Merckx was never able to link up with any of the really great riders (otherwise they probably would not have become really great). Roger De Vlaeminck and Walter Godefroot both politely declined, realizing that the presence of two captains on one ship was a sure-fire recipe for trouble.

While it is true that Vanspringel and Swerts were 'big names' when they were enlisted in 1971 and 1976 respectively, they had both just been through rough patches, and Swerts had already ridden for Merckx between 1968 and 1973 in any case. And they were not the most pigheaded or free-spirited individuals in the peloton. Anyone with that sort of temperament would at once cause an upheaval within Merckx's strictly run cycling family home. Rebellious, individualistic troublemakers like Martin Van den Bossche or Guido Reybrouck frequently clashed with the conventional Merckx, who was probably secretly jealous of the bravado that characterized these 'rather odd' fellows. Yet he certainly did not put himself out when it came to trying to keep them in his team.

VERBEECK, GIMONDI AND GHENT-WEVELGEM 1972

Roger Swerts had ridden in the service of Merckx for years without questioning the situation too often, but when he let his personal ambitions show more obviously the relationship between the two men soured visibly. "The closing stages of Ghent-Wevelgem in 1972 was characteristic of that," says Swerts. "After the second climb of the Kemmelberg, five of us were out in front: Gimondi with his teammate Tony Houbrechts, Merckx, with me as his domestique, and Frans Verbeeck. Houbrechts approached me and said that Gimondi was prepared to pay to win the race. I went to sound out Merckx. Eddy was not feeling at his best and knew he had no chance of winning himself, but he didn't want Gimondi to win (although in Chapter Eight Merckx denies this). Instead he wanted to return a favor for Frans Verbeeck. That year Verbeeck had helped Merckx win Milan-San Remo, by letting a gap open behind him on the Poggio which had brought the curses of the other favorites in the race raining down on him. At the time, I certainly didn't get on with Verbeeck at all. Let's just say I was out for his blood. As far as I was concerned, any one of them could win, except Verbeeck. Merckx, however, ordered me to lead out the sprint for Frans. If Verbeeck won I was to get BF 25,000, so, grudgingly, I gave in. But I had a plan of my own. Six-hundred meters from the finishing line I led out the sprint. Fuelled by my fury, I kept on going at full power in the hope that no one would be able to overtake me. I was already starting to sing inside when, 50 meters from the banner, Verbeeck came alongside and beat me at the last second. My blood was boiling. An hour after the end of the race Verbeeck was disqualified for straying off his line and pushing Gimondi out of the way. I was declared the winner. Merckx couldn't accuse me of doing anything wrong because, after all, I had done what had been asked of me."

Swerts felt himself being increasingly trapped in the muzzle of team discipline. "Merckx didn't like the way I was able to compete with him as a time trialist in 1972," claims Swerts. "The situation erupted during the Tour of Italy. On the days leading up to the final time trial, I kept a low profile in order to save my energy. In the evenings at the meal table, they regularly alluded to it. When I finished second in the time trial, only 33 seconds slower than Merckx, he was beside himself with anger. I was earning more than my other teammates at the time, and I could also command more money in the criteriums. As a result of that, the relationship between me and the others deteriorated rapidly. Merckx, too, eventually realized that he wasn't going to be able to keep me in the team any longer. I served out the remainder of my contract in 1973, but things weren't right any more between the rest of the team and me.

"That doesn't mean there were rows between Merckx and me, though. As a result of his dominance on the bike, Eddy was a real leader, but he never sought conflict. I had ridden for Raymond Poulidor for three years, but 'Poupou' never said anything and always seemed to be satisfied with things. Neither did he win much, though. With Merckx, on the other hand, everything was made clear right away. Nothing much needed to be said, but everyone was only too well aware of what was expected of him. Merckx was as hard as nails, and we accepted that because that's the way he was with himself, too. Not to mention the fact that we knew he won time and time again. Merckx managed to get the best out of most of us through the example he set, and through his encouragement. We were happy to ride for him, and you had the feeling that you were important by riding in his team. Merckx usually wanted to have his cake and eat it, but he also appreciated the work we did, even though it was not in his nature to make it abundantly clear."

THE SKEPTICISM OF JOHAN DE MUYNCK

Johan De Muynck was asked by Merckx to come and ride in his team on more than one occasion. "In the weeks leading up to the world championships in Mendrisio in 1971, I was riding with the strength of an ox," remembers De Muynck, savoring the taste in his mouth. "I was riding a training race in Geraardsbergen, in which we needed to take the Kloosterstraat climb several times. A leading group formed, made up of 11 riders: Merckx and eight of his teammates, Daniël Van Ryckeghem and me. Every time we came to the climb of the Muur, I shot off the front like a man possessed until finally the only man on my wheel was Merckx. He realized I was in great form and either didn't want to or couldn't get to the front during the final circuit. In spite of that, he took all the bonus sprints on the way and that made me really angry. In the final sprint, Merckx beat me by half a wheel. Not long afterward he asked me: "I take it you'll come and ride in my team next season, won't you?" My anger had not yet completely subsided and I rejected his offer out of hand. After that, Merckx asked me on another two occasions if I would ride for him. I declined both times. The mentality of the Molteni team was not for me. I was afraid that if I rode with Merckx I wouldn't be given enough freedom. I would have ended up in a straitjacket of servitude with permanent pressure to perform. For anyone riding for Merckx it was a case of working for him all the time and putting their own interests to one side."

▽ *Johan De Muynck: "The higher Merckx climbed, the more solitary he became. Even within his own team." (De Muynck leading the climb of the Kruisberg during the Tour of Flanders in 1974)*

De Muynck points to the servitude that Merckx's teammates were forced to show their team leader, which he drove firmly home to them. "The division of labor was something you just didn't talk about," says the 1978 Giro winner. "Anyone who had any ambition was best advised to leave it behind in the fridge. That's what Herman Vanspringel was to discover in 1971. Even after winning the national championship, there was no place for him on Molteni's Tour de France team. At the time that Tour was being raced, Herman won more than 10 races back home. I was put off by the fact that in Merckx's team it could not be said that there was a relaxed, friendly atmosphere. The leader's thirst for victory hung down on them like a lead weight. All this could only lead to Merckx becoming more and more isolated. The higher he climbed, the more solitary he became. It may be that this is an iron rule in sport and elsewhere in society, but it must have been absolutely bloody awful to have to live with such a thing. I would imagine that in his solitude Merckx must have done some really hard thinking. Mentally, he was a recluse. The standards he set himself were so high that he simply could not allow any sign of weakness to escape. From farmers to kings, everyone knew who he was. Everyone thought of him as being extraordinary, phenomenal and unique. He was a victim of their idolization. Where was left for him to be himself? In spite of all this, Merckx does like being among people. He likes to let himself go and can be really amusing. During his career, however, he had no option but to live with the brakes on. In retrospect, it may be said that he came to be surrounded too much by people who would sacrifice themselves for him and cast aside their own interests. As a result of that, he stopped getting any feedback, and he was never told what the actual situation was. He stopped having quiet, sober people he could trust assisting him, but ended up with subjects, flatterers and profiteers by his side. Everyone always agreed with him, everywhere. Eventually he couldn't put things in perspective any more, something which he found hard to do anyway due to his unbridled ambition. The black hole into which he sank after he retired was an extremely deep one."

When it comes down to it, it would seem that Merckx has most admiration for those who keep their distance from him and those who put him into perspective or challenged him. De Muynck claims that Merckx respected him because he felt he was different and therefore had a different set of values. Would Merckx's admiration for Godefroot and De Vlaeminck have been the same if they had said yes to his offer, and therefore in Merckx's shadow have taken off their mantles of champions? Patrick Sercu was another who dared to question the might of the Lord, and at first he had cause to regret it. Later, however, it was to win him Merckx's regard and friendship.

△ *"One of the things that Merckx and I had in common was our dedication to our profession," says Patrick Sercu. (The duo after their win in the Belgian Madison Championship in 1965. In the background Merckx's already ever-present guardian angel, Guillaume Michiels.)*

■ THE BOND WITH PATRICK SERCU

The earlier love-hate relationship with Patrick Sercu points to a contradiction in Merckx's character: he could only ever fundamentally respect another person if he was genuine, honest and dauntless: characteristics at odds with the subordination he assumed was present to a high degree in his teammates. The one-year-older Sercu was originally an opponent and just like any other, when newcomer Merckx gave as good as he got on the track in the Brussels suburb of Schaarbeek (the track was demolished in November 1966). Later on, Sercu formed a duo with Romain De Loof, while Merckx's regular partner was Jean Walschaerts. "My father, Berten Sercu, and Felicien Vervaecke – Merckx's race companion at the time – knew each other just like everyone does in such an enclosed world," says Sercu. "They were the ones who brought us together. I got on quite well with Eddy, although that is not to say that we became close friends right away. In 1963, I did my military service at the Little Château in Brussels, which gave me the chance to ride on the Brussels track more than ever. I started riding team races with Merckx, and every now and then I went to his house. It was a real 'rich-man's home' as we would have said in West Flanders. Eddy's mother, who radiated a homely, almost Italian warmth, always made sure everyone's stomach was well filled. His father was more withdrawn and timid. I got on well with Eddy, but it never went very deep. We were partners, no more than that. In any case, we only came into contact during wintertime. In 1964, the year of the Olympics, our bond was strengthened due to the training camps held at Raversijde and in Norway. We were also linked by having the same dedication to our chosen profession. When the others went out for the evening, we stayed behind in our hotel.

That created a certain sense of togetherness. Later that season, Eddy won the world title in Sallanches and I won Olympic gold in Tokyo, and a year later we made our debuts in the professionals together with Solo. As a result of the world sprint title I had won in 1963 at Rocourt Stadium in Liège, and that Olympic track title, it was almost inevitable that my career would be pushed toward the track, while Eddy went in search of success on the road. One year with Solo was enough for him, but I stayed with them for one more year. In 1968, we became teammates again with Faema, but my road-racing activities remained very limited that year. That was to change in 1969 when I decided to carve out a career for myself as a road racer. In 1970, I moved to another Italian team, Dreher. I still regret it somewhat that I left Eddy at that time. I would have definitely won more and bigger races if I had stayed in his team. We were once again reunited as teammates in 1977, this time with Fiat, and my 22 victories that year made it my best road-racing season."

Merckx was not at all pleased by Sercu's departure in 1970. The 'Cannibal' believes in the law of the 100 percent. In the same way that you cannot be sixty percent pregnant, he feels that you cannot be a 60-percent friend of somebody. "I was disappointed, yes," says Merckx. Although he avoided openly displaying his annoyance at Sercu's departure, there was outright rage in the way he raced against him."

"The 1970 Tour of Sardinia was my first stage race as a professional," Sercu remembers. "In one of the stages, Merckx had missed the decisive break due to a puncture, and I took over as race leader. I dreaded the remaining, hilly stages but thought that Merckx should keep a low profile. When I spoke to him about it one evening, however, he wouldn't have any of it. Over the next few days, he kept on attacking as though his life depended on it. I sat on his wheel and died a thousand deaths. I managed to stay the course, but it cost me blood, sweat and tears in the process. In that same year, I was riding at the front during the closing stages of Ghent-Wevelgem with Merckx, Roger Rosiers and Julien Stevens. If it came down to a closing sprint, I was the hot favorite. But even though he knew very well how much I wanted to win a major one-day race, Merckx won with ease as it turned out. At times like that you obviously called him everything under the sun, but you were left with a feeling of respect. Not long after that, on the track at the European omnium championship, I gave Merckx a taste of his own medicine. On that day, I was in no mood to do him any favors.

"When it comes down to it, what has kept us close in spite of all our disagreements has been our will to win and our insistence on sticking to our principles. As far as I'm aware, Merckx never gave away a single race. Whenever he rode, no matter where it was, he always

▽ *At first Merckx was not at all pleased with Sercu's departure, but in the autumn of Merckx's career the two came together again. "In 1977 with Fiat, I had my most prolific season," says Sercu.*

rode to win. My attitude was the same, especially when it came to the big races. I never gave a race away on the track. But, more importantly, we became friends at a time of innocence, when we were both snotty-nosed kids who hardly anyone had heard of. You don't let a bond formed under such circumstances be easily broken."

A COCOON OF CONCENTRATION

From the eye-witness reports of some of Merckx's other former teammates, one might come to the conclusion that there seemed to be no dialogue at all with the team leader. By its very nature, the sport of cycling does not allow much space for contact, and on top of that there was the cocoon of concentration that Merckx spun around himself. Communication was kept to a bare minimum and there was very little exchange of emotions. "Merckx inspired the team by his example, not by his words," says Huysmans. "And he finished the job off. As one of the worker bees, therefore, you were just left to do what was needed to be done."

There were two requirements: teammates were not to ask questions, and they were to keep any personal ambitions they might have under wraps. Merckx may well

▽ *Merckx spun a cocoon of concentration around himself. (The Molteni team at the start of the team time trial at Mulhouse during the 1971 Tour: left to right, Merckx, Bruyère, Swerts, Mintjens and Van Schil)*

declare that he helped teammates win on numerous occasions, but his physical dominance in the sport was so complete that most of his teammates imposed automatic censorship on their own will to win. Those who did not such as Swerts, Van den Bossche and Reybrouck felt as though their wings were being clipped and eventually went looking for other teams.

"I can remember one particular Montjuich Hill Climb in which I was riding at the front with Merckx and Swerts," says Martin Van den Bossche. "Merckx asked me, while we were on the climb, to give it everything I had. Swerts, being the lesser climber, was forced to drop off the back."

Merckx takes the opportunity to put the record straight on this: "In those days, the event at Montjuich comprised of a road-race, an individual time trial and a team time trial," he says. "If I were to have a chance of winning the final overall classification, we had to go hell for leather during the team time trial, too. You could hardly be expected, then, to go at the pace of those who weren't the best climbers in the team."

VAN DEN BOSSCHE AND THE CLIQUISH MENTALITY

Van den Bossche and Merckx never really hit it off, even though they often shared the same room during stage races. "A real ordeal, it was," laughs Van den Bossche. "At around half past eight at night Merckx turned out the light, and that was the end of my day, too."

Van den Bossche arrived in the Faema team in 1968 from the Romeo-Smiths team in the wake of Guido Reysbrouck, though certainly not at Merckx's request. And at first he was surplus to requirements – in view of the two-Italians-to-one-foreigner ratio that was in force – and he dropped out of the team picture. "For a while I rode races without a sponsor's name on my jersey," he says. "I always had to fight for my place in the team."

That year, Van den Bossche only regained his place in the first team just in time for Paris-Roubaix. His inclusion in the team for the Giro was only made at the very last minute, too, and only when it became so emphatically clear during preparations how much he would be needed. This is how Van den Bossche, the born climber, came to be something of a necessary evil Merckx was forced to put up with.

The Cannibal, it must be said, never went out of his way to keep Van den Bossche in the team. According to Martin "My contract in 1968 was for one year only and toward the end of the season the manager, Van Buggenhout, slipped a new contract into my hand. When I read it, I saw that the monthly wage was exactly the same as for the present season. I didn't say anything, but I tore it to shreds right there in front of Van Buggenhout, as theatrically as I could. 'Oh yes, of course, there must be a

His climbing helper, Martin Van den Bossche, could do nothing about the subservient mentality that had grown around Merckx. (Van den Bossche alongside Merckx during a training ride in 1971)

mistake in the amount that's been put down,' apologized Van Buggenhout right away, and he altered one or two things on it. It had been a nice try, all the same."

THE CLASH WITH VAN DEN BOSSCHE

An incident that took place in 1969 played a part in Merckx and Van den Bossche growing even further apart. On the climb of the Tourmalet in that year's Tour, Van den Bossche was pacing his team leader Merckx, nearly all the way up. When they were in sight of the summit, Merckx accelerated so that he would top the climb ahead of the hard-working Van den Bossche. (Merckx continued alone to win the stage by an enormous margin.) "That night I went to Merckx's hotel room looking for him," Martin remembers. "Only to say to him: 'Today a little rider expected a big gesture from you'. Merckx just gave a little smile."

"I still feel guilty about not letting Van den Bossche go over the top of the climb first that day," says Merckx. "But on the previous day he'd really got my back up. He came up to me and, as dry as a bone, told me that he had received an offer from the directeur sportif of Molteni, Albani, and that he would be leaving our team. Try to imagine the position that left me in: I was riding my first Tour and was still being haunted by the doping affair from the Giro when a very useful teammate comes telling me he's about to sign for someone else. I was feeling very edgy and I wanted to concentrate as much as I could on the race itself, and I wasn't sure of myself. I needed to be able to trust the whole team. It was a pretty inappropriate time for Van den Bossche to do what he did, and it really annoyed me. That is what made me think only of myself at the top of the Tourmalet. I knew I had done wrong, but in that situation, it proved to be stronger than I was."

When Merckx retired, Van den Bossche said: "To evaluate him as a rider is dead simple: there was no one better. As a person, though, he never reached that same level. Like everyone, he had his good side and his bad side. I cannot tell you the truth about him though, and I refuse to lie."

Time mellows man and loosens his tongue somewhat. Van den Bossche is reluctant to take part in any mudslinging, though he is prepared to say that he always found the cliquish mentality that surrounded Merckx difficult to bear. "A permanent band of yes-men emerged around Merckx," he says. "It was like holding court, almost. There was nothing I could do about this subservient mentality. I was full of admiration for Merckx, but I wouldn't offer myself up to him. Most of them couldn't get close enough to him. If he ordered a Trappist beer, everyone ordered a Trappist beer. As an individual, you might as well have been dead when you were next to Merckx. And that's not how I wanted to be."

IF YOU DO IT YOURSELF YOU DO IT BETTER

When seeking out the relationships that existed between Merckx and those people who worked for him, one comes across the same rather forced situation. Directeurs sportifs, soigneurs and mechanics were there to make it possible for Merckx to race at his optimum level, no more, no less. It was only his soigneur, Guillaume Michiels – whose name crops up in various places later in this book – who could count on Merckx's total confidence. Michiels, a former rider from Brussels, knew Merckx before he was five years old, and when he grew up he followed him selflessly wherever he went all around the world. After retiring from racing, Michiels became a coffin maker in the Brussels suburb of Evere and acquired the nickname 'The Grave', because he was so uncommunicative. Merckx was able to unload much of what he was thinking to Michiels, on the massage table or in the car. There were times when this man, who had seemingly been sculpted from a block of granite, was a tower of strength to Merckx.

▽ *Soigneur Michiels enjoyed Merckx's complete trust and expertly shielded him from the public when necessary.*

On the organizational and technical front, Merckx's wishes were very clear: he desired perfection. The assumption that Merckx would have preferred to have done everything for himself had it been possible is quite correct: he would have probably liked to have put his bike together himself or to have made his own sandwiches and to have chosen the hotels himself. If you do it yourself, you do it better. That can, however, prove to be a trap for perfectionists and they find it impossible to delegate. Merckx was not arrogant enough to walk into this trap, thanks in part to manager Jean Van Buggenhout, who regularly guided his protégé behind the scenes (see Chapter Eleven).

It was Van Buggenhout's idea to bring in Guillaume Driessens at the end of 1968 to be Merckx's directeur sportif, in order that this flamboyant, extrovert *comedia dell'arte* figure would provide a

Claudine Merckx got to know Guillaume Driessens at an early age. "Lomme had been soigneur for my father during some of the six-day races," says the daughter of Lucien Acou. "He was really good at pepping up riders. He could give weak, impressionable riders unbelievable lifts to their morale and motivation. Eddy, however, had no need for anyone to do this as he was motivated enough himself. And the way Lomme made a song and dance of everything was not to Eddy's liking. Eddy didn't go berserk with Driessens, however. Their split was more to do with the unequal treatment of the other riders in the team which made things go so wrong. It is well documented that Lomme had his own ideas about the presence and visiting rights of the riders' wives during stage races, but his rules were not the same for everyone on that point. Some wives were allowed to go on tours, others were not. Some of the riders became less and less prepared to put up with it."

counterpoint to the cool, maybe even melancholic Merckx. Van Buggenhout must have reasoned that Driessens would be able to 'sell' Merckx better. He forgot one thing, however, Merckx cannot stand play-actors, blusterers or jokers. The last thing the Cannibal could ever be accused of was laying things on a bit thick verbally. To him, it bore witness to a mentality that he did not appreciate in the least.

■ DRIESSENS, VAN LOOY AND MAERTENS

It is extremely rare for Merckx to speak out unreservedly against someone involved with the sport. Throughout all the conversations we had with him, each one lasting several hours, there were only three characters who were 'honored' in such a way: Guillaume Driessens, Rik Van Looy and Freddy Maertens. You will find out more about Van Looy and Maertens later, but for the time being we will concern ourselves with Driessens, a man about whom Merckx does not have a good word to say. "All that song and dance was just drivel, while all the time the organizational side of things was falling apart," he complains. "Everything Driessens did was like a big game to him. He enjoyed making people look like idiots. The 1969 Tour of Flanders was the crowning point of that. With more than 70 kilometers to go, I went away on my own. Driessens came driving alongside me and asked me if I'd gone completely mad. I can still see it now, mechanic Marcel Ryckaert, Marcel Daemers and someone from the cycling federation were sitting in the car with Driessens. 'Go screw yourself,' is what I screamed back in Lomme's face. And I carried on and won. Later, when I heard what Driessens had been jabbering on about at the finish, 'We've pulled it off yet again, we saw our chance once more and took it' and rubbish like that, well, it made me absolutely furious."

Merckx hated showing off and play-acting. As a child, he was taught that 'in the end

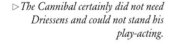
▷ *The Cannibal certainly did not need Driessens and could not stand his play-acting.*

the mask becomes attached to the skin.' And this was not to be the only '*petit bourgeois*' principle that was to determine his behavior. (see Chapter Seven)

The directeurs sportifs Merckx worked with were also not of the slightest use should he have needed his morale boosting. "I probably never had the right directeur sportif," he said, immediately after retiring. "Having said that, it would have been hard to find one who was right, in view of my nature. What the one had too much of, the other had too little."

Merckx was always able to motivate himself 100 percent, even for races like the Grand Prix of Zwankendamme. What, then, could a directeur sportif have been able to add on a tactical level, apart from reminding everyone that they were riding for Merckx? And Merckx certainly did not look to his directeurs sportifs to provide a shoulder to cry on. His upbringing had taught him that you should keep your feelings to yourself, a precept he had absolutely no trouble sticking to.

■ STEALING WITH EYES AND EARS

Merckx quite simply did not need that many people around him. According to the saying, 'solitude is a character facet.' That does not mean that Merckx did not pick things up from others. As a youngster, especially, he was constantly taking it all in with his eyes and ears. In his amateur days, he used to join local racers such as Guillaume Michiels, Emile Daems, Willy Vannitsen, Jose Thumas, Rene Van der Veeken and Roger De Koninck on their training rides. These were all wily professionals whom he observed closely and from whom he picked up the minutest tricks of the trade.

"I also have a lot to thank Vittorio Adorni for," says Merckx. "You couldn't really say we ever became good friends. He was too 'Italian' for that. But when we were teammates in 1968, he taught me in that year's Giro (which Merckx won) how you should go about tackling a major stage race. In the area of feeding is where he taught me so much. He passed on all sorts of seemingly minor things which, however, were to have a great bearing on the final classification."

During his career, one of the few occasions on which Merckx talked of 'a friend', was when referring to Italo Zilioli. But what he really meant by friend was someone like-minded. Zilioli was modest and cultured and never made a fuss, and he had no airs and graces. He was someone with whom Merckx could feel relaxed.

In the jungle that is world-class cycling, true friendship was impossible. One day someone was your teammate, the next day he was your rival. It was everyone for himself and God against everyone else.

▷ *Adorni taught Merckx how to approach a major stage race, at least as far as diet was concerned.*

1967

The initial blossoming

△ At Heerlen his first world title as a professional, ahead of Jan Janssen (l)
and Ramon Saez (r).

Team	Peugeot
Directeur sportif	Gaston Plaud
Teammates	André Bayssière, Jean-Claude Daunat, Raymond Delisle, Andre Desvages, Henry Duez, Jean Dumont, Charly Grosskost, Pierre Le Mellec, Désiré Letort, Michel Nedelec, Hubert Niel, Francis Pamart, Roger Pingeon, Christian Raymond, Jean Sadot, André Zimmermann (all France), Tom Simpson (GB)
Number of Races	113
Number of Victories	26
Major Stage Races	Tour de France -
	Tour of Italy 9th
Major One-Day Races	World Championship 1st
	Belgian Championship abandoned
	Milan-San Remo 1st
	Tour of Flanders 3rd
	Paris-Roubaix 8th
	Liège-Bastogne-Liège 2nd
	Amstel Gold Race -
	Tour of Lombardy 7th
	Het Volk -
	Ghent-Wevelgem 1st
	Flèche-Wallonne 1st
	Paris-Tours -
	Paris-Brussels -
Other victories	Baracchi Trophy (with F. Bracke), Critérium International...

"In my third year as a pro, I slowly started to reap the rewards of the hard work I had put in earlier. Although I was put in my place by Tom Simpson, a teammate incidentally, in Paris-Nice, by the time Milan-San Remo arrived I was as strong as an ox. On Capo Berta, I escaped with Gianni Motta. With one kilometer left to go, we were caught by Bitossi and Gimondi. Despite the massive effort I had put in already, I beat them in the sprint. On that day, I could hardly feel the pedals at all, and it was pretty much the same for me in Ghent-Wevelgem. I escaped with Willy Planckaert, who was on his knees by the time I finished with him. Even then, though, we were still caught by a group including Janssen, Sels, Fore and Vanspringel, and yet I still managed to beat them all in the sprint. In the Tour of Flanders, too, I was right in form, but that day I was held in a vice by Zandegu and Gimondi. In the Flèche Wallonne, I wiped the floor with everyone on the Mur de Thuin. Then in Heerlen, I crowned it all by taking the world title, in spite of having been immobilized for a few weeks with concussion after a fall in the national championship at Mettet. To me, 1967 was the year that showed I was gradually starting to reach the point where I was to get my maximum reward in one-day races.

"Against that, however, I knew I was not yet up to that same standard in the major stage races. That year, the Tour of Italy was the first major stage race I had ridden. I won two stages and just before the finish I was in third place overall, but then my health suddenly deteriorated. In the stage that went over the Tonale, I was seeing stars before my eyes. Ultimately, though, I was very satisfied with my ninth place in the final classification. It was gradually dawning on me that I probably had a future in stage races too."

The Rival

*"I would rather sit on a pumpkin which
is mine alone than together with a crowd
of people on a velvet cushion."*
(Henry David Thoreau)

"One man's breath is another man's death."
(Eddy Merckx)

"It's impossible for friendship to exist in the peloton, because in top sport, one man's breath is another man's death. This principle has never given me any problems. It's a golden rule of the sport. Were it any other way, it would be suspicious, because you would then be striking at the essential nature of the sport itself."

You are left in no doubt by Eddy Merckx that in professional cycling there is no room for sentiment. That is because sentiment is weakness, and weakness is mercilessly punished. "Certainly a champion like Merckx is solitary by definition," says Bernard Thévenet, who handed out crushing defeats to Merckx at the Tour de France in 1975 and 1977. "Communication between top riders is extremely difficult. You can't go and ask one of your rivals at the start of a race how he is feeling, because if you did you would be asking for information which would be useful in shaping your tactics. So you make sure your rivals don't know what frame of mind you're in, or if you have any doubts and worries. Anyone who wishes to be a champion must also be a champion in shielding and masking his inner self. Nowadays, if Merckx and I are ever having a go at each other, we painstakingly avoid painful subjects from the past. I never talk to Eddy about the 1975 and 1977 Tours, which were so disastrous for him, and he never says anything to me about the period between 1970 and 1973 when he rode everyone in France – me included – into the ground. Instead, we will talk about a relatively insignificant criterium that we still have fond memories of, and about minor innocent things from the past."

◁ *Bernard Thévenet said "Communication between
top riders is extremely difficult." (from left
to right, Roger De Vlaeminck, Eddy Merckx,
Luis Ocaña, Frans Verbeeck and Cyrille
Guimard before the post-Tour criterium
at Ronse in 1971)*

JINGLING MEDALS, RESOUNDING TITLES

It is a worldwide custom for a figure like Merckx, whose performances were of legendary proportions, to be honored by various bodies. Below is a selection of the medals, titles and recognitions he received:

• Officer of the Order of Leopold III (1974), Knight of the Legion of Honour (France), the Pope's Medal.

• Six times he was crowned Sportsman of the Year by the Belgian press. On three occasions he earned the title International Sportsman. The Belgian Federation of Sports Journalists nominated him as Belgian Sportsman of the Century.

• The renowned French monthly magazine, *Vélo* drew up its own points classification and proclaimed Merckx as the best cyclist of the 20th century. The points of the top ten: 1. Eddy Merckx (10,807), 2. Bernard Hinault (6,976), 3. Jacques Anquetil (6,030), 4. Fausto Coppi (5,260), 5. Felice Gimondi (4,052), 6. Francesco Moser (3,864), 7. Gino Bartali (3,575), 8. Louison Bobet (3,368), 9. Rik Van Looy (3,362) 10. Ferdinand Kubler (3,253).

• The Cannibal was the spiritual patron of the first two editions of the Perrier World Cup (1989 & 1990), and in 1989 received the Colombian Order of Sporting Merit.

• In 1976, a commemorative medal, E. Merckx, commissioned by Numismatica SA of Chiasso, Switzerland was struck. The quantity: 20,000 numbered 18-carat gold coins and 30,000 numbered silver coins.

GODEFROOT, THE NATURAL ENEMY

Men like Felice Gimondi, Roger De Vlaeminck and Walter Godefroot talk of Merckx in the same sort of terms: they had plenty of mutual respect, but they were never close friends of his.

"I was always one of Merckx's natural enemies," says Godefroot who, like the Cannibal, turned professional in May 1965. He developed into one of Merckx's fiercest rivals in one-day races. "In the amateurs, Merckx was still just another opponent. In my early races as a professional, I got to know my idol, Rik Van Looy. The first few times I rode with the Emperor, as he was known, I was so in awe of him that I didn't know whether I should call him mister or plain Rik. Rik put me at ease right away. What brought us together was the realization that in Merckx we had a common enemy. Together with Ward Sels, Gustave De Smet, Arthur De Cabooter and one or two others, we eventually formed a clan that would go for the throats of the coalition which had formed around Merckx – Georges Vanconingsloo, Ferdinand Bracke, Guido Reybrouck, Georges Vandenberghe and Willy Planckaert – particularly in the criteriums. That really was one tough bunch against another. We would ride one another into the ground, even for the most trifling prime. The knife was permanently between the teeth, and yet it was always played out in a very sporting spirit. Even after the eventful final sprint in *A travers belgique* in Waregem in 1966, in which Merckx closed the door on me too late causing me to tumble, I didn't lodge a complaint and relations remained on a healthy, sporting footing. In the G.P. Pino Cerami that followed, however, our rivalry was starting to be taken a little too far. In that race, I stayed on Merckx's wheel throughout. He finally got thoroughly sick of this and deliberately let himself slip off the back. But I still stayed with him. At one point, even I started to think it was all getting a bit too sordid, and I decided that from then on I was going to ride my own race."

NEVER GIVE IN

According to Godefroot, the media accentuated his rivalry with Merckx and sometimes even painted a misleading picture of it. "Often there was no objectivity whatsoever," he says. "After the 1966 *A travers belgique* I mentioned, the papers wrote: 'Neither of the riders deserves any blame, especially Merckx.' In 1967, I won Liège-Bastogne-Liège by beating Merckx fair-and-square in a two-man sprint. The massive headline in one of the papers the following day said: 'Merckx betrayed by cinder track'. Underneath, in small letters, were the words: 'Godefroot wins Liège-Bastogne-Liège'. It really made my blood boil when I read that. The Tour of Flanders in 1968 was a good example of the definite alliance which existed between Van Looy and me. Rik launched a counterattack on Merckx and I did the same on Reybrouck. When Ward Sels escaped, however, we didn't respond. As far as we were concerned, we would let anyone win, as long as it wasn't Merckx. Sels had the race wrapped up until he suddenly blew up in the final kilometer and left me to win the race in the sprint after all. From 1970 onwards, our rivalry became less bitter, but we never gave in to one another. Later on, other riders like De Vlaeminck and Verbeeck, would stay out of Merckx's way too much. I knew that in the mountains I had no chance of competing against Merckx, but at least on my own terrain I was never afraid to take him on openly."

Such an attitude is guaranteed to earn Merckx's tacit respect. He has always had a great deal of regard for Felice Gimondi, too, for example. That was not only because the Italian was the king when it came to taking his profession seriously – once, while out on a ride during a training camp on the Mediterranean, De Vlaeminck and Tony Houbrechts ordered coffee and cake, while the ascetic Gimondi made do with a cup of tea – but also because he rated his human qualities highly. Gimondi's 'purity', his total belief, his total correctness and his totally responsible attitude to his profession were all qualities Merckx found uncommonly attractive. It is as if he thought 'wouldn't the 'wicked' outside world be a better place if it were only inhabited by such people?'

▽ *The Belgian world championship team in 1965 pose for a photo call before the criterium at Zingem. (From left to right: Bernard Vandekerckhove, Arthur De Cabooter, Rik Van Looy, Walter Godefroot, Jos Huysmans, Roger Swerts, Eddy Merckx and Ward Sels)*

GODEFROOTS MISTAKE

Did Merckx have the strategic insight to weaken the opposition simply by getting one of his fiercest rivals to join his team? In 1970, he stated that he felt Herman Vanspringel would be one of his most dangerous opponents. By the following year, Vanspringel was riding for Merckx. In the same way, the promising Italian stage-race specialist Italo Zilioli was drafted into the team.

"In 1972, Merckx asked me to go and join his team," says Walter Godefroot. "That was after the world championship in Gap. We stuck around for a long chat that evening. I was ready to listen to his proposal, but I wanted to bring Wilfried David and Ronald Dewitte with me. Merckx was against the idea of Dewitte joining, however, because he felt that as a character he wouldn't fit in with the rest of the team. Because of that the whole deal broke down. I still regret never making the move. Along with my move from Salvarani to Peugeot, it was the biggest mistake I made in my career

RICE WITH CANDY SYRUP

△ *Merckx could never really stand the 'Emperor of Herentals', Rik Van Looy. "I got too much taunting and never a word of good advice."*

Someone who would certainly have no place in Merckx's ideal world was Rik Van Looy. The 'Emperor' and the 'Cannibal' could not stand the sight of each other. Through no choice of their own, they became teammates with Solo in 1965, Merckx's first season as a professional. While still an amateur, Merckx signed a contract with the margarine-producing sponsor, and later on when Van Buggenhout snapped up Van Looy, Merckx had no objections. "I was 19," he says. "The line-up of the team was the least of my worries. I just wanted to learn as much about the sport as quickly as I could."

His naïveté did him no good. Van Looy and one or two of his cronies were masters of the art of ridicule and would constantly keep on at Merckx. The young Merckx loved eating rice with candy syrup and he was mercilessly ridiculed for it. "They laughingly called me Jack Palance (the Hollywood baddie who Merckx resembled slightly)," says Eddy. "I was still fairly shy and I made it look as though it was all washing over me, but I was actually bottling everything up. Inside it really hurt me, all those taunts. But the final straw for me was when I realized that I was being completely left to my own devices. I never got any good leadership or received any good advice at all."

"The feud between Van Looy and Merckx was probably due to the way Van Looy treated Merckx away from races," says Jos Huysmans. "Van Looy knows exactly how to tease someone and you can soon get the impression he's being sarcastic. For Merckx it must have been really humiliating, and he's never forgotten it."

VAN LOOY TALKING ABOUT MERCKX IN JANUARY 1970

"Merckx is a great rider, but he's more vulnerable than you would think. Up to now, it's all gone wonderfully well for him. I wonder what would become of him if he were to be beaten fair and square a few times. In terms of morale, he is not very stable — he can't take defeat. On top of that there must be a question mark against his personal qualities if several teammates are leaving his team after a season when he won the Tour de France, and when they must have won a pile of money. I don't believe he is easy to get along with, either for his teammates, for those close to him or for journalists and supporters. With me, anyway, he behaves in a small-minded and haughty manner."

CONTROL OF THE MONEY

Joris Jacobs, for years the sports editor of *Het Nieuwsblad*, views the transfer of power between Van Looy and Merckx in a very matter-of-fact way. "What was actually behind it was the division of money from the national criterium circuit," he says. "The No. 1 rider was the boss and walked off with half the money. You must remember that in those days a large proportion of a rider's income came from these criteriums. Van Looy was finding it more and more difficult to keep it going with his legs, but he knew how to make the most of his bigger popularity. He was adored for his extroverted character and spontaneity. From that point of view, he was the direct opposite to Merckx. It was once written of Van Looy that on one occasion he had the nerve to relieve himself while riding in the middle of the peloton, causing all the riders behind him to scatter like flies. Can you really see Merckx doing that?"

The vulnerable Merckx was certainly not gifted verbally enough to offer any defense to all the teasing, and he realized early on that his stay with Van Looy could not last for more than one season. Merckx was quoted at the time as saying: "I feel like an outsider in Rik's family business, with Sels as his favorite, with his brother-in-law Hugo Mariën – who cannot possibly be an objective directeur sportif – and with Mrs. Van Looy. No, it's just too much."

Fortunately, Van Looy and Merckx rarely rode together during the 1965 season, but where they did, there was always the threat of a breakdown in communication. "The main reason we avoided each other was my military service," says Merckx. "It lasted from November 1964 until February 1966 (the first three months were spent training in Ghent; after that there was a year at the Little Château where Merckx served as an ordinary soldier at the medical examination centre and later on at the barracking service). I only made my debut on May 1, in the Flèche Wallonne. Van Looy was riding in the Tour of Spain at the time. The first big race we rode together was the national championship in Vilvoorde, which Godefroot won. We saw very little of Van Looy that day, and I finished second after being held in a vise by the teammates Godefroot and De Cabooter. I didn't get very much support from my teammates. It was a bitter pill to swallow, being only 19 and just missing out on the Belgian national jersey."

EVERYTHING FOR VAN LOOY

In Paris-Luxemburg that year, the only stage race Merckx and Van Looy rode in together as teammates, it became clear right away who was the boss within the team. "Everything was done for the benefit of Van Looy," says Merckx. "If he couldn't win, then he preferred that a rival win rather than a teammate. In that Paris-Luxemburg, I was in good form (second in the second stage and third in the third stage), but I didn't get any sort of protection. Immediately after the finish, I was summoned to go and eat with Arnold Standaert, the chairman of the Belgian Cycling Federation. I had to promise that if I was selected for the world championships, I would not ride against Rik Van Looy. 'Why would I want to ride against Van Looy, anyway?' I asked in astonishment. 'He is a teammate during the world championships, after all, isn't he?'"

As the Belgian standard bearer of the 1960s, Van Looy had the BWB eating out of his hands completely. This was a trump card the 'Emperor of Herentals' was to play on many other occasions. "During the 1968 world championships at Imola, I was saddled with Van Looy again," says Merckx, sadly. "Very early on in the race, he got involved in a pointless escape with Adorni, Stevens and another six riders. The Belgian team was left looking on and found it difficult to mount a chase, allowing the escapees to stay out of reach. Van Looy, however, was all too easily given the slip by Adorni, at a precise point that left us with no chance of doing a thing about it. The Italian, a teammate of mine with Faema at the time, became the World Champion. The following year, the federation asked me if I had any objections to

▷ *"Even in the 1969 world championships at Zolder, Van Looy ignored team instructions and rode the whole race on my wheel".*

▽ *Merckx and Van Looy (seen here in the E3 Grand Prix in 1968) were arch-enemies. In 1969 at Liedekerke, the hostilities burst into the open.*

Van Looy being selected for the world championships at Zolder. I said it made no difference to me, but added that I thought Van Looy should stick to the team plan more. When it came to the race, however, he spent the entire duration of it on my wheel. Unbelievable!"

■ DIRTY OLD GOAT

Van Looy got to Merckx so much that he actually succeeded in forcing him out of his shell to a degree. "I always had respect for someone like Jacques Anquetil," says Merckx. "When I caught up to him in the mountain time trial on the Turbie, during Paris-Nice in 1969, I didn't dare look him in the face. Three years earlier, also during the Paris-Nice time-trial, I caught Van Looy, who had started two minutes before me. As I left him trailing in my wake, I gave him a burning look right in the eye and continued to do so for several seconds – not without a small amount of satisfaction."

"Our rivalry reached a climax at a criterium in Liedekerke in 1969. Van Looy again put in no effort whatsoever. When I deliberately slipped off the back of the peloton he stayed in my shadow, even when we were lapped. When that happened I could no longer contain myself and I shouted at him: 'You dirty old goat'. Later that same day, we appeared for the start of an evening criterium we were riding at Rijmenam. I was still seething inside, and my condition didn't improve when I realized that he was once again staying on my wheel the whole time. As we came out of every bend I attacked with everything I had, until Van Looy was forced to let me go. The episode at Liedekerke was to cost us both an eight-day conditional suspension 'for displaying insufficient appetite to race.'"

Time heals wounds, it is said. But those who have wounded Merckx to his soul cannot expect total forgiveness. In a television debate broadcast on December 31, 1979, while in the company of Rik Van Steenbergen, Van Looy and Merckx really laid into each other once again. "The program was not transmitted live," says Merckx. "Just as well, too. They cut out the most-heated exchange of words. There was a lot of snapping at each other. At one point, Van Looy shouted out to me that I had never managed to win a world championship while he was still riding. 'And you mean to tell me that's something you're still proud of?' I retorted. You know, I've never really understood Van Looy. Why did he do all that? What was with all the childishness? Not only that but at times he was incredibly unsporting; for example, the way he pulled himself away from a teammate before going into a sprint. No, I'm afraid I never found him very appealing as a person."

DE VLAEMINCK: VAN LOOY SUPPORTER

Roger De Vlaeminck, on the other hand, clearly found Van Looy an appealing character. "Thanks to my father, who was a Van Looy supporter, Rik became my childhood hero," says De Vlaeminck. "He was the one in whose footsteps I wanted to follow. I had a very deep-seated admiration for Van Looy. That's one reason why I always tried to stop Merckx winning Paris-Tours, and it turned out to be the only classic he never won. I even sacrificed my own chances of winning to see to it that he didn't. My attitude was probably not one I should be proud of, but it's just that my veneration of Van Looy was absolute. As a result of that, Van Looy remained the only rider to have won all the classics."

△ Roger De Vlaeminck, here demonstrating his acrobatic talent to Merckx in late 1969, had too much ambition of his own to ride in the service of the Cannibal.

It was not surprising, then, that De Vlaeminck rejected Merckx's offer to him to join his team. "It came in 1968, when I was still an amateur," says De Vlaeminck. "I was riding in the Tour of Belgium and at the start of a stage Merckx, who was in training, came over to have a word with me. 'Let me know,' he said. I didn't take him up on it, though, because really I wanted to race against him. I don't think it would have worked out having two ambitious riders in the same team."

THE COLD WAR WITH LUIS OCAÑA

The relationship with Luis Ocaña went exactly the same way as with Van Looy, degenerating into a cold war between the two men that lasted several years (see Chapter Twelve). "I first came across Merckx during the Catalan Week in 1968," recalled the Spaniard. "He was already a major figure, and I was afraid to even call him by his first name. Although I had a great deal of respect for him, I didn't let that stop me battling against him with everything I had. The first time I did was in the Tour de France, where the climate and the mountains worked in my favor. I was always against the way many seemed to demonstrate a willingness to please and to lay down and die when it came to Merckx. I sometimes felt his fanaticism was uncalled for. In the 1970 Tour, any chances I had of winning the final classification were totally ruined by sickness. On the stage to Saint-Gaudens, I wanted to make up for it a little by winning the stage. While I was out on my own in front, Merckx mobilized his team. I wasn't feeling that great anyway, and had to dig very deep to hang on for the stage victory. At the time I thought to myself, 'I wish Merckx would go to hell'. From that day on, our relationship went downhill rapidly."

Merckx dryly responds: "Ocaña had won the Tour of Spain that year, and you try not to let a rider of that caliber stay out in front for a minute."

As will be discussed in greater detail in Chapter Twelve, something grew between Ocaña and Merckx that began to look suspiciously like genuine hate. In January 1973 Merckx – usually circumspection personified – really laid into the Spaniard. "Ocaña races too negatively. To him it doesn't matter if he doesn't win, as long as I don't. I was pleased to see him do so badly in the 1972 Tour."

Ocaña was also there during the closing stages of the world championship in 1973 at Montjuich, when he rode in a leading group with Gimondi, Merckx and Maertens, and where a chasm was created between the two Belgians that was never healed. At the time, all the newspapers were not only full of the details of how Gimondi won, but more particularly of how Merckx and Maertens had lost. Merckx's explanation for what happened is that at the request of Maertens – who claimed to have nothing left – he had kept a low profile. If that had been the situation, Maertens would have led out the sprint for Merckx. Yet Merckx only slowed down over the last few hundred meters. "Treachery!" screamed Maertens at the finish. "Merckx has sold it to Gimondi."

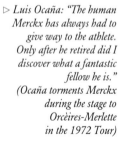

▷ Luis Ocaña: "The human Merckx has always had to give way to the athlete. Only after he retired did I discover what a fantastic fellow he is." (Ocaña torments Merckx during the stage to Orcèires-Merlette in the 1972 Tour)

"Merckx would never have sold a major race, least of all a world championship," said Ocaña, full of conviction. "At least I was never aware of him doing so and I never heard anyone else say anything. With two kilometers to go, it was clear that Maertens was sacrificing his own chances to help Merckx, because he was keeping the tempo very high. Gimondi was following him, then Merckx, and I was sitting in fourth position. When Gimondi took off, it was to my astonishment that I noticed Merckx wasn't able to go with him. Before I had time to get over the surprise, the gap had opened wide enough for Gimondi. If I'd had more belief in myself, I would have won the world championship in front of my own people, without a doubt."

At the time, Merckx claimed: "I couldn't feel my legs due to the nerves." He adds to that now: "The way Maertens led out the sprint was all wrong. You lead out a sprint by gradually increasing the tempo, not by suddenly exploding away. When he did it, he opened up a gap of about two to three lengths in no time. In that sprint he blatantly rode me toward an inevitable defeat."

I NEVER RECEIVED A CENT

Godefroot still vividly remembers that there were vehement discussions among the Belgian riders about the incident that evening. "I spent hours on end arguing with Merckx that night because I thought Maertens was right," he says. "When Maertens turned professional towards the end of 1972, I took him under my wing. I passed on my experience to him, a bit like a second father, because I had faith in him. I found it impossible to accept that Merckx could have been stabbed in the back by Maertens. In the end I didn't know who I ought to believe. At a later date, I got to know what the real Maertens was like, unfortunately."

"Maertens went right into my bad books that day," Merckx maintains. "I sank to the ground when I heard he had called me a coward. (vehemently) Never, not once, did I ever ask for or receive one cent from Gimondi. There is one thing I have never understood about Maertens: when I was a pro, Van Looy always used to ride on my wheel, but I never let it worry me and got on with my career. Then in 1973, along came Maertens. There was no way I was going to be stupid enough to play the game Van Looy had been playing with me and yet, to my great consternation, Maertens often used to follow me like a shadow! He never really accepted the responsibilities that go with being a top rider. And I can't stand the hypocrisy of someone who does all his mudslinging behind my back. Give me Ocaña any day, at least he came out and openly said that he couldn't stand the sight of me."

"Merckx had plenty of opportunities to sell races," his loyal helper, Guillaume Michiels, tells us. "In the closing stages of Milan-San Remo in 1967, Merckx had escaped with Gianni Motta. Motta kept on offering him money until he was blue in the face. From one hundred lira – which at that time was worth around eight francs – he upped his offer to six or seven million lire, or around half a million Belgian francs. Merckx turned it down."

"When I got offers like that, I pushed the pedals even harder," says Merckx. "So that they wouldn't have the breath to keep bidding."

▽ Large photograph: From 1973 there was a new name to challenge Merckx. Freddy Maertens left the Cannibal trailing in his wake in the 1973 Tour of Flanders, but could not get the better of Eric Leman.
Small photograph: Later that season all hell broke loose at the finishing line of the world championship at Montjuich. Gimondi was a surprise winner ahead of pacemaker Maertens and the slowing Merckx. From then on, things were never right between the man from West Flanders and Merckx.

MAERTENS: "MERCKX WOULD RATHER HAVE SEEN GIMONDI WIN"

When the paths of Eddy Merckx and Freddy Maertens crossed in the professional ranks, things went wrong almost from the beginning. When Maertens turned professional after the 1972 Olympic Games, he at once served notice that he would be a serious rival to the established order, headed by Merckx. "I belonged to the generation of Staf Hermans, Louis Verreydt, Staf Van Cauter and Marc Demeyer," says Maertens. "But from very early on, I had to do the dirty work myself. I had a great deal of respect for Merckx, but my own ambition took precedence. In areas where I thought I could get the better of Merckx, I did everything I could to beat him. The press were eager to play on that, with all the exaggeration that goes with it. I was hailed as the new Merckx by some. That was something I never actually said myself, but that was how I was pushed forward. Another reason was that my racing was geared toward Merckx, but there was nothing unusual in that. If you wanted to be at the front, you needed to follow Merckx. The unwritten law of the sport, which states that the older generation tries to resist the new crop of riders for as long as it can, was in full play. In 1973, I had to fight hard to win myself a place among the elite. In the world championship held at Montjuich that year, the relationship between Merckx and me was ruined forever. What happened in that race has always been festering between us."

Maertens stands by his view that Merckx tricked him that day. According to him, the explanation can be found in the commercial conflict raging between Camapagnolo and Shimano, two players of worldwide magnitude in the field of cycling accessories. "First of all, the story of the closing sprint," says Maertens. "I did indeed ask Merckx not to take on any more work. I promised that I would lead out the sprint for him, and that I did. At around two kilometers from the finish, I took over at the front and drove really hard. Over the final kilometer, I went harder still. Merckx, however, continued to hang back. I started to get a bit worried and I kept looking round, shouting to Merckx to come through. But he simply never came — probably because he was unable to. It is just not true that I led out the sprint too explosively. If I had, how could Gimondi — who wasn't exactly renowned as a sprinter — have got past me? When it dawned on me that Merckx couldn't make it, I kept going flat out, but it was too late. And apart from that, I was hindered by Gimondi. Anyway, I felt betrayed. Because of my youthful naïveté, I probably used language that was a bit too strong straight after the finish. Put yourself in my place, though, I was a young rider who had just missed out on the world title and who could have kicked himself over what had happened."

The real trouble was that money played a major role in the whole story. "The fact that neither Merckx nor I had won meant that everyone in the Belgian team could kiss goodbye to their win bonuses from Molteni or Flandria," says Maertens. "So the atmosphere in the Hotel El Rancho in Lloret de Mar, where the Belgian team was staying, was pretty unpleasant. Merckx had arrived back at the hotel before me. They say he was in tears when he got there. When the other lads had a moan about losing their bonuses, Merckx must have told them it was all my fault. So when I got there, I got the full works. Well, I wasn't going to take that. A meeting was convened and everyone was invited along, but Merckx did not show up. In the end, Vanspringel and Van Linden went and fetched Merckx. He accused me of counterattacking during the closing stages of the race. That much was true, but it was only so that I could fetch him, and therefore not have Ocaña and Gimondi on my wheel. 'Why didn't we carry on through, together?' I asked him. If we had both stayed at the front, one of us would surely have won, wouldn't we? Merckx simply did not dare to admit that he was worn out on the final circuit. That in itself was no bad thing. The only bad thing about it was that he never told me. If he had, I would have won. I am not saying Merckx gave away the world championship. If he had been feeling all right, then it would have been him that won. It's just that when he realized he couldn't win, he must have decided that Gimondi would make a better winner. And that's simply because Gimondi, like Merckx, rode with Campagnolo equipment. Shimano, for whom I was riding, was the up-and-coming rival of Campagnolo. On the Friday before the world championship race, Campagnolo's big boss called Walter Godefroot over to him and passed on the message that under no circumstances was the world championship to be won by a Shimano rider. That's the only explanation I can give to account for the way Merckx behaved."

"Ah, well," Walter Godefroot responds. "We did indeed go and familiarize ourselves with the circuit on the Friday and a car containing Tullio Campagnolo came riding alongside us. Campagnolo asked me who was going to win that Sunday. 'This one, here.' I shouted, pointing to Maertens. 'Oh God, no,' Campagnolo laughed. 'Not him. He rides with Shimano parts.' It was no more than that. It was just an innocent remark, which Maertens blew out of all proportion."

Anyway, after Montjuich, the atmosphere between Merckx and Maertens turned very sour. "The press, which for the most part took Merckx's side (Merckx, however, thinks that the very opposite was true) had, of course, a wonderful tidbit in the goings on at the finish at Montjuich," says Maertens. "On a sporting level, however, I did not get the chance to defend myself immediately. Two days after the world championship, during the criterium at Brasschaat, I tore open my arm in a collision with a post. I was out of action for weeks. And while Merckx was sweeping all before him in the autumn classics, I was forced to watch helplessly from the sidelines. Later on, I seemed to be the only rider who really dared to challenge Merckx. Roger De Vlaeminck, who in his early years had fought him openly, had long since buried the hatchet. And Jean-Pierre Monseré, who had threatened to become a formidable rival to Merckx, was killed in 1971. As far as Merckx and I were concerned, things were never right between us after that. But we didn't keep out of each other's way because of it. In November 1974, the newspaper, *Het Belang van Limburg*, called together Merckx, De Vlaeminck, Swerts and myself, along with our wives, for a chat. Afterwards, we went for a meal. We even danced among ourselves. But with Merckx and me, it was never more than superficial conversation. Merckx never showed any hard feelings about Montjuich, or openly wanted to take revenge. The 1973 World Championship, however, was always there between us like an insuperable barrier. I console myself with the thought that we gave Belgian cycling a rivalry that stirred the emotions of many people."

Maertens still fosters a silent admiration for Merckx's unbridled ambition (or as he puts it, his "addiction"). "It was incredible the way the man was so wrapped up in his profession," says Maertens. "Even in the criteriums he found it difficult to keep his will-to-win in check. I remember a post-Tour criterium in Verviers. I was out in front with Merckx, De Vlaeminck and Verbeeck. It was my 'turn' to win. With a kilometer and a half to go, Merckx dropped back so that he could get the speed going to attack in a way I sometimes still dream about. He shot by us like a rocket. I really had to 'grit my teeth' to get back to him and to floor him in the sprint. I was furious. 'What did you do that for?,' I asked him. 'You don't get anything for free,' he replied."

THE LOST REALM OF FELICE GIMONDI

Merckx sees more of himself in Felice Gimondi – who turned pro the same year as Merckx (1965) and called it a day in the same year (1978) – than in any other rider. "Due to sickness and injuries to teammates, I was catapulted straight into the team for the Tour in my first year as a pro," says Gimondi. "I had already come across Merckx when we were both amateurs. Our first confrontation was on August 7, 1963 at Alsemberg, a race I won, as it happens. We had to climb the Alsemberg twice. On the second climb, I managed to shake Merckx off. I didn't know at the time that it was him, as he had not yet built his reputation. The year after that we again came face to face, in the Olympic road race in Tokyo. In that race, Merckx launched a late offensive, and I was the first one to go and peg him back. It was not to be the last time we were to meet in the final stages of a major race."

▽ Felice Gimondi: "You don't have to be the absolute top dog for your life to mean something. That's what Merckx taught me." (Merckx and Gimondi in 1963 after their first sporting encounter with each other at Alsemberg, where Gimondi won ahead of Merckx)

Gimondi started his professional career with all guns blazing. In his first three seasons, he scored victories in the Tour de France, Paris-Roubaix, Paris-Brussels, the Tour of Lombardy and the Giro. He had the realm all to himself, until Merckx's career had fully blossomed. "His rise really affected me mentally," reveals Gimondi. "In 1967 and 1968, it was starting to become very clear that a time would come when he would enjoy an unprecedented dominance of the sport. My own rise to prominence had been rapid, but suddenly – mainly due to Merckx – I had to settle for much less. In the end, I managed to get the dirty swine Merckx out of my head and tried to take my chances as and when they came. Merckx taught me that you don't have to be a leader or the absolute No. 1 figure to reach personal goals in life. It is good to be able to gauge your own capabilities accurately and to make the most of them. Dealings between us were always carried out in the proper way. We would never dream of getting involved in illicit combines or arrangements. We always rode in a straightforward way, and we never rode with the sole intent of seeing the other one lose. He's a man after my own heart, that Merckx."

Learning the Italian way

△ *The first victory in a major stage race: the Giro. Different feeding methods picked up in his new Italian surroundings were in part responsible for it.*

Team	Faema
Directeurs sportifs	Yvo Molenaers (Bel), Mario Vigna (Ita), Jules Merckx (Bel)
Teammates	Vittorio Adorni (Ita), Luciano Armani (Ita), Antonio Bailetti (Ita), Giovanni Bettinelli (Ita), Emilio Casalini (Ita), Julien De Locht (Bel), Mino Denti (Ita), Noël De Pauw (Bel), Guido De Rosso (Ita), Lino Farisato (Ita), Robert Lelangue (Bel), Bruno Mealli (Ita), Ambrogio Portalupi (Ita), Guido Reybrouck (Bel), Giuseppe Sartori (Ita), Pietro Scandelli (Ita), Patrick Sercu (Bel), Luciano Soave (Ita), Joseph Spruyt (Bel), Roger Swerts (Bel), Martin Van den Bossche (Bel), Victor Van Schil (Bel), Luigi Zuccotti (Ita).
Number of Races	129
Number of Victories	32
Major Stage Races	Tour de France —
	Tour of Italy 1st
Major One-Day Races	World Championship 8th
	Belgian Championship abandoned
	Milan-San Remo abandoned
	Tour of Flanders 9th
	Paris-Roubaix 1st
	Liège-Bastogne-Liège abandoned
	Amstel Gold Race —
	Tour of Lombardy 3rd
	Het Volk —
	Ghent-Wevelgem 9th
	Flèche-Wallonne —
	Paris-Tours 8th
	Paris-Brussels —
Other victories	Tour of Catalonia, Tour of Sardinia, Tour de Romandie, G.P. Lugano....

"1968 was an important year for me because it was then that I signed with an Italian team. In that new environment, I learned an awful lot about care and preparation and feeding. Up to that time, I was the sort of rider who trained and rode races but thought that as far as everything else was concerned anything was all right. In actual fact, I had remained a rough diamond who was now being polished by Italian hands. It was with Faema that I took part in the first training camp of my career, from January 19 in Reggio di Calabria. On the run up to the previous road-racing season, I had ridden only in six-day races.

"The new approach clearly reaped its rewards. My racing weight went down to 72 kilograms (158 pounds). My climbing in particular was to benefit as a result. I won the Tours of Sardinia, Catalonia, Romandie and Italy comfortably. That final victory in the Giro was especially important because I won it almost effortlessly. I seemed to be flying. The crowning glory was, of course, that memorable stage over the Lavaredo where I made mincemeat out of everyone for 30 kilometers. In 1967, I had fully blossomed as a one-day racer, while in 1968 it became clear that I had a great future as a major stage racer.

"Yet, the early part of the season had been something of a disappointment. In the final stage of the Tour of Sardinia, I crashed and fell on my knee badly. The injury forced me to abandon during Paris-Nice, and as a result I was lacking condition for Milan-San Remo. I made up for it in the month of April by winning Paris-Roubaix — a race in which I had never performed very well in previous years ."

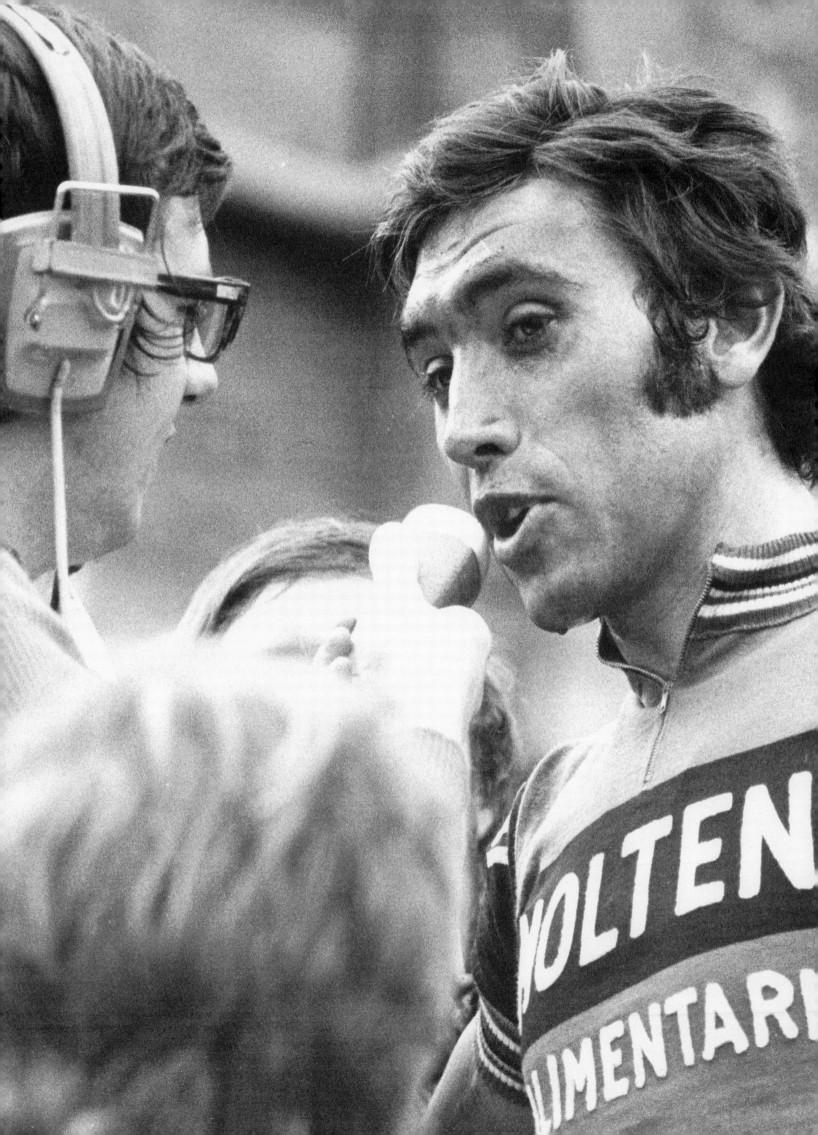

The Silent One

"There are people whose silence says much more than their words."
(Jean de Boisson)

"I cannot be artificial."
(Eddy Merckx)

The relationship between Merckx and the press was a troubled one indeed. There was such a gulf between what Merckx could do on his bike and what he said about it afterward that many questions were left unanswered. Like a pack of hungry lions, the press corps was always on hand, ready to pounce on outpourings from the Cannibal just to fill their pages or programs. Meanwhile, he continued chalking up the victories, winning almost a third of the races in which he started. Defeats for Merckx were news, too. The instructions reporters received were simple: during the cycling season there must be news about the top star on an almost daily basis. That inevitably led to problems. "What else is there to ask a man who has been interviewed a thousand times before?" the pressmen asked themselves. They were expected to come up with powerful articles. If Merckx were to tug at his earlobe three times, this was immediately held as grounds to write a report on an ear infection that was starting to give the international star problems.

Merckx was anything but a babbler, and his utterances never did anything to add any extra dimension to his incredible performances. Nevertheless, he took the time to be available for the increasing media interest, but because of his closed character he never made the most of it.

"It was always difficult to imagine what was going through his head," says his mother. "When he was still in the debutant category, the journalists used to come to me bemoaning the fact that Eddy rarely gave anything away. After a race, he always came straight to our car and disappeared into it immediately. I would say to him, 'Put on a balaclava so that no one will be able to recognize you or find you.' I urged him to do a bit more talking, but he would always say he just wanted to be left to himself. He was certainly no chatterbox, and that was something he got from his father, who was just as reserved."

THE SILENT HERO

"The presenter had prepared himself well and with one detailed question after another he tried to elicit some dramatic reaction or information from Merckx. But it was the same Merckx that we have come to expect from all the races, interviews and reports and in recent years from Tour radio commentaries: flat, boring, toneless, detached, showing no imagination, everything directed inward in almost deliberately frozen egocentricity, not conveying anything of the blood, the sweat, the tears, the strength, or the mighty, compelling stories of and about the legendary Flandrians. This whole fantastic cycling life Merckx has had only seems to have been possible thanks to his complete lack of any semi-tone or verve or any timbre in his character."
(from an interview on BRT at the opening in March 1987 of the exhibition of paintings and sketches by the Breton artist, Le Boul at City 2.)

(From the book *"Heldenlevens"* (The Lives of Heroes) (1987) by Martin Ros)

◁ *The silent man and the media: a difficult marriage.*

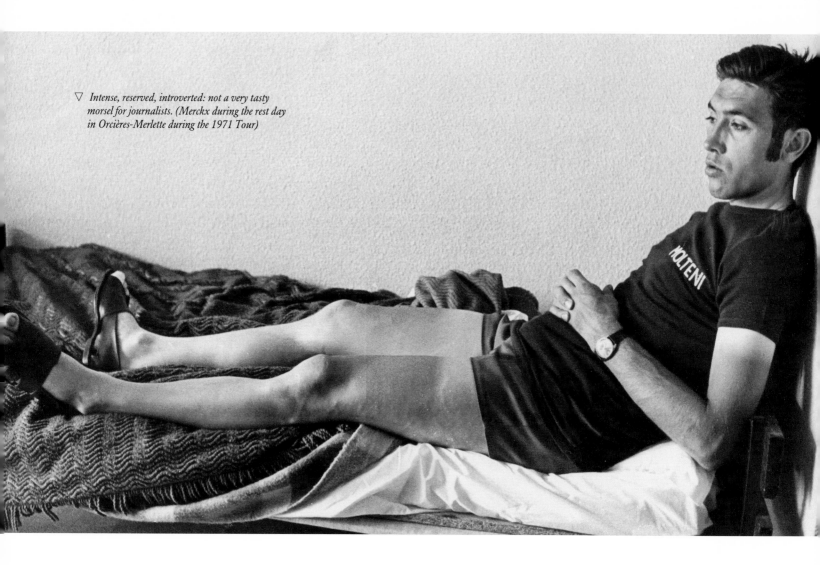

▽ Intense, reserved, introverted: not a very tasty morsel for journalists. (Merckx during the rest day in Orcières-Merlette during the 1971 Tour)

Merckx later expressly stated: "If I don't feel like laughing, then I won't laugh. I can't be artificial. I refuse to put on an act.

■ A VEIL OF SECRECY

Merckx's reticence was often mistaken for secretiveness. Joris Jacobs once wrote: "No matter what time of year, Merckx always succeeded in cloaking a part of his personality or his desires in a veil of secrecy." Jacobs, one of the figureheads of Flemish journalism, did not, however, find that Merckx's discretion handicapped him when it came to being able to carry out his own job. "The young Merckx was withdrawn, he was an introvert," he says. "In those days, journalists thought that they had the right to stake a claim on the star. Willem Van Wijnendaele was being quite serious when he spoke of a service that the riders should provide in return. "Because it is us who make them such big stars," was how he put it: that from the man who for years refused to speak to Van Looy because he wouldn't help him get one of his relatives a job with Flandria. In the journalists' view, the athlete was a piece of their property. The dour Merckx did not go along with that, however. He was 100-percent involved in his sport. He ate, slept and drank cycling, and there was no room left for anything else. Indeed, Merckx may not have been a talker, but there were two

△ Merckx in conversation with sports journalist Willem Van Wijnendaele, who was more interested in the Flemish cyclists.

great ways the press could gain from what he did offer. Firstly, the way in which he won was usually spectacular and warranted plenty of descriptive prose. Secondly, as a person he was impossible to define, which meant that journalists could allow their imaginations to run riot. What more could they ask for?"

The sports journalist Robert Janssens from the newspaper *Het Laatste Nieuws*, who followed Merckx's career from beginning to end, tries to sympathize with Merckx's formal bearing. "You have to realize that at the age of 19, when he won the world amateur championship in Sallanches, he was suddenly elevated to the status of national celebrity," says Janssens. "He had no idea at all how he was supposed to conduct himself in the new situation. He was overwhelmed by it. He couldn't understand quite why he needed to give answers to the most diverse questions. He would have liked to have a good chat, but he simply couldn't. His middle-class upbringing had taught him to do what was asked of him by his environment. But his nature was in direct conflict with this intent. He was not very well-disposed verbally, he didn't read much, and he used few words to express himself. Moreover, he didn't really need the press. He didn't race for the recognition or the glory, but above all just wanted to win for himself. Even without the press, he would have been just as tense, just as ambitious, and just as motivated."

THE PRICE OF FAME

Merckx confirms that. He has always regarded the massive interest in his person as artificial, exaggerated and sometimes even inappropriate. He still has trouble with it, even now. "I am still paying the price of fame," he says. "I'm used as a symbol and am always being forced to continue living my life in the past. I'm find it increasingly difficult to cope with that interest. I get asked to make the most trivial guest appearances. If I wanted to, I could spend the whole week going 'round putting in personal appearances. I find myself being gaped at like some display object. In time, that gets very tedious. Sometimes I think: I'll stop shaving for two weeks, then no one will recognize me. I don't want my life to be lived for me, I want to plot new courses for myself. I am not a God, and I find it hard to understand this worship I get from people."

The Brussels journalist Robert Desmet, another of the influential figures of Belgian journalism detected an internal conflict within Merckx. "Eddy certainly realized that he never gave enough of himself to the press," he says. "But he didn't have the nerve to stand up for what he thought. His bilingualism is a good example of that. He realized that he made mistakes in both national languages, but he carried on trying to do his best. Rik Van Looy, on the other hand, had the nerve to fob off French-speaking journalists. If they could not address him in Dutch, then they were wasting his time. Merckx was very unsure speaking into the mike, but Theo Mathy of RTBF, the French-language radio station, did a lot to help him. He never received the same sort of 'coaching' on the Flemish side."

THE KINGDOM OF THE IMAGINATION

Because the reality surrounding Merckx failed to provide them with sufficient good copy, some journalists gave free rein to their imaginations. Writer's block was overcome with the most fantastic stories. In that respect, the story concerning a certain Noëlla Maris is a striking example. This lady of mature years went to watch Eddy race in the criterium at Aalst. It was very warm there and very crowded. Noëlla started having trouble breathing and fainted. The winner, Merckx — who was returning from the presentation ceremony — witnessed this scene and, like a knight in shining armor, gave Mrs. Maris a kiss. And like Snow White, she then came around. To top it off, the bold Merckx gave her the winner's bouquet. "I have kept them ever since," added a touched Noëlla in the paper. Pure fantasy.

Merckx himself has no idea where or how this story came about. "Incredible what they sometimes dished up," he says. "During the Tour in 1969, it was written that in a certain hotel I had no faith in the cooking and that a soigneur was sent 70 kilometers to go and fetch fresh trout," he laughs. "Pure fantasy, too."

Do you want to hear another story? We will allow Roger Swerts to tell it. "Merckx was a supporter of the Racing White soccer team, while I was a fan of Beringen," says the man from Limburg. "One evening during the Giro in 1972, we were having a fundamental disagreement during our meal over the merits of our favorite teams. A couple of journalists watching from some distance away eagerly noted that Swerts and Merckx were openly arguing and that the split was close at hand."

If we were to believe the newspapers, Merckx shed tears at the drop of a hat. In the second stage of Paris-Nice in 1968, Merckx fell on his knee and he was forced to abandon. Reporters from the magazine *Sport '60* asked him if he would take back some of their photos with him to their editor's office in Brussels. In the papers, you could have read at the time: "When he looked at the photos he'd been asked to take to *Sport '60* in Brussels, big tears rolled down his cheeks." "Absolute rubbish," says Merckx. "You wouldn't believe all the things they dream up."

THE MARRIAGE TO CLAUDINE ACOU

Does or did Merckx consider himself a Fleming, a Walloon, a Brusselois or a Belgian? The Belgian press used to devote page after page on the community question. He set the cat among the pigeons with his marriage to Claudine Acou, one of the daughters of track racer Lucien Acou. On that day, December 5, 1967, the only language spoken at the Town Hall in Anderlecht and at the church in Sint-Pieters-Woluwe was French. Shameful. A number of the Dutch-language Flemish newspapers spent several pages letting rip about this provocative deed.

The background to the story is, nevertheless, banal. Claudine Merckx had picked up a wedding form, which was made out in French. Burgomaster Henri Simonet (who later went on to become a Socialist Minister), decided that that being the case, the custom was that the wedding must also be performed in French. The priest at Woluwe was acting in good faith too. He had asked Merckx's mother beforehand if he would also be required to give his sermon in Dutch. "Oh, don't take the trouble," she said in all innocence, not realizing what kind of fuss she would be stirring for her son.

"They raked my wedding up hundreds of times," sighs Merckx. "Ever since then, they have always been ready to pick me up on any blunders I make with the language."

From the hard line Flemish corner, they continued to have a go at him. The February 3, 1972 edition of *Het Nieuwsblad* wrote: "Little Sabrina, nearly two years old, but quick enough for one of three, pushed her doll into our hands and said: 'That's Tina, shut her eyes.' In Flemish. Who wrote that Eddy was bringing up his daughter in French only?"

In 1971, Merckx, along with several other top sports personalities, was received at the Royal Palace. He exchanged a few words with Queen Fabiola. "Immediately afterward a journalist asked me which language the conversation with the Queen had taken place in," growls Merckx. "What was actually said was of no interest to him."

During Merckx's career, there were many occasions when he apologized profusely for his aloofness, something today he tries to fight more than ever. "I'm probably not the easiest of people from a journalist's point of view," he said in January 1970. "Yet I have always tried to keep them happy. If I fail, it's because I'm very nervous, especially just before and after a race. That creates an impression of being absent-minded, of not being interested. I admit that I have not always behaved properly with the press, but I haven't done it in bad faith. Have I any right to begrudge others doing their job properly, if I make such an effort to do the same?"

■ THE BATTLE WITH THE SENSATIONALIST JOURNALISTS

The relationship did not get any better when Merckx was misrepresented by the press a number of times. "I was like death to sensationalist journalists," he says. "Sleazy journalism was the order of the day. I did not want to be used by them as a political football, for example. They tried to get me to say things about Belgian-language community issues. They were always ready and waiting to pick me up on the smallest thing."

After his heavy fall on the track at Blois in September 1969, Merckx was flown back to Brussels in a military aircraft. Certain sections of the media immediately started talking about preferential treatment, but according to Merckx: "They never revealed that the air force made urgent transport missions like that for 'ordinary' citizens, too."

Clashes also took place with journalists and photographers who did not keep their word, something which was a cardinal sin to Merckx. A crowning touch in that respect was the appearance of the book The Flandrians, by Stan Laureyssen, in which a photograph appeared showing Merckx's bare bottom.

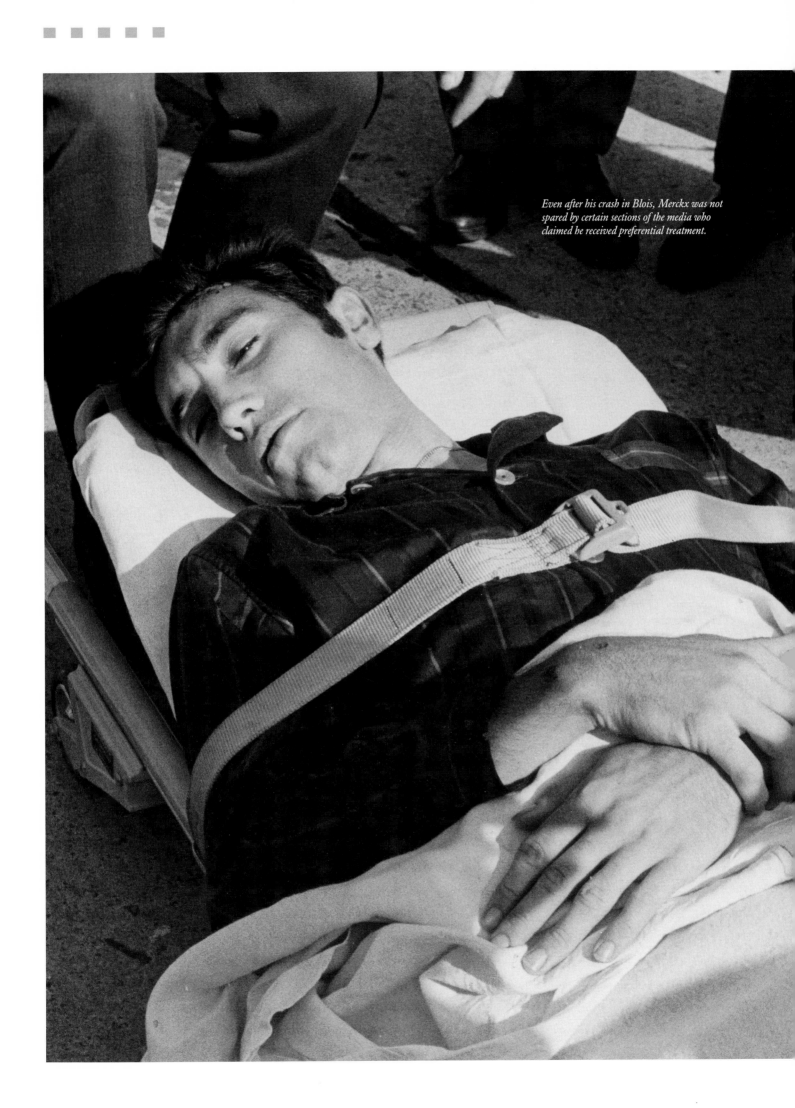

Even after his crash in Blois, Merckx was not spared by certain sections of the media who claimed he received preferential treatment.

In October 1973, posters went up all over Belgium showing a photo of Merckx with a bare bottom. They were to publicize the book *The Flandrians* by Stan Laureyssens, in which the photo was reproduced, in an eye-catching way. Merckx felt sufficiently offended by the photo to engage the services of a lawyer, Mr. Gooris (who was also a director of RWDM, Merckx's favorite soccer team). The French weekly magazine, *France-Dimanche* had used the photograph to show that on his thigh a suspicious black mark could be seen, which may have been the result of repeated drug injections. "Totally libelous," blasts Merckx. "That mark was a leftover from some fall or other."

The photograph was taken by an Italian photographer on October 12 in the changing rooms of the Vigorelli velodrome, where Merckx was preparing for his attempt at the hour record. Merckx let the photographer know what he thought of him and made him promise to destroy the negative. The photographer, however, sold it to a press agency. The photograph was distributed by ABC Press. The row erupted at the same time as the doping affair Merckx was having to deal with after the Tour of Lombardy in 1973, in which he was caught using ephedrine and had to forfeit his victory (see Chapter Nine).

In summary proceedings, Merckx's action against the publishers of the book containing the photo of his bare bottom was upheld by Judge Van Camp. Copies of the book containing the offending photograph could no longer be sold.

"The court may have come down on my side, but the whole affair cost me something like BF 120,000 ($4,000)," says Merckx. "On top of that, the author had got what he was probably counting on: free publicity. Ever since then, we have never taken the trouble to get upset by the rubbish that is spoken or written about you all over the place. It was a hopeless fight."

When in the presence of journalists, Merckx was rarely given any chance to be off his guard. "In the first place, you never knew who you could and who you couldn't trust," he says. "Fortunately, I built up a good relationship with some members of the press, but I will always remain on my guard. I remember a journalist who I got on quite well with challenging me to drink down a row of bottles of Tuborg beer as quickly as I could. I didn't really want to do it, but he kept pestering me until I gave in. You know what I'm like, if I'm challenged to do something I lose. To cut a long story short, I happily drank him under the table, but he had the presence of mind to take a photo of me without my knowing. Merckx with a stack of empty beer glasses in front of him would have made a sensational story, wouldn't it? I demanded the roll of film from him, at once. A similar thing happened to me over a photograph on which someone had caught me with a cigarette in my mouth. I had no objection of people knowing that I have the occasional cigarette to help me relax, but the press wouldn't have made that clear. It would have said: 'Merckx is a smoker.' As I didn't think it would be setting a very good example to young people, I made the photographer promise not to publish the photo. Yet, of course, it did get published, and there are hundreds more examples such as that."

■ THE INABILITY TO SAY 'NO'

Despite his sometimes-negative experiences with the press, Merckx continued to show a natural willingness to talk to them. It would have been virtually impossible for him to say no, and that, too, has cost him dearly in other areas (see Chapter Eleven). There were times, however, that the intrusiveness of journalists went a little too far for him. "I remember a winter's day in Paris, when I was there to collect the Super Prestige Pernod Trophy," says Merckx. "A journalist was hoping to conduct a lengthy interview with me, but I didn't have enough time to do it. I had an appointment to meet my directeur sportif, Robert Lelangue, at a restaurant in another part of Paris. The journalist decided to follow us, and even though we did several laps in thick traffic around the Arc de Triomphe, we could not shake him off. Lelangue drove our car to the side of the road, got out and went over to the journalist's car. He opened the car door and grabbed the ignition keys. We drove off and threw the keys out of the window a little further up the road."

Soigneur and confidant, Guillaume Michiels, tells me how a journalist went to Merckx's home when he was living at Tervuren, without having a prior appointment. "I lied to them, saying Eddy was not at home," says Michiels. "'In that case, I'll wait here until he is,' said the man, decisively. I left him standing in the foyer and went to inform Eddy. We hatched a plan to smuggle him out and he went to the garage and hid in the boot of my car. With Eddy hidden away, I drove off. Once we were around the corner, I let him out..."

Even after he had won the world amateur championship at Sallanches in 1964, many journalists remained skeptical about Merckx's qualities. Initially, there was even a little reserve, almost unbelievably obvious in comments made at the time. 'Was Merckx really so strong, or was it that the others were so weak?' they wondered. In 1968, Willem Van Wijnendaele made a comparison with the previous generation: "In 1951, Rik Van Steenbergen won stages in the Giro against the likes of Bobet, Coppi, Bartali, Magni, Koblet, Kubler and Astrua. Merckx is now doing the same thing against Gimondi, Adorni, Zilioli and Motta all of whom, at best, may be compared to Astrua. How would he measure up against riders such as Poulidor, Pingeon and Aimar in the major tours?"

"Back then, Flemish sportswriters had a clear Flandrian reflex present, which had been introduced by Karel Van Wijnendaele," says Joris Jacobs. "Anyone not coming from West or East Flanders needed to have a good set of credentials if he were going to be fully appreciated."

It is evident from Merckx's reading habits, or rather his virtual lack of them, that he would have been quite happy to live without the media. "I don't read much," he said in January 1971. "I know that's wrong of me, but I am quite often given articles that people think I might find interesting."

Because almost everything he heard reached him second hand, there were the occasional misunderstandings. "Much of what he heard was selective and laid on thickly," says cycling reporter Robert Janssens. "At my paper, *Het Laatste Nieuws*, my editor told me to mainly concentrate on Merckx's opponents. That's why I tended to go for interviews with Verbeeck, De Vlaeminck, Godefroot, Dierickx and that sort of rider. While familiarizing myself with the Tour route in June 1970, Merckx came up to me and asked: 'What exactly is it you have got against me?' I was taken aback. It seemed that comments made by his rivals that I had written in the paper were laid on more thickly by the time Merckx found out about them. No doubt he also came to the conclusion on the strength of them that the man who had committed them to paper was not to be trusted either. We discussed it until there was nothing more to say on the matter, and since then I have had one or two more brushes with him."

The basis for the relationship with the press was, as far as Merckx was concerned, mutual respect and trust. "That depended on who the journalist was," he says. "But I certainly never used the press. I never played someone up or rang up a journalist to find out something from them."

Joris Jacobs corrects this. "Toward the end of his career, as his halo began to slip, the press started to get at Merckx more," he says. "During the world championships at San Cristobal in Venezuela – which Moser won ahead of Thurau – Lomme Driessens had ordered Sean Kelly to ride on Merckx's wheel. This occurred in spite of the fact that Driessens was the official directeur sportif of the Belgian team. Merckx was furious

PASSIONS AND FEELINGS

"We cannot prove it with figures, but it is a certainty nonetheless: to achieve great popularity, a champion needs more than just a string of victories. It is the fan's love of the sport that works in his own favor and at the same time keeps the wheels of his professional turning. Triumphs and worthy performances may be highly regarded by an expert minority, but the wider public demands a human background with virtues and shortcomings, passions and feelings."

(From 'Eddy Merckx, Van Libramont tot Heerlen' (1970), Louis Clicteur and Lucien Berghmans)

about it and wanted it to be made known in the Belgian press. The magazine, *Sport '70*, had a real go at Merckx, and he asked us if we would put the record straight and also put down in *Het Nieuwsblad* that Driessens was a villain. I asked him why he was ringing me to tell me this. 'I trust you,' he said. 'How can we put something straight which appeared in another publication?' I asked. 'If you openly come out with what you think about Driessens, then we can print that,' I said. Merckx thought that would be overdoing it a bit, though, and he didn't want to get involved in any rows."

NO MAN IS AN ISLAND

Even the great Eddy Merckx was often used as a football by the press. "It is a power which the press has that you cannot begin to challenge as an individual," he says. "I knew all about the game, but I never wanted to get involved. After the world championship at Montjuich in 1973, I could have summoned the press in order to give my version of events and to counterbalance what Freddy Maertens was saying. I knew, however, that it was a waste of time. My time as a major subject was running out. I had been at the forefront for too long and they were starting to get bored with me. The arrival of Maertens was a like a breath of fresh air for some journalists. At long last, Flanders had a new figure, a highly promising young rider who was going to make it. At Montjuich, I was the traitor who had sold the title to Gimondi, while the naïve young Maertens was the poor sucker who had fallen for it. If I had come forward with an explanation at the time for the ever-eager press, I would without any shadow of a doubt come up against a wall of prejudice. That's the reason I kept my mouth shut. I did get my revenge in the following Paris-Brussels, when I left everyone trailing in my wake. I was aware of how the press had dealt with Van Looy at the end of his career. They are just as ready to blacken your name as they were to praise you. I knew my turn was coming and was ready for it. What all of this meant was that I endured it all and said nothing."

△ *The Cannibal was hardly a bookworm.
(Merckx browsing through the papers with teammates Mintjens, Rottiers and Delcroix during the 1975 Tour)*

It is a known fact that he who reaches the top is lavished with praise, while he who stays there too long engenders resentment.

The Year of Blois

△ *Merckx makes his initial move on the Ballon d'Alsace during the 1969 Tour. De Vlaeminck has already been dropped, and the same fate awaits Altig shortly.*

Team	Faema
Directeurs sportifs	Guillaume Driessens (Bel), Mario Vigna (Ita)
Teammates	Frans Brands (Bel), Tino Conti (Ita), Julien De Locht (Bel), Guido De Rosso (Ita), Pietro Di Gaterina (Ita), Lino Farisato (Ita), Frans Mintjens (Bel), Englebert Op de Beeck (Bel), Adelio Re (Ita), Guido Reybrouck (Bel), Pietro Scandelli (Ita), Patrick Sercu (Bel), Luciano Soave (Ita), Joseph Spruyt (Bel), Julien Stevens (Bel), Roger Swerts (Bel), Bernard Van de Kerckhove (Bel), Georges Vandenberghe (Bel), Martin Van den Bossche (Bel), Victor Van Schil (Bel), Valère Van Sweevelt (Bel), Herman Vrijders (Bel).
Number of Races	129
Number of Victories	43
Major Stage Races	Tour de France 1st
	• Points classification 1st
	• Mountain classification 1st
	• Stage victories 6
	Tour of Italy disqualified
Major One-Day Races	World Championship abandoned
	Belgian Championship abandoned
	Milan-San Remo 1st
	Tour of Flanders 1st
	Paris-Roubaix 2nd
	Liège-Bastogne-Liège 1st
	Amstel Gold Race 3rd
	Tour of Lombardy -
	Het Volk 12th
	Ghent-Wevelgem 1st
	Flèche-Wallonne 5th
	Paris-Tours -
	Paris-Brussels -
Other victories	Paris-Nice, Paris-Luxemburg, Super Prestige Pernod...

"When you look at my honors list, your immediate impression is that 1969 must be considered a great year. I had a brilliant early season, winning Milan-San Remo (for the third time), the Tour of Flanders (my first), Ghent-Wevelgem and Liège-Bastogne-Liège. Strangely enough in Milan-San Remo, at the foot of the Poggio, I almost rode straight on toward the finish, because I was feeling a stinging pain in my right knee. By the time we reached the top of the Poggio it had disappeared, thankfully.

"On top of this series of classic victories, 1969 saw my first victory in the Tour de France, 30 years after Sylvere Maes. I can hardly claim to be unhappy about the season, then. Yet two incidents overshadowed everything positive that had happened. Firstly, there was the doping affair in the Giro. It felt as though the whole world was crashing down on me in Savona. It was the greatest instance of injustice I experienced in my whole career. I was therefore enormously motivated when I started the Tour. Just like in the early season and in the Giro, I could hardly feel the pedals. My victory in the stage from Luchon to Mourenx-Ville-Nouvelle, over the Peyresourde, Aspin, Tourmalet and Aubisque remains one of my best performances. A solo of 130 kilometers in the yellow jersey, everyone and everything ridden into the dust: I was never able to match such a feat in my career, unfortunately. The reason for that was my crash on the track at Blois on September 9. From then on, things were never the same. My back never recovered from it and climbing, especially, never felt the same as it had before. From that moment on, the word 'suffering' came into my vocabulary on an almost daily basis."

CHAPTER SIX

The Star

"For many people, admiration begins
at the point where their comprehension
comes to an end."
(Fliegende Blätter)

"I always rode for myself."
(Eddy Merckx)

THE UNNATURAL GESTURE

When greeting his supporters, Merckx had something of the haste of the proverbial elephant in a strawberry field. As an introverted young man who chose the solitude of racing his bike above the merrymaking of a social event, he had a natural aversion to crowds and their intrusive interest. "I have an image of Eddy from right after the first of his Tour de France wins in 1969, which will always stick with me," says his wife Claudine. "Eddy came into a restaurant that was teeming with supporters. Probably because he felt obliged to do so, he stuck his hand into the air in the most unnatural gesture I have ever seen anyone make. He just didn't look right doing that sort of thing. You had the feeling that had he been left to himself, he would never have made such a gesture. He probably felt compelled to do something euphoric, or his manager, Jean Van Buggenhout, may have asked him to. But he had no sense of spontaneity, and he never made a show of his emotions."

I t is not always so great being a star. The public demanded more of Merckx – a three-time World Sportsman of the Year – than he cared for. Yet glory and fame were only marginal motivations for him. He did not need his ego to be massaged by celebrations, tributes and other ceremonies of honor. "I always rode for myself," he says. "I never won races to make the supporters happy. You win races for yourself, to reap the rewards of your efforts and sacrifices. After a race, though, I was happy for the supporters, but they were never the driving force behind my career. I was never in love with the sound of applause. You can end up becoming a slave to it. Any man who is so desperate for recognition will be left with no life at all after he's retired."

People in Merckx's immediate circle claim that his relative indifference to the response of the general public was not out of a sense of false modesty. "It was an inner urge which always motivated Eddy to race," says his wife, Claudine. "He wasn't looking for recognition. He was looking for satisfaction within himself."

Former teammate Jos Huysmans also finds it impossible to imagine a Merckx wallowing in his success. "You can rest assured that he did not need the press and the public," he says. "At least he didn't in the beginning. I am convinced, however, that later on, he became aware of the effects his performances were having on people." Merckx admits this to a certain extent: "As a young pro, the applause left me cold. Later on, I was drawn to it more. At least when I waved to the crowds it was spontaneous. That was something I never did when I was younger."

◁ *"I raced for myself. Never for the applause or the pats on the shoulder." (Merckx is given a regal reception in Brussels after his Tour victory in 1971)*

■ TENNIS AND HOCKEY

When Merckx was riding in the youth categories, there was only limited interest in him. "The district I was brought up in, Vogelzang, was not very cycling-minded," he says. "The people who lived there were generally quite well-off, and tennis and hockey were more their kinds of sports. Cycling was regarded as a sport for ordinary people. There was nobody in my neighborhood who especially followed me or who let my success go to my head. I never even had a supporters club, for that matter. A victory never got me into an exuberant state. During the winter that followed my Belgian title victory with the newcomers in 1962, there was a celebration in the Cheval Blanc Inn right in front of our shop. I never went mad about them, though."

Even when Merckx won his world amateur title in 1964, interest remained fairly limited. "When you became a professional, you suddenly had luxury like you'd never known before," he says. "I certainly wasn't the great white hope everyone was looking for. Van Looy, who in 1963 was deprived of the world title in Ronse by Beheyt, soaked up most of the attention. There were other people around like Emile Daems, Willy Vannitsen, Jos Hoevenaars, Ward Sels, Jef Planckaert and others too numerous to mention, but the last time a Belgian had won the Tour de France was 1939. Cycle-loving Belgium was definitely not a desert for the sport, though, and in the Tour we were regularly up there near the top, and we won many stages. My eventual

▽ *Merckx had a certain aversion for crowds and their intrusive interest. (Merckx at the start of Milan-San Remo in 1976)*

introduction to the professional game in May 1965 was not exactly earth shattering. As a result of my military service, I had less chance to train, and in my first race, the Flèche Wallonne, I abandoned. The severity of that race came as a real shock to me. I originally wanted to ride Liège-Bastogne-Liège too, but after my sobering experience in the Flèche Wallonne I put my plans aside. It was certainly no big drum-beating start, even though I was the current world amateur champion."

The absence of a supporters club, which was remarkable for someone of his caliber, prevented Merckx becoming self-satisfied. "Learning was a tough experience," he says. "I kept having to draw on inner strength. Looking back on it, that was a great advantage. I also never had to be dependent on anyone else, other than my parents. Due to my not having a supporters club, they had to dig deep into their pockets to pay for my racing equipment. I am still very grateful to them for having done so."

■ AN AVALANCHE OF INTEREST

When Merckx was enjoying one success after another as a pro, the weight of interest in him descended like an avalanche that caught him unawares. This new star, the man who gave Belgium its first overall victory in the Tour de France since Sylvere Maes in 1939, became public property. And as is always the case, the public kept on asking more of him.

"It would be impossible to do everything the supporters ask of you," sighed Merckx in early 1970. "I try to keep them happy during the race itself by always putting all I have into it and coming up with good results. Anyone who writes to me to ask for a photo or an autograph can count on receiving my personal attention."

Merckx found out all about the flip-side of fame. The telephone rang from dawn until dusk, he was recognized everywhere, and he lost any privacy he once had. "In 1971, I spent a holiday on the Canary Islands, but from the very first day, I was hunted down," he says. "I took the supporters' intrusiveness in my stride, but there are limits. Some of them disturbed me at meal times and expected me to immediately put down my knife and fork to give them the autograph they wanted. It's at times like that when you have to be most watchful of what you do or say. If you react too enthusiastically and no one is put off, you get the whole lot going again. If you let someone down or read them the riot act, you'll soon find yourself getting a reputation for being awkward and cocky. It's always one extreme or another."

Merckx was not the only one who had to put up with supporters descending on him. His wife, Claudine, also had her fair share. "In 1972, a man from Verviers came knocking at our door," she tells me. "He asked me whether Eddy could give him any

THE EUPHORIA
AFTER GHENT-WEVELGEM 1973

Merckx's army of supporters was extremely enthusiastic about his performances in those days. But the man himself let very little passion show. He was too unemotional to do that; he did not let his feelings show through enough. Merckx greeted his victories with a resignation that left the outside world bewildered. There was hardly any sign of emotion. "I was too wrapped up in what was coming next," was Merckx's same answer when he was asked why he always stood so impassively on the podium.

"There were two occasions when I showed my exuberance," Merckx says now. "One was in Montreal in 1974, when I was tremendously happy with my third professional world title. The other I will always remember was Ghent-Wevelgem in 1973. After that race, I was even quite excited when I was standing on the podium."

What could have been so special, then, about that particular Ghent-Wevelgem? "That year, I hadn't won a single big race," says Merckx. Indeed, he had 'only' won the Het Volk season-opener and had missed out in Milan-San Remo and the Tour of Flanders. Within three weeks of Ghent-Wevelgem, the Amstel Gold Race, Paris-Roubaix and Liège-Bastogne-Liège had been added to his honors list for the season.

▷ *Merckx's exuberance after the world championship at Montreal in 1974. (Raymond Poulidor (l) and Mariano Martinez join in the celebrations.)*

▷ *Eddie Stichnoth with the offending poster on which Merckx's bare bottom is seen (see page 60). For years Stichnoth has been collecting things that have anything to do with Merckx. You can admire items from the collection on pages 72 and 73.*

work, and I told him I thought it was unlikely we would be able to help him. With that, he became angry and said that in that case the least we could do was pay for his train fare — a 300-franc return ticket!"

△ *Some supporters make no secret of their preferences.*

■ SUPPORTERS IN THE GARDEN

Supporters ask for the most bizarre of things. "If you let them into your house, you'd find they would still be sitting there two hours later," says Claudine. "There was one woman who claimed that she was having some trouble because of us. The telephone company had given her the old telephone number we used to have in Tervuren. In return, she asked Eddy if he would go and visit her one afternoon. She had a nine-year-old son and he gave his friends a real surprise by letting them spend half a day with Eddy. He was always being asked for lots of money for charities, sick children and anything else you care to name. At first I used to answer all the letters we received, but eventually I stopped. I once supported a good cause and the following week I was inundated with begging letters. A woman who had gone bankrupt wrote to ask us for 3 million francs, promising to pay us back when she could. When we lived in Kraainem, some supporters forced their way into the garden. They started pulling down Eddy's jerseys from the clothes line. Luckily, I had seen it and I was able to stop them before anything else untoward happened. There were people who got in through the back gate and peered through the windows to catch a glimpse of Eddy. When that happened, Eddy went upstairs because he never dreamt of scolding anyone. On a rare occasion when we went out to a restaurant for a meal, some people came over and just sat down next to us. Eddy gave his customary indifferent reaction, but that only meant that the people started babbling away to me. It wasn't long before they found out that was a waste of breath, too."

These forms of unhealthy interest may all have been quite innocent, but Merckx's success also attracted malicious types. In February 1975, some paintings, antique pistols, crystalware, silver and other valuable items were stolen from their villa in Kraainem. Among them were medals and trophies. The paintings were by artists such as Miro, Albert Saverys and Jacques Maes. "With the exception of one or two medals, nothing was ever found," says Merckx, the pain in his voice still audible. "I estimate that I lost around two million francs (about $60,000). The Saverys alone was worth at least half a million. Not that it was ever our intention to make money from the paintings, but it was a blow, nevertheless."

WE'LL SIMPLY SMASH YOU DOWN

In his racing, too, Merckx had to pay a high price. He was a favorite target for supporters of his rivals. "I sometimes had to put up with the crudest forms of insults," says Merckx, mystified as to why. "They would sometimes shout: 'Do you think you're God, or something?' There were also threatening letters. In one was written: 'If you come to ride in Evergem, we'll simply shoot you down.' I brought the Detective Division of the police in. I did, of course, ride in Evergem in the end, because I feel that if you give in to threats like that, the people behind them have got what they wanted."

During the 1970 Tour, the race organizer, Felix Lévitan, received a threatening letter that said: 'You have made the Tour for Merckx. Look out, we're going to get Merckx – somewhere near the top of a mountain in the Pyrenees. You can go and tell him that.' Lévitan didn't attach too much significance to the letter, but the gendarmerie accompanying the Tour were told to pay extra attention on the way.

Along the way, a lot of unpleasant things happened. "People spat in my face and stones were thrown at me," says Merckx. "Minor irritations, that's all they were. Not only did I fail to understand why they were doing it, but it made me pretty angry, too. On more than one occasion, I felt like turning around and grabbing the perpetrators by the scruff of the neck. To me, what they were doing was entirely unwarranted, squalid even. I might have been able to understand it if I had been some sort of upstart who won races using underhand methods, but there was nothing controversial about my success: I was simply the best. So what was the reason, then, for all this unsporting behavior?"

In interviews with Merckx from his racing days, these incidents hardly receive a mention. "I knew there was little point in complaining about it afterward," Merckx says now. "They would dismiss it as nonsense or take it as being an excuse. The way some spectators behaved so unsportingly did make me

▽ *An exuberant and spirited female fan cheers Merckx toward victory in the wind and rain of Paris-Roubaix in 1970.*

mad, but it breathed even more fire into my belly. The more people annoyed me, the faster I rode. That, then, was my answer: my way of taking down these spoilsports a peg or two."

Merckx was also aware that after years of dominating the sport, interest in him was bound to be wearing a bit thin. The fans had become so used to it that when Merckx carried on winning, it was regarded as nothing more than inevitable. "I think what the public is looking for is new names," said Merckx at the start of the 1974 season. "They soon get used to the old ones. What else have I to offer the supporters beyond what I've already given them?"

When his career was snuffed out like a candle in 1978, he never wanted a farewell race or final tribute. "They can be pretty distressing, those farewell events," is Merckx justification for that. "You're expected to trot out again and show yourself for one last time, and then to say goodbye. I think it's pathetic really. It's better just to put it all behind you."

◼ SEVEN THOUSAND CARDS

Generally speaking, reaction to Merckx was positive among the legions of supporters. Not that Merckx had the type of charisma that grabbed people by the throat right away. His performances, however, were so super-human that any right-minded cycling fan has admiration for him at the very least. Nor was Merckx ever the subject of heated argument. He was not controversial like someone such as Rik Van Looy, who you were either for or against. Merckx came across as too flat, either to make you mad or to want to praise him to the skies. To the mass of cycling fans, he was a superhuman rider and not just a man made of flesh and blood.

"During hard times, the support the fans gave me was heart-warming," says the Cannibal. After he was found positive in the 1969 Giro, he received no fewer than 7000 cards and letters of support. "The reception I received in the Grande Place in Brussels on July 26, 1969 after my first Tour win was unforgettable, too," says Merckx. "You would have had to be made of stone to remain unmoved by all those thousands who have turned out especially to see you."

▽ *Merckx's reply to the thousands of letters of support after Savona in 1969.*

Your moral support and sympathy have consoled me and fortified me in the most painful hours of my career. I am very grateful to you and will do everything I can to keep your faith in me.

Eddy Merckx

THE GOOSEBUMPS OF VINCENNES

One of the most powerful memories of Merckx's career was the time when he secured victory in the 1969 Tour on the velodrome at Vincennes. "I will never forget it, the crowd of thousands who were chanting my name when I rode into the velodrome in yellow," he says. "I experienced everything all at once: goose bumps, cold shivers and tears in my eyes. It was a real emotional release. All the effort, all the suffering evaporated away from me there and then. The sudden realization that everything had been worth it. And the injustice of my doping charge in the Giro had been set to rights."

The name Eddy Merckx was used to promote the most unlikely products. Here is a sample of the many commercial collectors' items designed to satisfy the supporters' collecting mania and to push up sales.

BERNARD VANHOUTTE: 530 DAYS OF CUTTING AND PASTING

Bernard Vanhoutte, a metalworker from the West Flanders village of Moen, fell under the spell of Merckx so much during the television coverage of the 1964 World Championships from Sallanches, that over the following years he clipped every press article that had anything to do with his idol and stuck them in albums. "I was taken by the doggedness with which the man plied his trade," says Vanhoutte, who adorned the entire top floor of his house in Kerkstraat in a Merckx rug. "In the evening of every working day, I sat going through the newspapers, cutting out anything that had something to do with Merckx." A quick calculation reveals that during Merckx's 14 seasons as a professional, Vanhoutte must have spent 12,600 hours with scissors and glue. Or to put it another way: 530 days of 24 hours — in all, a year and a half at it. "After the Tour, in particular, it was a big job," Vanhoutte remembers. "I usually couldn't keep up with it. As Merckx was riding into the Vincennes velodrome, I was still busy working on him climbing the Tourmalet."

Merckx had become a part of Vanhoutte's life. So it was a high point for Vanhoutte when he was given the chance to shake the hand of the brand new world champion, Merckx, in the Town Hall at Avelgem in the presence of the mayor. "Not many could say they have done that, here in Moen," he says, with a lump in his throat. "I had arranged it through Jean Van Buggenhout, who I had informed about my collection. I also had a quick word with Merckx in Moorslede, at Zwevegem and at the track in Ostend. On each occasion, the impression he made was of behaving politely but being detached, and he was not a great conversationalist."

A selection from the collection of Merckx articles has been used for exhibitions. "In 1971, I was offered BF 100,000 (about $3000) for my collection," says Vanhoutte. "But I refused it. I didn't do all this collecting to make money from it."

Vanhoutte's involvement became so great that he started to display psychosomatic complaints when things were going badly for his idol. "I was very concerned by the doping affair in Savona," he says. "I wrote a letter to him right away to drum some courage into him. It made me slightly ill, too. At my work, they could see right away that I was not very well. I found the whole business so unfair."

Vanhoutte has moved to another house in Moen since we spoke to him and there is no trace of any pictures or souvenirs of Merckx to be found anywhere. "There is just one photograph of him hanging in my office," says Vanhoutte. "The time for all of that has long gone. It is now obvious, though, that in the year 2000 Merckx will be proclaimed Sportsman of the Century."

Cécile and Maurice Heleven were without doubt the most dedicated supporters Merckx ever had. In 1959, the Helevens opened a grocer's shop in Diepenbeek near Hasselt (just like Merckx's parents, see the next chapter). It was as ordinary cycling fans that they went to watch the Tour of Limburg for amateurs in 1963, an event in which a certain Eddy Merckx won two stages and final overall victory. They were impressed by his performance, but no more than that.

"In 1967, we went to watch the national championship at Mettet," says Cécile Heleven. "Merckx had a heavy fall that day, and we just happened to be by the Red Cross tent when we saw Eddy being led away, still groggy. It was then that we wrote to Eddy for the first time, to send him our wishes for a speedy recovery. Eddy's mother replied to us, that same week, enclosing a signed photo of him. Since then we have kept in touch, and nothing could stop us being at races in which Eddy was riding."

△ Hard-core supporters, the Heleven family, followed Merckx whenever they could. The children's clothing was specially adapted with the favors of their hero.

You can say that again. Even with a shop that was open six days a week, from half-past six in the morning to eight o'clock at night, the Helevens went to watch Merckx every Sunday. The fact that they had to drag their five, later six, and eventually seven children (four boys and three girls) with them, was not going to stop them. The children were always dressed for the occasion, with the corresponding sponsor's jersey and the obligatory riders caps on their little heads. "The girls ended up being even more fervent supporters than the boys," laughs Cécile Heleven.

Providing Merckx was not riding in another part of the world, they wanted to be there to watch him. And whenever their idol landed at Zaventem airport, a Heleven was inevitably on hand to present him with a bouquet. Maurice Heleven also attended every world championship in which Merckx took part. "I was there at Montreal in Canada and at San Cristobal in Venezuela," he says. "There is, however, one glaring gap in my 'honors list': the world hour record in Mexico. I missed that because they never announced in advance how many days Eddy would be spending making the attempt. After only three days he succeeded in breaking it. God, and to think I wasn't there to see it..."

In winter, too, the Heleven family hit the trail with diapers, baby-food containers and all the other accessories they needed to be able to look after the numerous offspring. If Merckx was riding a six-day event somewhere, they paid him a visit. One particular trip, to the Cologne Six Days, which was ridden at the turn of the year, is etched into their memories for ever.

"It must have been before 1970, because we only had six children at the time," says Cécile Heleven. "We set off on our 'break', but because the weather was so bad, we didn't get very far at all. There was snow on the ground and it was dangerously slippery. We decided to drive to Tongeren and then catch the train from there to Cologne. At Tongeren station, we were told we would have to go to Guillemins station in Liège and buy a ticket there. So we slid over to Liège, where I got out of

◁ *The Vanhoutte family whose love*
of their idol even went as far as
the bedroom.

the car and went into the entrance hall to buy the tickets. While this was going on, Maurice was looking for a place to park the car. It must have taken him quite a while, because just as we got to the platform we saw our train pulling out of the station. The next train was a Trans-Europe Express, for which we had to pay a hefty supplement on each of the eight tickets. Then when we got to Cologne we were forced to take two taxis to get to the velodrome."

"Once there, we were soon spotted by Merckx, and he came over to see us as soon as he could. He said that he was having trouble, as he was finding it impossible to sit down without being in pain. 'I probably won't make it all the way through,' he then told us. It amazed us the way he gave his all that evening, especially in some of the sprints. It later became apparent that he had won a children's bike in the sprints, and he gave it to us as a present. That gesture was typical of the man. Although he didn't give much away with what he said, it only served to make his deeds stand out more."

◼ A DAY AT THE SEASIDE WITH CLAUDINE

"Merckx has a heart of gold," says Maurice Heleven. "He was always straight with us and respectful. He never acted too big for his boots. I got the impression that he was rather grateful, and that he felt privileged to have been given all the talent he had. As great as he was as a rider, he was as big in his heart. He never let us see anything negative about him, even when he was completely drained after a race. We are not the type of supporters who hunt down their idols like wild animals immediately after the finish of a race, so that they can be in a photograph with him. We usually saw Eddy after he had changed into his clothes."

THE TRUE SUPPORTERS

Mere mortals who are able to turn in out-of-this-world performances can expect admiration that sometimes goes too far, and in certain cases starts to resemble worship. Without wishing to go into the psychology of the supporter who identifies with his or her idol to an excessive degree, and as a result loses all sense of reality and perspective, one must assume that some of them - in their immeasurable admiration - step over the bounds of what is acceptable. They sometimes become the victim of it, like André Debrycke who in July 1975 experienced the same dramatic collapse Merckx did during the Tour stage to Pra-Loup. Debrycke, then 59, was no longer able to control his emotions and burst into tears and slumped to the ground: he had died of a cardiac vein rupture.

The elderly Mrs. Lauwerijs from Hekelgem was also in a very bad way during that same Tour. When she watched Merckx being destroyed on her television she, too, became unwell. An urgently summoned doctor brought her back to her senses with sedatives, but she was ordered not to watch the Tour again on the television. Over the next few days Mrs. Lauwerijs turned her chair around and sat with her back it, listening to the commentary only. Mrs. Annie Moreels from Limburg wrote to *Het Nieuwsblad* — which in 1975 was giving its readers the chance to air their views on Merckx — to tell them that she could only get her three-year-old toddler into the bath if she promised to let him put on his little Eddy Merckx jersey afterward.

A priest, Albert Heinkens, also had a thing about Eddy Merckx. The pastor from Maria-Aalter made a habit at that time of referring to the performances of Merckx from the pulpit, regularly holding him up as an example. When Merckx's career was on the decline, Father Heinkens preached: "Dear parishioners, Eddy Merckx is a great man in victory, and he is also a great man in defeat."

▽ *The loyalty of the Heleven family was unconditional. Wherever Merckx rode in Belgium, the nine-strong clan was there, along with the babies' bottles and diapers. In the photographs, from left to right: Ingrid, Eddy, Ronny, Marc (at back), Kathleen, Myriam and Patrick together with mum and dad show off a yellow jersey from Merckx's Tour victory in 1971, kept in a glass frame. Maurice and Cécile Heleven also assembled an impressive photo collection, spread over something like 45 albums.*

Eddy after he had changed into his clothes."

"What has always impressed me about Eddy is how uncomplicated he and his family are," says Cécile Heleven. "He has never changed and has never forgotten his roots. We got on well with Claudine, too. In July, when Eddy was hard at it in the Tour, we used to invite her to come and spend a day with us in an apartment at the seaside. While there, she would cook a meal for the whole bunch of us. During the season, she always let us know what Eddy's riding schedule was, especially when any amendments were made to it. In all humility, I would go as far as to say that we became confidants of the Merckxes. Many people have come and asked us if we could arrange something with Merckx, like finding out if he would be available to make an appearance at a golden wedding anniversary party, or a school party or an opening. We never took it any further for them, as we are not opportunists. We didn't become supporters of Eddy to make ourselves feel important. Many people who live near us think that Eddy is the godparent of one of our children, but that is not the case, and we never asked Eddy to be one. We put our hearts into being supporters, particularly when we discovered what fine, warm people the Merckxes were."

1970

No More Snow

△ *Merckx sets the tempo on a climb in the 1970 Tour.*
A handful of rivals are able to hang on (for the time being).

Team	Faemino-Faema
Directeurs sportifs	Guillaume Driessens (Bel), Mario Vigna (Ita)
Teammates	Etienne Antheunis (Bel), Joseph Bruyere (Bel), Pietro Campagnari (Ita), Julien De Locht (Bel), Francesco Desajmonet (Ita), Pietro Di Caterina (Ita), Lino Farisato (Ita), Fernand Hermie (Bel), Joseph Huysmans (Bel), Roger Kindt (Bel), Frans Mintjens (Bel), Willy Monty (Bel), Adelio Re (Ita), Pietro Scandelli (Ita), Willy Scheers (Bel), Joseph Spruyt (Bel), Julien Stevens (Bel), Roger Swerts (Bel), Georges Vandenberghe (Bel), Arthur Vande Vijver (Bel), Victor Van Schil (Bel), Italo Zilioli (Ita).
Number of Races	138
Number of Victories	52

Major Stage Races		
Tour de France		1st
• Points classification		2nd
• Mountain classification		1st
• Stage victories		8
Tour of Italy		1st

Major One-Day Races	
World Championship	29th
Belgian Championship	1st
Milan-San Remo	8th
Tour of Flanders	3rd
Paris-Roubaix	1st
Liège-Bastogne-Liège	3rd
Amstel Gold Race	8th
Tour of Lombardy	4th
Het Volk	7th
Ghent-Wevelgem	1st
Flèche-Wallonne	1st
Paris-Tours	-
Paris-Brussels	-

Other victories	Paris-Nice, Tour of Belgium, Coppa Agostoni, Montjuich Hill Climb, Critérium International, Super Prestige Pernod...

"In 1970, my sharpness was no longer there, strange as that may sound looking at my results. But the snap of before had gone. That was entirely due to my crash in September 1969 on the track at Blois. It was no longer possible for me to achieve my previous level of consistency, and my success rate started to decrease. I was still able to dominate, but no longer in the same emphatic way. The one exception was Paris-Roubaix when it felt like old times that day. But climbing, especially, was no longer the waltz it had been to me before.

"That season, I made the mistake of failing to really properly tackle the effects of my fall in Blois. At the start of the season, I was like a madman trying to adjust my saddle all the time to ease my back pain, I messed around with pedals and experimented with frames, but what I failed to do was to bring in any osteopaths or physiotherapists. In those days, it would have been unusual to have done so. Luckily, before the Tour, I had the opportunity to thoroughly familiarize myself with the mountains, thanks to the contract I had with RTL (Radio-Télé Luxembourg) for that purpose. It was enough to give me sufficient climbing rhythm to be able to impose my will on the Tour.

"In 1970, I also won the Belgian road championship for the first and last time as a professional. I found the course in Yvoir to be just testing enough to make the difference in my favor. The fact that it depended on the course was another indication of how things had changed from how they used to be, because at one time I could have bossed races on any kind of terrain. From 1970 onward, however, I had to rely on races sapping enough energy out of others so that I could beat them as a result of my superior condition. That's the reason why I found it was getting harder and harder to win events such as shorter stage races. Blois 1969 may have had a dramatic effect on me, but I am still grateful that my career, or my life even, did not come to an end there and then."

CHAPTER SEVEN

The Cub

*"Hidden inside every real man is a child
who wants to come out and play."*
(Friedrich Nietzsche)

*"If they had awarded certificates for living
on the street, I would have passed
with a distinction."*
(Eddy Merckx)

It is impossible for anyone trying to discover another person's character to avoid digging up their past. We are all molded by our background and our upbringing, and that was no different for Eddy Merckx.

Jules Merckx, Eddy's father, who died of a heart attack in 1983 at the age of 63, was an inscrutable, edgy man with a complex character and an unbridled lust for work. "My father was nervous and introverted and someone who suffered with his stomach, characteristics which I have inherited to a greater or lesser degree," says Eddy. "My stomach won't stand very much either. I can't drink strong coffee without getting stomach cramps. My father was a man of few words. His life consisted of work, work and more work. I sometimes wonder how he kept going all those years. In the morning, he had to go into Brussels for the early-morning market to buy fruit and vegetables. He did this every day during the summer, and in the winter, he did it three or four times a week. The shop was open every day, even all day Saturday and Sunday morning. My father came from a family of 11 children and they were not very well-off. He was actually a trained cabinet-maker, and at home he did lots of jobs around the house. It was probably all of this working with the hands that I got my adjusting bikes from."

In the best post-war tradition, Jules Merckx was also a strict father. "Firm but fair," is how Eddy's mother more specifically puts it. "He possessed a great deal of wisdom, he knew about a person's soul and had a bit of the homespun philosopher about him. He thought about things a great deal."

"Yes," says Merckx. He used to use some of those sayings you remember for the rest of your life. About greed for example. 'The more things you have, the more things you want.' Or: 'In life, there will always be someone who is your superior.'"

EDOUARD LOUIS JOSEPH MERCKX

Edouard Louis Joseph Merckx was born in the village of Meenzel-Kiezegem on June 17, 1945, at 11 a.m. officially (although according to his mother it was at 11.45: 'Just before meal time, which explains my permanent hunger' says Eddy), the eldest child of Jules Merckx and his wife, Jenny Pittomvils. In August 1946, the Merckx family left the rural Meenzel-Kiezegem to move into a grocer's shop in the Place des Bouvreuils in Sint-Pieters-Woluwe, a suburb of Brussels.

On May 23, 1949 Eddy was presented with a brother and a sister in one go when the twins Michel and Micheline were born.

The little Eddy Merckx was sent first of all to the municipal nursery school on the Chasse Royal in Oudergem. Staying in the same commune, he went on to elementary school, which he always went to on his bike. At the junior school in Etterbeek, he followed a course in Latin for the first three years, after which he switched to modern humanities (in the option known as academic A). He tried every possible sport and joined the juniors of the White Star soccer club (a team which later merged with Racing Brussels to form Racing White), for whom he usually operated as an inside forward. Over time, however, he became increasingly interested in cycling. In 1961, he rode his first official race in the debutant category. The 13th race he took part in, at Klein-Edingen on October 1, was the first one he won. At the beginning of 1962, he won four of the first five races he rode in and during the Easter holidays that year, he decided to leave school and devote all his time and energy to cycling.

◁ *Edouard Louis Joseph Merckx was king of the street before becoming king of the peloton.*

STALE CHEESE

Eddy Merckx is a product of an old-fashioned, conformist and authoritarian upbringing that was the generally accepted norm until the 1960s brought about a moral revolution. In the '50s, there was little room for dialogue, rebellion or openness in the relationship between parents and children, and punishment and a sense of guilt were important instruments for keeping offspring in check. "I got a lot clips round the ear," remembers Merckx vividly, though immediately adding: "They were well-deserved, because I was a fairly naughty boy who didn't know what to do with his energy."

In those years of recovery after World War II, 'good' and 'bad' were clearly differentiated. The cinema was still forbidden territory for youngsters – because all you can do there is pick up germs – was Jules Merckx dictate. Leaving something on your plate at meal times was regarded as a deadly sin. "You ate without grumbling about what came out of the pot," says Merckx. "If you left anything on your plate at lunchtime, you were sure to find it on your plate again at teatime."

Forbidden fruit, of course, was a great source of attraction, and it was great to 'commit a sin' (sneakily) for the sake of it. A classic case of silent rebellion in those days was smoking on the sly. "Those forbidden cigarettes were great," says Merckx. "The brand we smoked most was Zemir. On one occasion, I must have inhaled a little too much, because I started to feel a bit woozy. When my father came home he saw right away what had been going on. He took me to stand in front of the mirror. 'Take a look,' he said. 'Can you see it? You look as white as a piece of stale cheese.' Before I had chance to say anything back, I got such a whack on the head that my ears are still whistling from it."

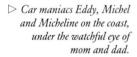

▷ *Car maniacs Eddy, Michel and Micheline on the coast, under the watchful eye of mom and dad.*

■ RED QUIFF

If Jules Merckx was the embodiment of the strict, fair and all-knowing father figure, then Jenny Pittomvils – from whom Eddy inherited his brown eyes and long eyelashes – corresponds to the archetype of the warm, protective and understanding mother in whose arms it was easy to forget sadness and misery. She was the woman who doggedly held the purse strings together and who made sure that there was at least one warm meal on the table each day. With the instinct, the obliging nature and the dexterity that most women possessed at that time, she guarded over the peace of the household. Middle-class morality in those days dictated that everything had to appear to be 'peace and quiet' to the outside world, and the social fabric was held together by an enforced uniformity. Deviant behavior such as girls wearing short skirts, boys growing long hair or sporting a red quiff was social heresy. Answering to the norms of appearance and conduct was one of the iron rules of the '50s, and it was mothers who were the chief guardians of this rule.

It was the most unruly and rebellious individuals who came into conflict with this social harness most regularly, of course. And that was true of Merckx, too, even though it was manifested in an innocent way. He has had to wrestle for the rest of his life, however, with this internal conflict. And yet, as will be described later, this developed into one of the primary sources of mental energy during his cycling career.

△ *"What am I going to do with him?" despairs mother Merckx once more. (Photograph taken on June 17, 1951)*

The Brussels suburb of Vogelzang was not yet fully developed at the time of Merckx's youth, and the adjacent Europawijk village did not exist at that time. This hilly district to the south east of the city was a paradise for adventurous children. Nearby was a wood and a thicket, and there was wasteland in abundance. In the ponds of Woluwe they could fish for sticklebacks, frogs and tadpoles, while on the steep streets they could make wild descents on their bikes, their bogies or their mopeds.

Merckx was the king of the castle in this environment. "Eddy always wanted to be outside, on the street. That's the way he expended his energy," says his mother. "To Eddy, school soon became like a prison. Studying was frightening to him. If he did pick up a book at that time, he would usually go and read it by the dormer window. From there he could at least see what was happening down below in the street. I once called in the help of Madame Gaspard, a retired governess, to try and get Eddy to spend a little more of his time with his nose in a book. After a few weeks, though, she too was almost in a state of despair. 'Mrs. Merckx, he's gone back to studying in the tree,' was how she put it. Many was the time I said to my husband: 'Jules, what are we going to do about that boy? What's going to become of him?'"

1. Already armed, ready for the 'Wild West' life that was to come later.

2. Bon viveurs on the terrace of the Cheval Blanc Inn at the time of a county fair in 1950.

3. Flower parade in Vogelzang in 1954.

BEING SAVED FROM THE CRANE

As a child, Merckx was an energetic and enterprising little fellow. The street was his natural environment. "Once, when they were doing roadwork in our street, I climbed up the hoist arm of a crane, before letting myself down the cable and into the grabber," he says. "As I couldn't go back the way I had come, someone eventually had to come and get me out. No, they weren't particularly happy with that little adventure, I can tell you."

THE YOUNG LAD WHO SHAVED OFF ALL HIS HAIR

It is clear that Merckx soon developed his own will from the following anecdote. "It must have been when I was around seven or eight," says Eddy. "I had to go to the barber shop on the Chaussée de Wavre. I wanted to have my hair cut really short, but while I was still there I saw the results in the mirror and for some reason or other did not like what he had done, so I asked him to cut the rest of it off. I must have been inspired by the shaven-headed prisoners who worked in the area at the time, doing drainage work. At first, the barber ignored my request, but I kept insisting and refused to get out of the chair. In the end, he gave in. When I got home, my mother was scared out of her wits and she burst into tears. Needless to say, I got a clip around the ear from my father."

"I rang the barber and asked him what had got into him," Merckx's mother remembers. "But madam, he wouldn't leave until I shaved his head," the man said. What made it doubly bad was that it was Eddy's birthday and we were expecting some of his friends round that afternoon. It wasn't exactly the way you would have wanted him to look to welcome people."

7. Snapshot from a fully-blown 'artistic' photo session.

8. Standing intently by father Jules' Plymouth.

9. Merckx and his playmates in the garden of his parents' house.

10. A young Eddy on the Place des Bouvreuils setting the pace during the Vogelzang festival, in front of the Cheval Blanc Inn.

11. Anxious look, carefree childhood.

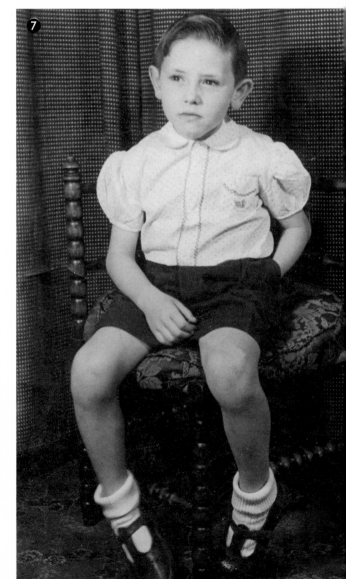

4. *Under siege for the first time, but certainly not the last.*

5. *Fun in the snow for the kids of Jules and Jenny Merckx.*

6. *Flower parade in Vogelzang in 1954 with sister Micheline and brother Michel. "I still remember Michel being mad because he had to play an injured person," Merckx laughs.*

A MEMORABLE BEATING

Merckx received one of his most memorable pastings after an afternoon fishing in one of the ponds in Woluwe Park. "I wanted to go and catch some tiddlers and tadpoles there with some friends," he remembers. "Two boys from across the road wanted to come along as well, but because they were a pair of troublemakers we said 'no.' After we had gone, the two of them took their revenge by going to my house to tell my parents they'd seen me in the company of a strange man. At first, my mum and dad didn't pay much attention. However, I got so involved in the fishing that I forgot to go back home by four o'clock as I had been told to. At home, they started to get very worried and the police were informed."

Earlier that day, in the nearby suburb of Oudergem, the police had arrested a weirdo — as he was referred to. And not too far away a blood-stained knife had been found.

"Unaware of all this, we returned home at around seven o'clock that evening," says Merckx, "pleased as punch, with our catch in a bowl. As we were coming out of the park someone shouted to me that I should get home as soon as I could because, I was told: 'Your parents are looking for you.'

I didn't know what was going on and was mystified when I saw a group of people hanging around in front of our shop. When I went indoors my father didn't need to say a great deal to let me know what was happening. He literally kicked me up the stairs. I still remember a woman in the shop shouting, horrified: 'But Mr. Merckx, really!' To which my father replied, in a loud voice: 'Madam, it's my family.'

"I was given an unbelievable beating. It was due to the shock my father needed to work out of his system. The worst thing about it was that I had to stay in my attic bedroom for the rest of the evening, while outside I could hear the other children playing. I really didn't think I'd deserved it."

■ No Bookworm

Merckx went through elementary school with the Marist brothers, and after that came three years of lower middle school (Latin) in the Athaeneum in Etterbeek. "I didn't like studying, and I was certainly no bookworm," says Merckx. "I needed to keep moving. Where we lived, I played basketball for hours on end. In the elementary school, I used to play a lot of football, too, and I later signed up with a team called White Star. The park in Woluwe was an ideal place to play, to mess around and to get up to no good. That was my life. I just needed to be outside. If there had been a certificate awarded for being on the streets, I would have passed with a distinction. And there would be loud applause on top of it. I also loved to play cards, mainly in our garden. 'Hunt the Heart' was my favorite. And at the Cheval Blanc Inn I often used to play tennis. There was a billiard table there, too, and I was drawn to it even though I didn't have the money to play on it very often. If I had to stay in my room and study, I could never concentrate. The noises of the street constantly distracted me. Yet if I found something to be exciting, I was a keen student. I got through my first two years of Latin without any problem. My memory was good and I didn't have any trouble with tenses or that sort of thing. But from the third year onward, we were given more complex Latin texts to translate and I had a lot of trouble with them. I was conned into having to retake a Latin exam. For me, that was a signal. I convinced my parents that I didn't need Latin, claiming as a reason that 'I didn't want to become a doctor or a chemist.' At the start of the 1960-1961 school year, I had to switch to the science course. That was a real setback, what with Maths and English as part of the course. Moreover, it was during that period that I started to go mad on bike riding, and my performances at school soon started to go rapidly downhill. By the end of the year, I was given a 'failed' mark in every subject. I had to retake the whole year. It was getting harder all the time for me to sit still on those school benches. It led to me having frequent clashes with the teachers. I know only too well how it feels to have a ruler come crashing down on my knuckles. At around that time, it was also becoming a foregone conclusion to my parents that I would end up taking a certificate in physical education."

At the time, it seemed to be the only honorable way to make the best of Merckx's energetic nature.

△ *Street urchins in a warm, safe environment.*

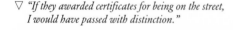
▽ *"If they awarded certificates for being on the street, I would have passed with distinction."*

△ *Merckx could never get too enthusiastic about school life. (photograph from his first year: Eddy is in the next to last desk in the middle row)*

NOT A CITY BOY

Merckx has already told us that his father lived to work. Underpinning that was the work ethic of the postwar years of rebuilding. No one questioned having to toil from morning till night and it was seen as a virtue. Anyone ducking out of it was stigmatized as a lazy good-for-nothing who would get their just desserts at a later date. Happiness came as a result of hard work, and he who didn't slave was not worthy of salvation.

"For my parents it was, of course, also a question of survival," thinks Merckx. "We weren't really well-off. I regularly had to help in the shop (although to set the record straight, his mother later tells me that it was difficult getting him away from the street). In the evenings, I had to stack shelves, or on Sunday morning I had to deliver bread rolls. During the holidays, I delivered the orders. I also went with my father on several occasions to the early market in Brussels. That always seemed like an expedition, because our involvement with the capital was very small really."

While on this subject, a misconception needs to be cleared up. It is often said that Merckx comes from Brussels. The fact that he spent his youth in the suburb of Sint-Pieters-Woluwe does not in any way signify that he was a city boy: quite the opposite. Although it was a residential community, it was hardly urbanized at all at that time, and it looked and felt more like a rural village than part of a bustling, urban capital city. The district around the Place des Bouvreuils was a community in which everyone knew everyone else, and in which anyone from further than five kilometers away was regarded as a foreigner. There were very few cars, and television had not yet acquired

▷ *The six-year-old lover of life giving the impression he was a bookworm.*

▽ *Visits to his grandparents in Meenzel-Kiezegem were special days. In the countryside a whole new world opened up for him.*

the power to tie people down to their homes. Anyone looking at their photograph albums from those days cannot help but get an attack of retro-romanticism. Prints from that time make one have sepia-tinted reminiscences of starched sheets, grazed knees, bread rolls on Sunday, waffle feasts, secret dens in bushes and the smell of duckweed and incense. "If I was to be allowed to carry on talking about my youth, we would probably still be here tomorrow," says Merckx, savoring, in his words, the bittersweet taste of bygone days.

ON THE SCHOOL TRIP

School trips were the absolute high spots of adventure, especially if they were to places in far-off lands. "In my case, the most exotic destination was Valkenburg in the Netherlands," laughs Merckx. "That was the only time I ever left Belgium. I remember that there was a huge big dipper there and I only had enough money for one ride, and it turned out to be a disaster, of course."

The wealthy, inexhaustible surrounds of Sint-Pieters-Woluwe were sometimes exchanged for the fantastic natural world on his grandmother's farm in Meenzel-Kiezegem, where he regularly went on a Sunday. "It was a large farm with cows, pigs, a horse and lots of outbuildings," says Merckx. "The work I did there was mainly in and around the stables, but I didn't mind it. At least I wasn't sitting there surrounded by the same four walls."

Merckx remembers that from his other grandmother, on his mother's side, he learned to knit. "I once managed to knit a piece the size of a towel," he says. "For reasons I'm still not sure of to this day, I called it my 'Cack'. It was a source of comfort to me, and I always took it to bed with me. When I used to announce that I went to bed with my cack, I got some funny looks from strangers."

The pinnacle of pleasure each year for Merckx were the summer holidays. It was then that the family headed off —without father Jules, who only allowed himself two days holiday a year — for a week in Blankenberge, a place which felt like it was at the other end of the world. "There was water and sand and lots of space," says Merckx. "In other words, it was a heaven on earth. Later on, when I became obsessed by bike riding, I was allowed to go and train there on the local track. What more could anyone wish for?"

▽ *Blankenberge, a heaven on earth every year. There is no mistaking the family tendency to put on a bit of weight. (Eddy is 12 years old here)*

'YOUR BACKSIDE IS MUCH TOO FAT'

One of the relatively more inexplicable elements in Merckx's young life was his love of the bike. There was nothing unusual in him learning to ride a two-wheeler, as that is what nearly every toddler got from his parents when he reached a certain age. What was more remarkable was the fact that he became so mesmerized by racing bikes. No objective explanation can be found for this. There was never any member of the family who was fanatical about some cycling idol or other to encourage him to go into it, and there were no cycling magazines lying around at home. The rather elitist Sint-Pieters-Woluwe was not in the slightest bit cycling-minded, the sport being considered by most of the population to be a preserve of ordinary people. There was actually one rider, Guillaume Michiels, whose mother and brother often helped out in the shop, and who Jules Merckx went to see ride on the odd rare occasion. Yet Michiels, who was later to become Eddy's confidant, never tried to get the youngster to take up the sport, and he says: "Quite the opposite is true. When Merckx was about

10 or 11, he said to me in deadly seriousness: 'I want to be a rider eventually, too.' I laughed in his face. 'Your backside is much too fat,' I said. 'In five years time, you won't even be able to get through the shop door.' Years later, when he was selected for the Olympic Games in Tokyo in 1964, Merckx suddenly raked that up again. 'Do you know what,' he then said. 'My backside was too fat then, but now I can go to the Olympic Games.' It had already become apparent that you are well-advised not to challenge Eddy Merckx."

CYCLING IS NOT A JOB

Merckx, alert and restless as a youngster, discovered the bike in the same way as he found out about basketball, soccer, tennis and several other sports: on the street. For some reason or another, however, it was cycling which provided him with the most attractive way of expending his excess energy.

"At junior school, I was asked on several occasions what I later wanted to be," says Merckx. "I always answered as though it was obvious: 'cyclist'. The teacher would then reply: 'But that's not a job.' I played soccer for White Star, I played basketball with the young kids and I played tennis. But I could not get cycling out of my head, though I wouldn't be able to give you an explanation why, right away."

In a presumptuous attempt at psychoanalysis, one might adduce that the young Merckx was able to throw off the straitjacket of his strict upbringing on his bike, and that it was only when sitting on the saddle that he could sample the complete freedom which he found so hard to achieve in normal life. Must there, however, always be an explanation for each step that anyone takes? What determines one's destiny? Is it a convergence of circumstances, a coincidence or a plan? Why does someone become a concert pianist, while someone else spends their whole life fascinated by gorillas? What was driving Thomas Edison to find it so necessary to discover the light bulb? Why did Merckx want to become a cyclist, whatever it took? In the final, chapter we will try to find an answer to that question.

'ATOM BOMB'

"When I was four years old, I had a little bike with thick tires," says Merckx. "I went on the craziest little rides near where I lived. Strangely enough, people used to shout to me: 'Are you riding the Tour de France, laddie?' The local nursery school I went to was in Oudergem, on the 'Chasse Royal', close to the main road to Wavre. Next to the school there was a candy shop which sold the famous 'atom bomb', a round lollipop which tasted better than anything else in the world. With one franc in my pocket, I once made my own way there on my thick-tired bike. In my parents' shop, we had as many candies as we could wish for, but none of them compared to the atom bomb, of course. Hence my expedition, which was not without its own dangers. The road to Wavre was busy with cars, and there was also a tram track. Once having negotiated all the traffic, however, I got to buy the wonder lollipop."

"One other time I was sent flying on that bike," Merckx continues. "My mother was out walking my younger twin brother and sister, Michel and Micheline, in the push chair. I must have been about five at the time and I went with them on my bike. When a moped came riding by, I tried to follow and overtake it. But suddenly my chain slipped and I could no longer keep up with him. I went flying over the handlebars and landed right on my face, which ended up covered in blood. I still remember swooning and thinking: I've just died."

Later, Merckx always used to go to school on his bike ("The journey back was tough, with the steep climb of the Avenue du Kouter being the first thing you came up against") and he regularly raced in his neighborhood against his friends ("The first one to that lamp post, that the sort of thing"). With the skill he had inherited from his father, the young Merckx knocked together a bogie. He spent much of his time taking his bike to pieces (when he was eight he got his first second-hand racing bike) or giving the frame a new coat of paint.

△ The Tour de France on fat tires.

From the age of 12, his interest in news about cycling grew noticeably. "I didn't actually know very much about the classics," Merckx admits. "They were ridden on a Sunday and that was the day I was usually at my grandmother's in Meenzel-Kiezegem. The Tour de France, however, came during the summer holidays and we could listen at home on Radio Luxembourg to the live commentary. I also followed it on the radio when we were away in Blankenberge. We were most interested in the performances of the Belgian riders, of course. The one who I particularly looked out for was Stan Ockers."

▽ At the age of 12, Merckx rode a number of unsanctioned races such as this one in Meenzel-Kiezegem. "I was dropped in that one, I remember it well," says Merckx.

"In 1956, when Eddy was 11, Ockers was killed in tragic circumstances," says his mother. "I was afraid to tell Eddy, as he admired Ockers so much. When he did eventually find out, he had a good weep." Merckx confirms this: "Yes, I really was devastated when a friend broke the news to me on the way to school."

■ THE CURSED ESSAY

When Merckx started out retaking the third year of the science 'A' course in September 1961, it seems he had already decided that he was going to see out his time at school. In the exams that Christmas, he even got marks of 75 percent. "Then a different French teacher took over, and it wasn't long before we didn't see eye to eye," he remembers. "We all had to do an essay for him, but I kept putting off doing mine. (Merckx has trouble trying to remember what the subject of this cursed essay might have been.) I also used to stay off school on a Tuesday afternoon, with a letter of permission from my parents, so that I could ride medal races on the track in Brussels. Nothing came of that essay, and on the day before the Easter holidays I was hauled in front of the headmaster to be given a real roasting. 'What's this bike racing all about?' he raged. 'Do you think that will get you anywhere in life? And what's happened to your essay?' He carried on like that. I could forget any plans to return to school after the holidays if I didn't have that essay in my satchel. I thought: 'What a disaster this is', because I still hadn't written a single word of it."

It was at that point that Merckx decided to put everything he had into cycling. In the debutant class, he had already won quite a few races and he believed in what he was doing. But his parents were likely to be the formidable obstacle that he would have to get past. "Circumstances went in my favor somewhat," he says. "At around that time my mother needed an operation and that gave me the perfect reason for volunteering to work in the shop. It also provided an excuse to give school to explain why I would have to give up my studies. The headmaster still tried to persuade my parents otherwise – they were even prepared to let me postpone my exams until September – but it didn't do any good. The battle was won, I was going to become a cyclist."

◁ *His victory on July 15, 1962 in the national debutants championship at Libramont removed any last resistance his parents had toward his choice of profession.*

HOW DO YOU WIN OVER YOUR MOM AND DAD?

You are 16 years old and you are the oldest son of hard-working shop-keepers who don't have the time to worry about something like cycling. You are having to take your first year at secondary school again, and you tell your parents that the school can go to hell as far as you're concerned because you want to become a cyclist. In such a situation, you can hardly expect your mother and father to break out into enthusiastic applause. And that is what Eddy Merckx discovered during the Easter holidays in 1962.

In his mission to persuade them, the young Eddy intuitively went about it in the most proper way possible. First of all, he sweet-talked his mother. After that the paternal fortress, which was also displaying serious cracks — Jules could hardly hide his fatherly pride when Merckx won his first races — would then automatically capitulate.

Mother was indeed not very happy at the decision of her headstrong son to give up school. "In the months leading up to it, I cried a lot because I was afraid that Eddy was taking the wrong road by going with cycling," she says. "Every mother wants her child to have a decent future, and what did cycling really have to offer?

"During the Easter holiday, Eddy came and asked me: 'Mom, would you

really not be able to take it if I packed in school?' I answered with a question: 'Would you be really unhappy not racing your bike?' I wanted to know. Eddy said that his heart was no longer in school, and that he would really love to become a cyclist. 'But if it makes you unhappy, I will stop cycling at once,' he said to me.

"I think it was his compliant attitude that broke down my last resistance. I asked him one more time if he really knew what he was getting into, if he was really convinced. 'There are thousands of racing cyclists, but only Van Looy and Van Steenbergen make decent money out of it,' I said, without knowing very much about the sport. Eddy confirmed, however, that there was nothing he would rather do than race his bike, so I gave him my blessing. 'Do it then, if you can't live without it,' I said, with pain in my heart. 'You'll get my full support. But don't blame us later for not making you continue your studies.'

'What about Dad,' asked Eddy, who I knew was going to be racing in Halle on May 1. So I said 'When you're in Halle, think about what we have said here today.' On the evening of May 1, Jules rang me from Halle. Eddy had won the race by almost four minutes. That's when I knew. When Eddy became Belgian debutant champion at Libramont on July 15, Jules's last resistance was broken, too."

1961-1965

◁ *Victory in the Flèche Halloise in 1963.*

World Title and almost Olympic Gold

Debutants: 1961

Number of Races	14
Number of Victories	1
Victories	First victory on October 1, 1961 at Lettelingen

Debutants: 1962

Number of Races	55
Number of Victories	23
Victories	Belgian national championship at Libramont...

Amateurs: 1963

Number of Races	72
Number of Victories	28
Victories	Tour of Limburg...

Amateurs: 1964

Number of Races	72
Number of Victories	24
Victories	Brussels-Opwijk, World Championship at Sallanches...

Amateurs: 1965

Number of Races	5
Number of Victories	4

Turned professional after this.

"I rode my first official race in the debutants category on July 17, 1961 in Laken, where I came sixth. There was certainly nothing stunning about my early races, and I had to wait until October 1 to chalk up my first victory, in Lettelingen.

"The early part of the following season gave me a headache because of my school obligations, but after the Easter holidays I made a firm decision to go for cycling. Things then progressed fairly quickly. In July, I became the national champion at Libramont. That removed any doubts my parents were still harboring.

"It would be wrong to think that I became an absolute high-flier as an amateur from 1963. I was a decent rider but there were certain lads, generally a little older than me, who could leave me standing. I continued to grow, however, and I made sure I never pushed myself too hard. During my time as an amateur, I didn't ride one single stage race outside Belgium. Félicien Vervaecke, my first race advisor, kept me in check.

"It was toward the end of 1964 that my first real breakthrough came, with my world title win in Sallanches. Shortly after that, I was selected for the Olympic Games in Tokyo and had hopes of becoming Olympic champion, too. There was a lack of communication in the Belgian team, however, during the closing stages of the race.

"That was when Van Buggenhout signed me up for the following season with the Solo team. That was where I was to find out all about, and soon get fed up with, Rik Van Looy."

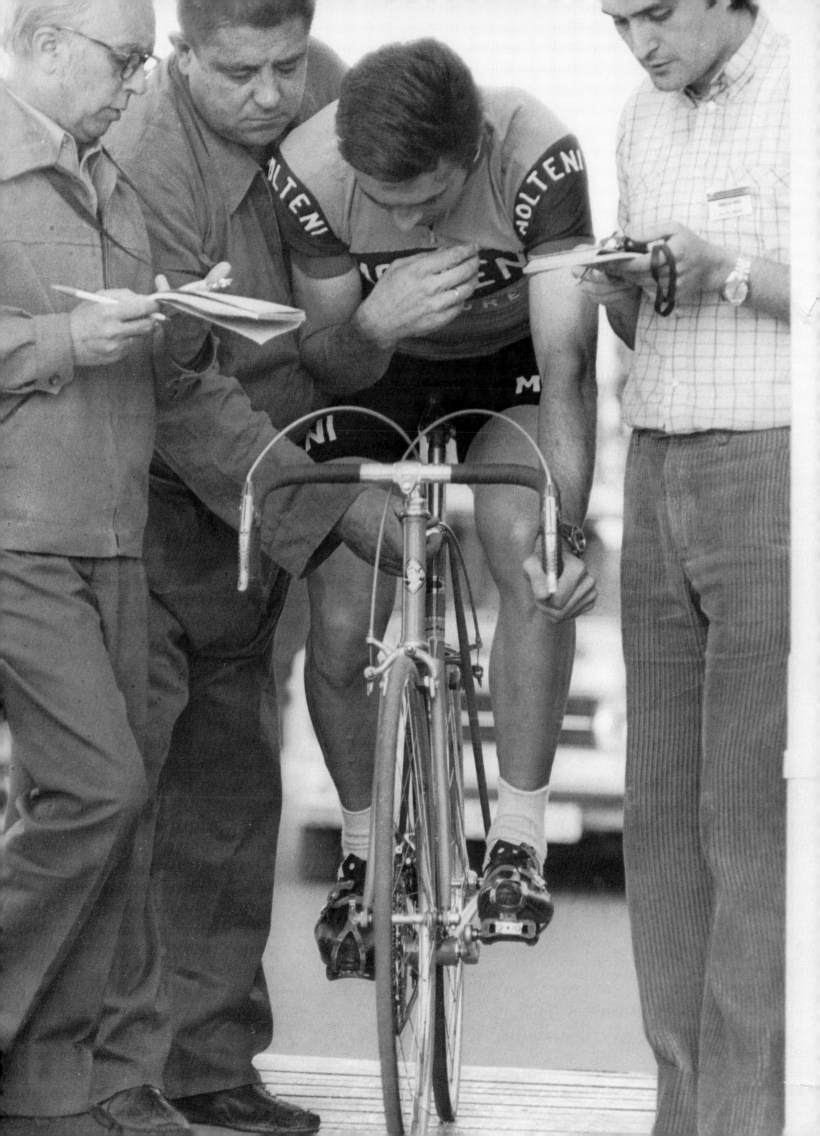

CHAPTER EIGHT

The Thinker

"To be fair unto others, one needs to be honest to oneself."

(Jean-Jacques Rousseau)

"Honesty is the best policy."

(Eddy Merckx)

'**H**e who lies deceives. And he who deceives, ends up in prison." This was one of the many precepts that penetrated into the soul of the young Eddy Merckx. Those wishing to learn more about Merckx cannot escape his Catholic upbringing. In the early post-war years, dogmas were still being firmly drummed in, and the boundary between good and bad was well-defined and indisputable. It was the era of the catechism, of the Ten Commandments, of the acts of repentance, belief and love, and of the profession of faith that was recognized as being eternal and always ("I believe in God the Almighty Father, Creator of heaven and earth, and in Jesus Christ..."). For some people this religious information went in one ear and out of the other, but in Merckx's case some of it stuck. The Catholic church valued highly such virtues as loving thy neighbor, forgiveness, virtue, respect, and this sense of responsibility that was crucial in determining the behavior of Merckx the rider. It was from these that he derived such principles as sportsmanship, integrity, loyalty and propriety.

◁ *Merckx: a life founded on rock-solid principles.*
(Merckx crosses himself before the start of the time trial during the Vuelta in 1973)

THE THEFT OF THE MOUSE GAME

There are few sins a young lad brought up a Roman Catholic can commit worse than stealing and lying. That was what the seven-year-old Eddy was to discover in his first year at school. "One day, I saw a game on the teacher's desk; it was a maze with a small mouse sitting in it," he tells us. "At a moment when it was unguarded, I grabbed this fascinating thing from the desk and put it in my trouser pocket. When I got home, my mother asked me where I had got it. 'Someone gave me it,' I said, with a face that gave away to anyone in the vicinity that I was lying. My mother knew at once. I had to come clean right away and admit that I had committed a sin."

"I was absolutely furious," says his mother, the memory still fresh. "That's the worst thing you could ever do, steal," I shouted at him. I took him straight back to the school on the Chaussée de Wavre. With tears of rage pouring down my face, I explained to the headmistress what had happened. She calmed me and said: 'Don't worry, after all it's only a game.' To which I said: 'But this is a question of principle.'

From that day, Merckx has been only too aware of it, and he was careful to make sure he passed on the principle to his own children — successfully it would seem. "I lied once myself, too"," says Axel Merckx. "It was about something really trivial, I can't even remember what it was now. But my father thought what I had done was very, very bad. All those scruples frightened me to death. Since then, I have never lied again."

And without being prompted further, Axel adds: "My father made something very clear to me at that time: you have to listen to what you're told, and learn something from it. It's all to do with having respect for your parents, for their experience, and for their wisdom."

THE MEETING WITH POPE PAUL VI

"In May, Mary's month, we went to pray every evening at the image of Our Lady in our street," say Merckx. The weekly visit to the church was never questioned and was part of the social pattern. Merckx's mother remembers that her energetic toddler at first found it a hellish test because he was forced to sit still. "As Eddy grew older, he became more serious and was always very well-behaved during the church service," she says.

Merckx never made a show of his belief, but he never dispensed with it entirely. "In 1963, I rode a few races with Merckx in East Germany," says Roger Swerts. "They were at Dresden and Sepnich. I still remember on the Sunday in that one-horse-town the way Eddy moved heaven and earth to be somewhere near a church. Nothing was going to stop him attending the mass."

When he turned professional, it became almost impossible for him to continue to carry out his religious duties on a Sunday. "Yet for a long time I quibbled about it," laughs Merckx. "In 1965, my first year as a professional, I had to take part in the Grand Prix Parisien, a team time trial over 125 km. It started quite early, meaning that on that particular morning I went to mass at seven o'clock."

Swerts was also present in 1970 when the Molteni team, with its leader, Merckx, visited Pope Paul VI. "For Merckx, that was a very moving experience," witnesses Swerts.

"It did indeed make a great impression on me," says Merckx. "To me, it was totally different to a reception before the King, for example. At the time I was very religious, and I still am, for that matter. It's just that doubts have been cast on my faith in the church, as I believe we have been taken for fools for too long."

Merckx stresses that his show of faith was not a motivation, as it may have been for other stars. "Before every race I crossed myself, not to be in God's good books, nor to improve my chances of winning," (he says laughing), "but simply because I believed in God."

△ *During the Giro in 1970, Merckx had an audience with Pope Paul VI. "It made a deep impression on Eddy," remembers Roger Swerts.*

'I WANT TO BE ABLE TO LOOK MYSELF IN THE MIRROR'

As it happens, Merckx has trouble with the word 'God'. "It's a name for something that's impossible to grasp." he says. "I believe in a great principle that is directing the world, but beyond that I have no questions. I do derive a few values that are important to me from my belief. Materialism is definitely not one of them. Attaining wealth should certainly not be the main aim in life. People will say: it's easy for that Merckx to talk, with all his millions. What I am talking about, though, is a mentality – greed especially – which has affected more and more people in recent years.

◁ *"I am very religious, but that has never been my motivation." (Merckx takes time out for prayer before the start of a Tour stage)*

Shopping for example, the acquisition of goods does nothing for me, I even try to avoid it. Throughout my career, I never knew much about money. My wife looked after all that. Even now, I try not to have much to do with money matters. Shares and debentures leave me cold. I'm just not interested in it. That's because I'm convinced that there are things that are more important. Peace of mind, for example, is one of them. I want to be able to look myself in the mirror. And that can only happen if I think that what I do is proper, honest and fair. I need to know I am doing good things."

"I am certainly not a philosopher," Merckx still says. "But I know that religions must exist, otherwise society will explode. People must have a mutual belief, and they need to more or less stand behind the same values. If they don't, you'll end up with anarchy."

■ HONESTY IS THE BEST POLICY

As we pointed out at the beginning of this chapter, Merckx needed to have a clear conscience. It was one of the most important principles he retained throughout his upbringing. This could only happen if you were righteous, honest and fair. Merckx says that this is his greatest property. "I always try to do the decent thing," he says. "I am as straight as I can be and want to be honest. I couldn't bear it if I couldn't look someone in the eye. Honesty is the best policy. That's also true in cycling, in the business world, everywhere. I don't believe in deceit, swindling or dirty tricks.

THE POWER OF NEW SOCKS

Merckx not only had religious belief, but he was also superstitious. "It never reached an unhealthy level," he says. "In 1963, I won the Tour of Limburg as a member of the provincial team. After that, I always wore my provincial team jersey whenever I was riding an amateur race. After turning pro, I developed another custom that has something to do with superstition. I always wanted to start each classic with new equipment: new jersey, new race shorts and new socks. It made you feel as though you were starting out every race from scratch."

▷ *Roger De Vlaeminck: "You never sprinted dirtily against someone like Merckx." (De Vlaeminck and Merckx side by side in the 1969 Tour on the climb of the Kloosterstraat in Geraardsbergen)*

THE SPRINT IN EEKLO

The principle of righteousness is so deeply ingrained in Merckx that he has no trouble at all remembering every occasion he erred. In Chapter Three, we discussed his misplaced anger at the top of the Tourmalet when he prevented his own teammate, Martin Van den Bossche, winning. But he did a bad thing on one other occasion, he admits. "It was in 1975, in Eeklo," he remembers. "It was a criterium. I am still sorry about what happened that day. During the final sprint I clearly strayed from my line, knocking Godefroot to one side. Afterward, I apologized to him, but it was too late to do any good. I just shouldn't have done it in the first place."

On this subject, the testimony of Roger De Vlaeminck is significant. "During sprinting I thought nothing of using a shoulder or elbow to hold off an opponent," he admits. "When Merckx was sprinting alongside me I never did, though, because I knew he was a fair sprinter."

Those who want to achieve something in life must work for it. A deceitful person will perhaps achieve success in the short term, but in the long run he gets into a hole. You can deceive someone once, but not 10 times. Being able to sleep at night is precious to me. I don't want to go to bed thinking: 'How many people have I deceived today.' And I don't want to get up thinking: 'How many will I deceive today.' I have a clear conscience."

"Eddy has a heart of gold, but he will not tolerate wrongdoing," says his mother. "He cannot stand injustice. Rather like me, for that matter."

It is just as well he is, because otherwise his career might have taken a completely different course. Jenny Pittomvils dishes up an unlikely story from 1964. The board of selectors of the Belgian Cycling Federation tried to leave Merckx out of the team for the Olympic Games in Tokyo and for the world championships in Sallanches.

THE FALSE ELECTRO-CARDIOGRAM

"The squad was called together for a training camp on the coast," Mrs. Merckx tells us. "On the way there, they had to stop off and take a medical in Ghent. Afterward, Eddy came back home dejected. 'Bad news,' he said. 'I'm not in the team because they've discovered something wrong with my heart.' This amazed me, because our own doctor, Dr. Fesler, had never mentioned anything of that nature. 'Eddy's got his father's strong heart,' he would always say. I had my suspicions about all of this, but I didn't let Eddy notice. A few days later, he fell badly and damaged his elbow. I told him to go and see Dr. Fesler to have it looked at. When he was on his way to the surgery, I rang the doctor to inform him of this strange result from the medical in Ghent. He was astonished by it, too, and promised me he would examine Eddy. When he couldn't find anything abnormal about his heart, Eddy was extremely happy. I contacted Oscar Daemers who was responsible for the Belgian team and asked what this heart problem would mean. Daemers claimed that an electrocardiogram had brought to light irregularities in the rhythm of Eddy's heartbeat. 'Our own doctor hasn't found anything unusual,' I added. 'Your doctor must be a quack, then,' replied Daemers, claiming that out of a misplaced sense of motherly pride I was refusing to see the reality staring me in the face. I swore that the health of my son was sacred to me. 'You're putting your son on a pedestal,' Daemers said. 'He might have won one or two minor races, but he won't be able to ride in more demanding ones. And he is certainly no climber. He can't even climb a mole hill.'

"Daemers almost talked me into believing him and giving in. Then he let something slip with a careless remark. 'Anyway, we can probably still do something for him. I'll get him selected for the 100km team time trial,' he said. Now I didn't know that much about cycling, but I realized that there was something not right about this. The team time trial is one of the most difficult disciplines it's possible for a young rider to do. If Daemers was intending to select Eddy for this event, there certainly couldn't have been anything wrong with his heart. By his sudden concession, Daemers had indirectly admitted it. I told him so, too. 'You stubborn old woman,' he roared, and brought our talk to an abrupt close. I rang Dr. Fesler again to ask him if he wanted to speak to Dr. Marlier, the man who had examined Eddy in Ghent. Fesler demanded a new examination, at which he was to be present. Dr. Marlier owned up right away and informed Dr. Fesler that he had been under instructions from Daemers to make out a negative report. When he told me that, I threatened to lodge a complaint with the Order of Physicians. Eddy, who was unaware of any of this, was immediately summoned to take another medical in Ghent. This time it miraculously transpired that his heart was in perfect working order again. Eddy was as pleased as punch, of

△ It was Merckx's mother's fight against injustice that made sure of Eddy's place in the Belgian amateur team for the world championships in 1964.

▽ After his struggle to be selected in 1964, and in spite of an alleged heart problem, Merckx won a resounding first world title in Sallanches.

course, but I was still not happy. I wanted him to be allowed to ride in the road race and not to have to take part in the grueling team time trial. I hardly knew anyone involved in the sport, but I had heard the name Jean Van Buggenhout being mentioned on a number of occasions. I rang him up and told him the whole story. He would see what he could do, he promised. He then managed to persuade members of the federation's selection committee to choose Eddy for the world road race championship and for the Olympic road race."

What happened next is history. In Sallanches, where he would never have been riding without the efforts of his mother, Merckx won the world championship. "I'll never forget it," says Mrs. Merckx. "The first telegram we received after Sallanches was from Oscar Daemers. 'Congratulations, Mrs. Merckx. Fortunately we took your advice,' it said. I nearly fell through the floor."

How would Merckx's career have progressed without the behind-the-scenes work his mother did on his behalf? That question remains unanswered. But in any event, history has left Merckx – who was later informed of the full facts – with an enormous sense of indebtedness to his mother. Who knows, perhaps that was one of the great motivations of his career.

DUST AND ASH

He who believes is humble. That, too, was made clear to Merckx at an early age. Next to God you are a mere worm. Everything and everyone eventually turns into dust and ash. That realization inevitably leads to modesty. Notice that when Merckx crossed the finishing line or was standing on the podium, he never made any degrading gestures, thumped the air with his fist, or let out any primal screams. After his world amateur championship victory at Sallanches, the success was not allowed to go to his head. "A few days after his victory, I asked Eddy to help with some housework," says Mrs. Merckx. 'Who, me?' The world champion?' he said, half in jest and half seriously. 'Out there you might be the world champion,' I said, pointing outside. 'But here at home you're worth the same as Michel and Micheline, no more and no less."

Throughout his entire career, Merckx was tempted to 'sin', but he never gave in to it. The more he came to dominate, the less he wanted to profit from his position, because that would have meant rejecting some of his sacred principles – in other words, committing a sin. And that would have triggered off the scruple mechanism, a very real part of the religious doctrine of the Catholic church. Sports journalist Joris Jacobs provides a telling example of this.

"At the beginning of the 1967 Tour of Italy, I made an appointment with Merckx to interview him during the rest day," says Jacobs. "By chance, we were staying in the same hotel that day, which was a good thing. ' I'll have plenty of time after breakfast,'

Merckx had promised me. When the day arrived, we were both sitting at our breakfast tables when, suddenly, I saw journalists from a rival weekly newspaper approaching Merckx. After a little while, they all left the dining room together. I waited awhile, but there was no sign of him. I went outside and what did I see: Merckx sitting in the garden with 'the opposition.' I went over to him and asked him if he had forgotten our appointment. 'I'll wait inside for two more minutes,' I said, enraged. A little later, Merckx came in to offer me an explanation. 'I made an agreement with that paper to give my impressions on a daily basis,' he said. He must have been getting thousands of francs for it. Having to give way to them had made me pretty angry. I said to Merckx: 'Look, you're still young and maybe you don't understand it yet, but to me if a man gives me his word he should stick to it. I'm not in the mood to do that interview now, anyway.' And I left it at that. When I contacted my editorial office that night, I was told that Claudine Merckx had rung them earlier to apologize for Eddy's behavior. Merckx had wanted to make sure that the matter was put right. That's typical of him. Others wouldn't have given a damn about it."

THE WEDDING LIST

Merckx's lack of pretension can be seen from the wedding list he and his bride-to-be, Claudine Acou, drew up at the end of 1967 in a Brussels department store. "Included on it were: a siphon at BF 2,000, cutlery BF 1,250, a soup tureen and accessories BF 1,000, a toaster BF 1,325, a casserole BF 425, a toast rack BF 440, a coffee mill BF 995, and a service BF 450." (a total of about $250)

(From *Het Nieuwsblad*, December 5, 1967)

PROTEST CULTURE, NARCISSISM AND YUPPIEDOM

The scruples model of the Catholic religion was echoed in the code of conduct of the *petit bourgeoisie* at that time. Much of what one did and, to an even greater extent, much of what one abstained from was for the sake of appearances: one had to be continually conscious of the fact that society had expectations and made judgments about you. It was best that one lived like that. Merckx was part of this so-called silent generation from the period of postwar reconstruction. There was no sort of protest culture of the 60s, narcissism of the 70s or yuppie greed of the 80s. As grocery shopkeepers, Merckx's parents must have had to behave in an exemplary manner.

▽ *No one can say that his conduct was negative. Even after his struggle up Alpe d'Huez during the Tour in 1977.*

DOLF

For fear of what people might think, one omits offensive or insulting language. The story of Roger "Dolf" Swerts is a fine example of where this has had to be done. "At the beginning of 1968, the team was holding a training camp in Reggio de Calabria," Swerts tells us. "To keep the atmosphere relaxed, we drank some champagne one particular evening. After a couple of glasses, I was three sheets to the wind. At that moment, a bus full of German tourists came into the hotel. I went and joined them and started singing German songs with them. That's where my nickname saw the light of day, and from then on I was known as 'Dolf' to my teammates. Merckx used to call me it, too, but only when we were alone. When there were any outsiders in the vicinity he would always call me Roger."

They must have had to conform to their customers' requirements. On top of that, Vogelzang, where he lived, was the sort of neighborhood where everyone's comings and goings were closely watched. The need to live up to expectations was forced home to Merckx at an early age, certainly not the sort of character trait you would expect from the confirmed individualist. He was scared to death of his behavior being seen in a negative light. Robert Janssens of the newspaper *Het Laatste Nieuws* gave us a telling example.

"In the 1977 Tour, Merckx was totally wiped out at the end of the stage to L'Alpe d'Huez, which had taken in the climbs of the Madeleine and the Glandon," says Janssens. "I saw Merckx in his hotel shortly after the stage finish and he looked awful, a wreck. He said he felt terrible, too, and that he'd had enough. He told me that he would be packing it in and that this was going to be his last season. The next morning, Merckx's soigneur, Jos Janssens, came to see me to tell me that Eddy wanted to talk to me. It was very unusual for Merckx to summon a journalist to him. 'I told you one or two things yesterday, about stopping and things like that,' he said. "Well, I've changed my mind since then. The reason I got such a pasting yesterday was that I was sick. I'll be back next year for the Tour, not just to ride it but to win it.' All of this, of course, was big news. Unfortunately, however, there was no paper the following day, July 21 (Belgian National Day), and the day after that Merckx repeated his intentions to my rivals from other branches of the media. Otherwise, I would have had a brilliant scoop. Returning to the point, what was obvious is that Merckx hadn't wanted me to spread false information about him on the basis of his first statement."

■ OVERSTEPPING THE MARK

His ethical sense of values inspired Merckx to be extremely sporting. "I'll never forget his gesture in the 1975 Tour de France," says Bernard Thévenet, winner of that year's event. "In the high mountains, I had put some time on Merckx, and I knew that I had nothing more to fear in the climbs. But Merckx was also extremely good on the descents, while that was something which I was pretty inept at. On every descent, he attacked. During the 17th stage, which finished at Morzine, I punctured at the top of the Col des Aravis. This might have been the signal for Merckx to turn up the heat and take back the yellow jersey. Instead, though, he stayed where he was and waited until I had returned to my place at the front. I take my hat off to him for having such a fine attitude."

Strangely, not only is Merckx unable to recall this incident, but he has this to say: "I would be amazed if that's what I actually did," he says. "Puncturing is all part of the game. Although I don't think you should profit from a crash, I think anyone who doesn't attack when an opponent has punctured is guilty of taking the principle of loving thy neighbor a little too far."

Merckx may well have tried to fight for correctness, but there were limits to his

△ *Because of his sportsmanship, Merckx's teammates were not allowed to give him a push. Even if there might have been exceptional circumstances...*

aspirations. He was prepared to overstep the mark, especially in a situation where his virtue turned out to be a serious handicap. "When I was riding for Peugeot, I more or less rode the Tour of Italy in the service of Merckx," says Roger Pingeon. "During the climb of Mount Etna, Eddy twice asked me to push him, so push him I did."

Merckx protests vehemently. "You should have seen the things that went on in Italy in those days," he roars. "I was 21 and riding my first major stage race, and I was being confronted with the most outrageous practices. The pushing went on as if it were going out of fashion. For kilometers on end, people were hanging on to the back of the team cars. It's quite likely that I got a push, too, but it was a rare exception. Later on, I always refused pushes. Just ask my teammates. They may have offered to give me a push, but I always refused them."

DE MUYNCK AND THE BANANA

The respectable upbringing Merckx received also determined the way he behaved toward his rivals. Usually, he spoke of them respectfully. His sporting mastery did not tempt Merckx into displaying unwarranted megalomania or condescension. "In the Tour one year, Merckx was totally dominant yet again," says Johan De Muynck. "But I didn't want to get dragged into the apathy of the rest of the peloton and I kept on attacking. Eventually, this was clearly starting to get on the nerves of Merckx's teammates. I had an altercation with Vic Van Schil, who stuffed a banana into my hand and said: 'Here, eat this banana and settle down a bit.' Merckx, who had spotted what was going on, intervened immediately and reprimanded Van Schil."

**JACQUES GODDET
AND THE CORTISONE ACCUSATION**

There was never a great deal of love lost between Jacques Goddet and Merckx. The former Tour de France chief did, of course, have enormous respect for Merckx as an athlete, but when the French cycling magazine *Vélo* asked Goddet what he considered to be the 10 greatest exploits during his time as the Tour organizer, Merckx did not even rate a mention. Or did he? Goddet did mention Luis Ocaña's foray in 1971 on the stage to Orcières-Merlette, when he put something like ten minutes into Merckx. "Ocaña would certainly have won that Tour had he not fallen during the descent of the Col de Menté," Goddet still maintains. If Merckx reads that, all hell will break loose.

One way of getting Merckx infuriated is to read him a passage from Goddet's book *L'Equipée Belle.* In it, he insinuates that Merckx may have used cortisone toward the end of his career. "I remember that Merckx put on a couple of kilos in weight when he retired," said Goddet in an interview with the magazine *Sport '90,* published on February 5,1992. "Not that cortisone was a banned substance in those days, it's just that the famous always have trouble coping with the first signs of decline. It is a very difficult time for many athletes, and it explains why so many of them look for artificial ways of seeing them through their problems."

Merckx is still absolutely incensed by Goddet's remarks. "When I won the Tour for the fourth time in a row, I can still remember the way the Tour organizers celebrated it with a forced sense of merriment," he says. "They had had enough of me, they were afraid that I might ruin everything for them. I think it is very small-minded of Goddet to attack me in such a way so many years later."

ANARCHY IN ITALY

Roger Pingeon confirms that there was anarchy in Italy at the end of the 60s. "In Italy, it was common practice for riders to organize pushing for their team leaders," says the 1967 Tour de France winner. "Teammate one pushed the leader from kilometer A to kilometer B, then the job was taken over by teammate two. And it carried on like that. Felice Gimondi was one of the few Italian stars who wanted nothing to do with it. That's probably another reason why Merckx has such respect for him. For Merckx, propriety embodied, constantly having to confront that sort of cheating must have been very frustrating."

It is typical of Merckx that he rarely made anything of that situation in public. That does not mean to say that he did not react to it, he did – but it was mostly with his legs. The worse the cheating, the more unrelenting his 'revenge'. "I would never want to resort to cheating as some sort of weapon," says Merckx. "Because if you do you're as bad as those you are criticizing."

When necessary, Merckx tried to see that justice was done. "In 1976, he rode a poor Giro," says Johan De Muynck, who was the race leader when teammates De Vlaeminck and Ronald De Witte headed home. "I was left stuck out there on my own. Merckx helped me out when that happened. Before the start of the penultimate stage, he warned me about the descent to the finish in Bergamo, the home town of Felice Gimondi, who was 25 seconds behind me. In one of the first bends of the descent I took a tumble, but Merckx waited for me and brought me back up to the front. It proved to be wasted effort because in the following time trial I lost my Pink Jersey to Gimondi by a very narrow margin. The final stage was an insignificant criterium in the streets of Milan. My situation was utterly hopeless, yet still Merckx spurred me on. At the start of the stage he kept saying, 'It's not over yet'. Unbelievable, that fire in him."

Merckx acknowledges helping De Muynck in that race. "I would have rather seen a Belgian win it than a foreigner," he says. "And certainly rather than an Italian. That was because I resented the Italians' unsportsmanlike behavior. The irregularities within the peloton went far too far. Yet everything illegal the Italians came up with was ignored."

PEDAL FIRST, TALK LATER

It was a waste of time trying to make 'arrangements' with Merckx. That is not to say he didn't have plenty of opportunity to profit from them. Merckx was usually close to where the 'winnings' were, where there was money to earn, where chances of victory could be converted into real money. Moreover, with his impressive and rapidly growing honors list, it was barely possible for Merckx to increase his market value any further by winning more races. 'Selling' races was all the more attractive.

Yet Merckx did not go in for it himself because he had moral objections to such practices.

"You can only negotiate with Merckx after you had earned his respect by using your legs," says Walter Godefroot. "Pedal first, talk later. He wanted nothing to do with combines and arranged results, however. Agreements were tacitly reached, they simply went with the job. By agreements I mean, of course, natural coalitions: the tacit agreement that in a leading group everyone does his share of the work to make the break succeed, and that the eventual winner puts in a bit of money in gratitude."

Roger De Vlaeminck sketches a similar picture. "If Merckx thought he could win, then he did everything he could to try and achieve it," he says. "Merckx never gave anything away. Everyone knew that. For the first five or six years of my career, we hardly had any contact with each other at all. Toward the end of his career we did start to negotiate with each other, but it wasn't for money. It was a question of giving and taking. We were all in the same boat and we all had a vested interest in getting ahead as quickly as possible. Take this from me anyway: real champions do buy the odd race, every now and then. But they don't sell them. Never."

Merckx swears to all and sundry that he never did any trading where the prize was victory. "I have never sold a race," he says, forcibly. "Yet I had plenty of chances to. You should hear how much Gimondi offered me to be allowed to win the world championship in Mendrisio in 1971 (Merckx and Gimondi having escaped on the last-but-one circuit). I came to an agreement on one occasion only, and the word agreement is something of an exaggeration. And still it went wrong, as it happens. It was in the 1972 edition of Ghent-Wevelgem. As we approached the final stages, there was a leading group of five: Gimondi and his teammate Houbrechts, me and my teammate Swerts, and Frans Verbeeck on his own. I was dead on the saddle and knew that I didn't stand a chance of winning. As far as I was concerned, I was happy if Gimondi won, as I was in no fit state to do anything about it. In the

▽ "Real champions may buy a race every now and then, but they certainly never sell them," says Roger De Vlaeminck. (Merckx and De Vlaeminck have a chat during the Circuit Het Volk in 1973.)

sprint, however, Gimondi was hindered by Verbeeck, who was disqualified, and as a result Swerts won the race."

This scenario is entirely at variance with the version given by Roger Swerts (see Chapter Three). According to Swerts, he was told by Merckx to guide Verbeeck to victory in return for services rendered by him in Milan-San Remo a few weeks earlier. Verbeeck is alleged to have left a gap open on the Poggio, which worked to Merckx's advantage. "Rubbish," is Merckx's response to that. "People are always looking for the most sensational explanations, but they forget to think of the most obvious ones. During the descent of the Poggio in 1972, all that happened was that Frans simply couldn't stay with me.

"That's all there is to it. Unfortunately, that's probably too unspectacular to be believed."

■ THE CART HORSE OF YVOIR

Roger De Vlaeminck, on the other hand, has let it be known that he occasionally gave races away. "When I look back on it now, I'm sorry I did," he says. "I would never do it nowadays. Merckx was right to want to win all the time. It didn't exactly make him the most popular man in the peloton, but at least you knew where you stood with him."

It does not always seem to have been so clear-cut between De Vlaeminck and Merckx. After the 1975 World Championship at Yvoir, there was a big row because, according to De Vlaeminck, Merckx had not kept his word. "All I wanted was to finally win the world championship," says De Vlaeminck. "I reached an agreement within the Belgian team. If I were to win, Merckx would get BF500,000 ($16,000), Van Impe BF250,000 ($8000) and the rest of them BF50,000 each. During the race Merckx — who had fallen — said that he was not feeling fit and that he would be riding in my service entirely. But he failed to close the gap opened by Hennie Kuiper with his late escape, and it was the Dutchmen who rode off to the title. I am still disappointed about it." Merckx's face goes a little red when he is reminded of this event. "It's true that I wasn't feeling 100 percent after my crash," he says. "I offered my services to De Vlaeminck, and during the toughest climb on the course he was hanging onto my shorts. I remember Gerrie Knetemann riding up to me and saying: 'Is that you, the great Merckx, the favorite, riding like a helper?' On the final circuit, Roger hung on to my shorts again. With all my working like a cart horse, I was completely worn out. It all left Roger to finish the job off, but he failed to do so. Immediately after the race, Roger was full of praise for the way I had worked for him. It was only on the following day that — driven to torment by it, no doubt — he suddenly pointed an accusing finger at me. I always felt that it was wrong of him to do that."

As a rule, you could only count on Merckx's support if it coincided with his own interests (in winning). "To a certain extent I have Merckx to thank for the green jersey I won in the Tour in 1974," says Patrick Sercu. "I won three stages and finished second five times. Merckx, however, had won eight stages as well as the prologue. In Besançon he led out the sprint for me, although it's likely that he didn't do it intentionally. For safety's sake, he made sure he was the first onto the track, and that gave me a great closing position. In doing something for his own benefit, then, he had indirectly worked for my benefit."

On the last stage, Sercu almost lost the green jersey. He was relegated from first place to third – and not, as is usually the case, to last – for hindering Staf Van Roosbrouck in a dangerous sprint. It left him with enough points, however, to stay just ahead of Merckx on the points classification.

■ NEVER AN EYE FOR AN EYE OR A TOOTH FOR A TOOTH

The way the outcome of the 1973 World Championship at Montjuich was settled was one of the biggest slaps in the face Merckx ever had to contend with (see Chapter Four). "I can still see him sitting in the Belgian team's equipment van like a beaten dog," sports journalist Robert Janssens remembers vividly. "Not a word crossed his lips. I swear to you that he sat there for at least half an hour with his head in his hands. I followed him to the doping control and he remained silent there, too. It wasn't the defeat that had made him so dejected – he had been beaten before. The reason he was so despondent this time was Freddy Maertens's dishonesty. That's what he couldn't understand. It was a good hour before he uttered his first words."

Claudine Merckx can recall how tense her husband was before the start of that particular world championship. "I was almost certain he was going to win that day," she says. "He was absolutely disgusted at Maertens's behavior."

It is remarkable that Merckx never talked of getting his revenge. It was a motive that never seems to have inspired his conduct during races. Again, that points to his great moral integrity. In the 1976 World Championship at Ostuni, for example, he worked to protect Maertens's escape, helping him win the title. "In such a situation, the interests of the Belgian team would take precedence over my private feelings towards Maertens," he says. "In any case, seeking revenge only leads you into making mistakes. I never rode with the intention of seeing to it that someone else would lose."

Claudine endorses this: "Eddy has never been able to understand the negative attitude of some riders. Whenever Axel has complained about it, Eddy always says that such an attitude showed a person's

▽ *Merckx never talked about gaining revenge. But with his legs he made it clear what he thought about certain matters. (Merckx drops rival Maertens during the Amstel Gold Race in 1975.)*

ignorance. 'If they choose your wheel, it's because they can't do any better', is what he told Axel."

"I couldn't live like that," says Merckx. "I thinks it's a sad attitude. Where is the pleasure in messing it up for someone else, while you're getting nowhere yourself?"

Merckx was not even prepared to apply the principle of 'An eye for an eye, a tooth for a tooth' toward Rik Van Looy, who, nevertheless, was regularly on his back like a shadow. In the 1969 Tour, the Kaiser of Herentals, by then 35, wanted to get his own back on the flat run up and win a stage for his sponsors, Willem II. Partly due to the efforts of Merckx's troops, Van Looy, however, was not given any freedom. During the stage to Nancy, Van Looy attacked at the feeding station. Julien Stevens, who was in the yellow jersey and who had been riding in Van Looy's team the previous year, wanted to get a reaction going but was ordered to stay calm by his leader, Merckx. A couple of days prior to that, on the strength of the banners lining the road as the race passed through Belgium, Van Looy had declared: "You see, I'm still more popular than Merckx." The Cannibal retained his positive attitude, however, 'because that's just the way I am', he says.

▽ *Merckx regularly called his rivals to account. But it was always in a sporting manner.*

The Year of Pain

Team	Molteni
Directeurs sportifs	Guillaume Driessens (Bel), Marino Fontana (Ita)
Teammates	Etienne Antheunis (Bel), Marino Basso (Ita), Giuseppe Bellini (Ita), Joseph Bruyère (Bel), Luigi Casteletti (Ita), Jos De Schoenmaecker (Bel), Jos Huysmans (Bel), Frans Mintjens (Bel), Giacinto Santambroggio (Ita), Jos Spruyt (Bel), Julien Stevens (Bel), Roger Swerts (Bel), Guerrino Tosello (Ita), Romeo Tumellero (Ita), Martin Van den Bossche (Bel), Julien Van Lint (Bel), Victor Van Schil (Bel), Herman Van Springel (Bel), Rini Wagtmans (Neth)
Number of Races	120
Number of Victories	54
Major Stage Races	Tour de France 1st
	• Points classification 1st
	• Mountain classification 3rd
	• Stage victories 4
	Tour of Italy -
Major One-Day Races	World Championship 1st
	Belgian Championship 5th
	Milan-San Remo 1st
	Tour of Flanders 76th
	Paris-Roubaix 5th
	Liège-Bastogne-Liège 1st
	Amstel Gold Race -
	Tour of Lombardy 1st
	Het Volk 1st
	Ghent-Wevelgem 3rd
	Flèche-Wallonne -
	Paris-Tours -
	Paris-Brussels -
Other victories	Rund um dem Henninger Turm, Tour of Belgium, Dauphiné Libéré, Midi-Libre, Paris-Nice, Tour of Sardinia, Baden-Baden, Super Prestige Pernod...

△ *A hard-fought victory over Georges Pintens, his second in Liège-Bastogne-Liège. It gave the media plenty to write about.*

"As in 1970, I showed signs of vulnerability in 1971 that were not there previously. In Liège-Bastogne-Liège, I was overtaken in the closing stages by Georges Pintens, and in the Tour de France I was embarrassed by Luis Ocaña. The back pain I was suffering as a result of my crash at Blois was playing me up. Riding my bike, previously a pleasure, was becoming more and more like a cross to bear. I won that year's Liège-Bastogne-Liège and I won the Tour, but they were both achieved in a manner that showed my increasing vulnerability and my fragility. From that point of view, 1971 was a low point, even though I won nearly half of the races I took part in. My preparations for the Tour were not ideal, either. I didn't ride the Giro that year, and that was always the best way of preparing for the Tour.

"It was only toward the end of that season that I had my back problems looked at seriously. I called in osteopaths and physiotherapists and I started treatment that would get my pelvis back to something like right. For that purpose, I had to work on my flexibility by doing gymnastic and stretching exercises, and it was an approach which bore fruit, as in 1972 much of the trouble had disappeared."

"My problems didn't stop me winning Het Volk for the first time early in 1971, and I also won the Tour of Lombardy for the first time later that year. And in Mendrisio I won the world pro championship for the second time. Yet there is one word which describes that year best of all: painful."

1971

The Victim

"One doesn't stumble over a mountain,
one stumbles over a stone."
(Indian proverb)

"I sometimes used to sit on my bike,
weeping with the pain."
(Eddy Merckx)

Nature was kind to Merckx. The Cannibal had an iron constitution and he was, so to speak, built to race bikes. Morphologically and physiologically he had everything he needed to become a top champion. In relation to his total height, his legs are long and his trunk is rather short. This is a plus point because, after all, the legs are the cyclist's engine, while the rest of his body may be regarded as something of a dead-weight. When it came to heart and blood, too, Merckx had a head start. He displayed a unique type of ability to recuperate. At examinations in Turin and the Sports Academy at Cologne, he put in efforts that astonished the watching experts. It appeared that Merckx was able to continue performing with abnormally high levels of lactic acid in his blood. Academically speaking, he should have been in no fit state to continue at such times, but he was always able to give the pedals one more turn.

Could this then be the explanation of the essence of Merckx, the exceptional racer? Imagine that is the case. Imagine that the uniqueness of an athlete can quite simply be determined by biochemistry. The alchemy of success, however, is more complicated than that, and also contains mental factors. According to certain academics, ultimately these mental factors must also be explained biochemically. Other books, though, have been written which go into that subject. Champions are the product of countless qualities feeding off one another, which bit by bit must be present in minimal doses. If just one of these basic qualities is missing, or if the various properties do not complement each other in precisely the proper manner, mediocrity may be the outcome.

One of the capacities it is essential for a cycling champion to possess is the ability to overcome suffering. Reaching the top of the mountain may be one thing, but climbing up out of a valley time and again is another. At that level, too, there was more than one occasion when Merckx produced daring exploits. He has had his share of suffering: not only physical pain, but mental torment, too.

△ *All too often they discovered – like Zoetemelk did here during the 1975 Tour – that the Cannibal was, so to speak, designed to be a cyclist.*

◁ *Merckx has had his fair share of suffering: both physically and mentally. (In pain after being punched in the kidney on the Puy-de-Dôme in the 1975 Tour.)*

A WEAK, VULNERABLE YOUNG LAD

With the health of a delicate hothouse flower, you would never become a cycling champion or even a cyclist, period. Merckx was exceptional on an athletic level, riding an incredible number of races each year in which he repeatedly had to dig deep into his reserves. The pressure – overuse some would say – must have been enormous.

In sport, the one thing which remains for a champion when all else has gone is his honors list. What tends to be forgotten with the smooth passage of time is what he had to go through at the time to achieve that success. With the great champions in particular, the temptation is there, strangely enough, to assume that everything was plain sailing. In Merckx's case, winning was such a normal occurrence that people thought he only had to open his mouth to catch a bite of something. The pain he suffered, the crashes he was involved in, the sickness and the doubts he wrestled with, and particularly the way he got over the knocks are hardly ever mentioned or discussed nowadays. Merckx attributes his impressive career, nonetheless, to two factors: talent and character. The latter not only refers to the tenacity he needed to keep forcing victory, for the call of victory gives wings to the exhausted rider. Suffering, but knowing that one is going to win, is totally different to suffering at the back of the peloton. It is different to the difficult return to action after a period of inactivity after injury or sickness. There is also no public around when the apprehensive rider starts out on his umpteenth training ride in rain, cold and wind, worried about whether his knee will stand up to the strain this time.

AN OPEN LUMBAR VERTBRA

During the early years of his life there was nothing to suggest that Merckx would develop the body of a sportsman. His ability to stave off illness as a toddler was not particularly impressive. "Quite the opposite," says his mother. "When he was just a tot, he seemed to be prone to catch any illness going. He got that from me. If there was an outbreak of flu in the neighborhood, it was certain that I would get it. When Eddy was three or four, he had to put up with one throat or ear infection after another. It made me really worry, and I asked the doctor when it was all going to end. I even feared that he would grow into a weak, sickly young man. 'Wait till he's seven or eight', the doctor told me. 'By then the worst of it should be over.' Fortunately the doctor turned out to be right."

Merckx continued his development in a normal way, but when he was irrevocably affected by the cycling virus, his body found its own way of protesting. "The first few years I raced, I suffered very badly with cramps," he says. "I regularly used to be kept awake at night by it. My mother then put a bar of Sunlight soap in my bed next to where I lay. It would help, people said at the time (he laughs). They were probably classic growth cramps. I was a slow grower, even though I was sturdy. For a long time, though, I was smaller than children of my own age. It was only after I had already

▽ *During his early years as a young racer, Merckx suffered terribly with cramps. And in 1964 he had problems with his back. Here is Merckx on his 16th birthday on June 17, 1962 before the debutants race at Sint-Laurens-Berchem.*

started racing that I suddenly grew. All the convulsions growing brought with it were, however, cured in time."

The back problem Merckx suffered with in 1964 was a different matter completely. "I am deformed, actually," laughs Merckx. "One of my lumbar vertebra did not completely grow into a closed position. In 1964, I had won quite a few races when I went on a training camp with Sercu and Walschaert to Norway. We did a lot of skiing there. The day after we arrived home, I took part in a race. After 50 kilometers my back locked. It came as a fright: My muscles totally contracted. I got into a real panic because I had visions of my career coming to an abrupt end, there and then. For weeks on end I was hardly able to win a race. Willy Vannitsen then recommended me to a doctor who manipulated me using a syringe 20 centimeters long. Spine-chilling, it was. The problem disappeared, though, and from then on I've never had any trouble with that particular back complaint."

THE DRAMA IN BLOIS

Merckx's career did indeed live on, but it almost turned into a nightmare on September 9, 1969 when, during a derny-paced exhibition race on the track at Blois in France, Merckx was involved in a particularly nasty crash. "I knew beforehand we had precious little appetite for it," says Merckx. "The weather that evening was terrible, there were hardly any spectators, and Anquetil was still showing the traces of the previous day's extravagance. He had drunk a little too much, and as his wife was driving him to the hotel he felt sick. Jacques opened his door so that he could hang his head out of the car, while his wife, Jeanine, drove over to the side of the road. In doing so, she lost sight of a kilometer post in the grass shoulder and the open door smashed into it, leaving Jacques sitting there with his head jammed between the door and the car body. This left Anquetil with a headache big enough for two at the start in Blois. The derny race was running normally until fate took a hand in the closing stages. The pedal of the pacemaker, Reverdi, who was pacing the Czechoslovakian, Jiri Daler (the Olympic pursuit champion at Tokyo in 1964), broke off. Neither my pacemaker, Fernand Wambst, nor I could avoid hitting the pacemaker and rider sprawled out ahead of us, and we both crashed to the concrete. I was knocked unconscious and only came around on the operating table, where I needed to have a head wound stitched."

Merckx was luckier than Wambst, who was killed instantly. Guillaume Michiels saw the tragic scene from close by. "I was watching the race from the central area," says Michiels. "The track at Blois was only 250 meters long and not very wide. Wambst was the only pacemaker with any experience. At the start of Merckx's heat, Wambst let himself slip back to last place so that he could get back up to everyone else during the second half of the race. Eventually, there was only one pairing ahead of Wambst and Merckx: Reverdi and Daler. Then a pedal broke off Reverdi's motorbike. The bike shot off up to the perimeter fence where it went tearing along the advertising

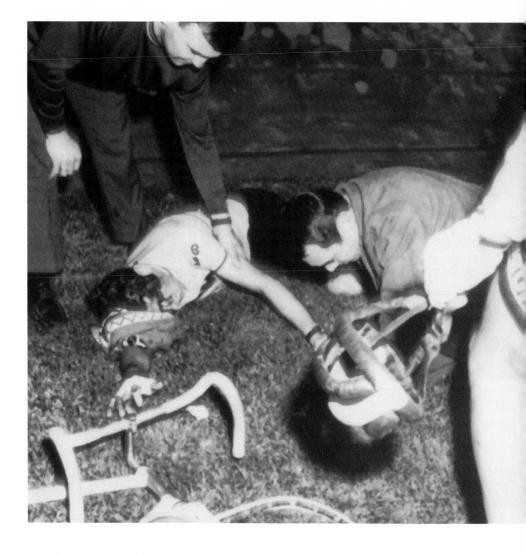

▷ *September 9, 1969: fate takes a hand. Merckx lies motionless at the side of the track at Blois, while Guillaume Michiels leans over him. Cycling was never to be the same again.*

BACK ONTO THE DERNY

On September 9, 1969, Claudine Merckx was four months into her pregnancy with the couple's first child, Sabrina, when Merckx crashed on the track at Blois. She was informed on the telephone by Guillaume Michiels of the tragic events in which pacemaker Fernand Wambst lost his life.

"Eddy was worried about the possible shock Claudine would have to get over and expressly asked me to play down the situation," says Michiels, who that same night drove to Brussels to collect Claudine and Eddy's mother and take them to Blois.

"I was especially worried when Eddy rode on the track," says Claudine. "When I was five, I saw my father fall behind a derny in Brussels. I can't remember a great deal about the actual incident any more, but I can still clearly remember what was said about it afterward. So I wasn't very happy when I could see in Blois that Eddy had still not completely come to. On the way back to Belgium we got it through to him that Wambst had died. The news absolutely shattered him. Yet he was well aware of the risks involved in the sport. He also knew that after Blois he would have to be back on his bike as quickly as possible to overcome the shock. As it turned out, one of his first races back was a derny race at the Ghent Sport Palace." sportpaleis."

hoardings for a good 15 meters before sliding back down. Wambst took a gamble and tried to avoid the whole mess by riding underneath it, but just at that moment Reverdi slid down and he went right over him. Merckx, in the meantime, was trying to escape by going above it all, but in doing so he hit Daler. Eddy smashed down onto the concrete, five meters from where I was standing. He was unconscious and bleeding heavily from a head wound. It was only in the hospital that he finally regained consciousness. He asked how Wambst was. 'He's the same as you,' I lied."

At first sight, it looked as if the damage to Merckx was not so bad, after all. He suffered a light concussion and needed to have stitches inserted to a gaping wound on his forehead. "It could have been even worse," says Merckx, "so I can't complain. But having said that, that fall did have a negative influence on the rest of my career. At first, my left leg was given the wrong kind of recovery program. Instead of patiently following a therapeutic course of treatment and exercise, I chose to get back to riding as soon as I could and to combat the pain with injections. That did nothing to eradicate the causes, of course. The fall had cracked one of my vertebra, and some of my nerves were trapped. Some time later, acupuncture and limbering exercises brought some comfort, but the worst thing, the back pain, kept coming back. It was later discovered that the fall had caused my pelvis to become slightly twisted, leading me to experience increasing problems, especially when climbing. Before then, climbing had almost been a pleasure. Now it had become almost a source of torment.

Sometimes, I sat on my bike weeping with pain. The joy I used to experience in my work was no longer there. In 1970, although my condition was the same as it had been before, I no longer had the power, and I was still not back to my old self in 1971, either. It was not until the autumn of 1972 that I started to occasionally feel as invincible as I used to. Had it not been for Blois, my career would have certainly had a lot more shine, I can assure you of that."

"Eddy often used to tell me that Blois had made him lose 50 percent of his strength," says Guillaume Michiels. "That's an exaggeration, of course. I do know, though, that before September 1969 no one ever rode away from him on the highest climbs. After then, it happened on a number of occasions."

■ IF YOU ENJOY DOING SOMETHING

The blow Merckx received in Blois was not the only time he suffered, as like any other rider he occasionally came to grief – though he was usually able to ride away unscathed. Merckx usually took up a position at the front of the peloton, where there is less chance of a crash taking place. "I would estimate that throughout my career I hit the asphalt about 80 or 90 times," he says. "And in all that time, I only had one serious break of a bone. That was in 1963, when I was still an amateur and broke a finger just before the Championship of Brabant. In Paris-Nice in 1972, I suffered a break of a vertebral projection in a crash."

It is not the intention here to detail all the physical suffering, be it large or small, Merckx had to endure during his career. Briefly, though, in his time he had to put up with operations on his posterior for a cyst; in the 1967 Belgian championship at Mettet he was concussed in a crash; the early season in 1974 was a complete write-off for him due to a combination of illness and bad luck. He repeatedly struggled with his knee problem. He has also had trouble with flu, hot feet, infections of the air passage, and many other ailments.

None of the suffering was serious enough for Merckx to ever question whether he was in the right profession. "If you really enjoy doing something, you are only too happy to put up with the suffering", says Merckx, with a shrug of his shoulders. "But that chronic pain after Blois, that could have broken me."

■ THE SAVONA DOPING AFFAIR

Something else that may have broken him was the doping affair in 1969 during the Tour of Italy. His positive sample in Savona had an enormous impact on Merckx. His trust in mankind was seriously

▽ *"Anyone who enjoys doing something puts up with the suffering." Did his rivals think the same during the 1972 Giro.*

▷ *Feeling the pain after the infamous
stomach punch during the 1975 Tour.*

THE STOMACH PUNCH
ON THE DE PUY-DE-DÔME

One of the most talked-about incidents
Merckx was ever involved in was the
memorable punch to the stomach he
received on the Puy-de-Dôme during the
Tour de France in 1975. A few hundred
meters from the finish, a French supporter punched Merckx who was in yellow at
the time. He was already having breathing difficulties, but he made it to the finish, just about on his last legs. "It was
because of that punch that Eddy lost the
Tour," insists his mother.

Merckx's initial reaction to it was that a
crime had been committed. Legal proceedings were set before the court at
Clermont-Ferrand, and the case was
heard at the end of November that year.
The blow had been administered by the
55-year-old Nello Breton, who claimed
he had acted involuntarily and had
been pushed. Breton was found guilty
and given a conditional discharge.
"Damages of one franc were awarded,"
Merckx informs us. "I'd never actually
asked for damages, though, as they
weren't going to do me any good. It was
all a bit too late really, wasn't it."

After the stage up the Puy-de-Dôme,
there was a transfer to Nice, where the
riders spent a rest day. A day later, they
set off on the 15th stage to Pra-Loup,
where the winners and losers of that
Tour would be decided. Merckx made a
purposeful uphill attack on the Col
d'Allos, but blew up like a second-rater
on the final climb of the day. The
Cannibal had only one explanation for
this dramatic collapse: the blood-thinning medication he had been administered to cushion the effects of the punch
in the stomach had weakened him. He
was not to win the Tour for a sixth time,
as a year later he was forced to miss it
due to a swelling in his groin, and in
1977 he was to finally bow out.

tested by it, because it was all too clear to him that he had been the victim of a plot.
Several factors point to that being the case. Firstly, we will set out the course of the
events that took place.

For the first nine days of the 52nd Giro, which started in Garda, the winner of the
first stage, Giancarlo Polidori, rode in the Pink Jersey of the leader. Merckx himself
had already shown what he was capable of by winning the time trial in Montecatini
and the road stage to Terracina. He announced his imminent ascendancy even more
emphatically by taking the leader's jersey at the end of the ninth stage. For a few days
after that it ended up on the shoulders of Silvano Schiavon, but after the 15th stage,
a 49-kilometer time trial to San Marino, the stage winner, Merckx, was once again
sitting firmly on the throne. It was clear that yet again nothing was going to stop the
Cannibal, who had won the Giro the previous year showing crushing dominance.
That had led to a feeling of great frustration among the rival Italian teams, especially
among the sponsors who hardly got a look in on the podium or in the media. In
1969, too, it was looking as though it was going to be all Merckx and Faema.

Following the time trial, a rest day was scheduled, and on Sunday June 1, the transfer from Parma to Savona took place. The stage started under a dark cloud, when dissatisfied workers from the Salamini factory blocked the start, much to the annoyance of some of the riders, like Rudi Altig who angrily went for the demonstrators with his bicycle pump. The stage was ridden at a snail's pace of 37 kph, but in the best Italian tradition it caught fire in the final kilometers. A few kilometers from the finish Roberto Ballini escaped. Faema's sprinter, Guido Reysbrouck, asked Merckx if he wanted the team to lead the chase after Ballini so that he would have a chance of taking the final bunch sprint. To which he said he did. Two kilometers before the line, Merckx was slightly knocked by a television-camera motor bike which ran into his back wheel. He just about managed to stay upright and it was just as well, too, because if he had not, he would have had the whole peloton riding over him.

Ballini held on and won the stage. A quarter of an hour later, Merckx reported to the dope control for the ninth time during this particular Giro. Afterward, he was taken to the Excelsior Hotel in Albisola, where the team stayed overnight.

The following morning in room 11, which he was sharing with Martin Van den Bossche, Merckx woke to prepare for the day's stage to the nearby Celle Ligure. The two riders were lying on their beds in their racing shorts, waiting for the signal from the team management that it was time to leave.

"There had already been one or two uninvited people coming in," says witness Van den Bossche, taking up the story. "We were getting pretty fed up with it. 'Wait a minute,' I said. 'The next person who walks in here is really going to get it from me'. I picked up a cushion ready, and when there was a short knock and someone opened the door, I scored a direct hit.. in the face of team manager, Giacotto."

Vincenzo Giacotto, who was accompanied by the organizer of the Giro, Vincenzo Torriani, did not share the joke, but that had nothing to do with Van den Bossche's clowning. He had bad news for Merckx. "When Eddy heard that he had been found positive and had been thrown out of the Giro, it was as though he had been struck down by the hand of God," says Van den Bossche, who fled as soon as the media rush into the little room began.

An analysis of Merckx's urine sample that Sunday afternoon by Dr. Cavalli of the medical committee of the Italian Cycling Federation had shown traces of phencamphaminum, a banned substance which is present in the pick-me-up Réactivan. A year earlier, a number of riders, including Felice Gimondi and Vic Van Schil had been found guilty of using the same product during the Giro.

▽ *Tears of defenselessness against the 'wicked world.'*

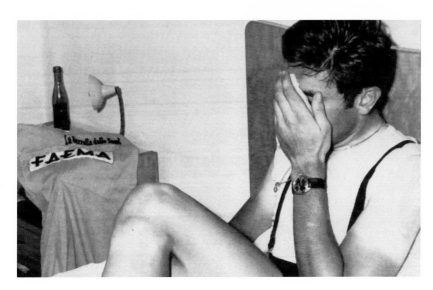

Torriani, the race organizer, was now informed, and Professor Alexandro Genovese, a respected pharmacologist at the University of Milan, was summoned to Savona. There, on Monday June 2, at 7 a.m., he carried out a second analysis. He too came across the gas chromatograph phencamphaminum. At 10 o'clock Merckx was given the bad news and all hell broke loose. The pink jersey wearer was suspended for a month and was thrown out of the Giro with immediate effect. This meant that there was no chance of taking part in that year's Tour de France, which was to begin on June 28.

There was all hell to pay. Team sponsors Faema were the first to react when they remarkably threatened to sack Merckx. He wanted to prove his innocence as quickly as possible, however, and that same day, together with his teammates, he produced new samples in the presence of three journalists. Merckx wanted to serve a writ, but directeur sportif Giacotto did not think that was necessary. The new samples were examined by Professors Franco Lodi and Emilio Marozzi at the Institute for Medicine of the University of Milan. Between these samples being taken and the production of the official ones there had been a gap of 16 hours. Because the concentration of phencamphaminum was so high in the official sample, there should still have been unmistakable traces of the substance in this sample. That, however, was not the case. At a later date, Merckx underwent a further examination by Professor De Vleeschouwer from Ghent University, for which he voluntarily doped himself with Réactivan. From this test, it appeared that the substance remained traceable for a long time.

Irrespective of this, Merckx was forced to quit the Giro. There was uproar both at home and abroad. The Belgian sporting world was shocked and insulted. A sociological study carried out by the University of Liège on June 3 clearly showed that the doping affair was having just as great an impact on the country as the assassination of President Kennedy or the first man on the moon. Belgian politicians also felt moved to respond to this disgraceful episode. Questions were asked in parliament. At the insistence of two Ministers of Culture, the Belgian government demanded a thorough investigation and a vindication of Merckx. The chairman of the International Cycling Union, Adriano Rodoni, set up an investigation himself, but came to the conclusion that sabotage could not have taken place. Nevertheless, there are many signs that hint at the existence of a plot.

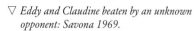

▽ *Eddy and Claudine beaten by an unknown opponent: Savona 1969.*

■ THE PLOT THEORY

The doping affair around Merckx needs to be looked at against the background of his incredible domination of the cycling scene. His rivals tried to beat him by every sporting means possible, but Merckx remained unassailable. The obstinate way he would not enter into the occasional deal aroused ever more resentment, not only among his opponents but also among their team sponsors, who were seeing very little return for their sizeable investments.

"In the 1968 Giro, there was an unusually ferocious battle between our team and the other Italian squads", says Martin Van den Bossche. "The rivalry with Felice Gimondi's Salvarini team was particularly fierce. The Italian opposition was pulverized by Merckx, and not unnaturally their sponsors were not happy about it. In 1969, they were being threatened with more of the same medicine. I can imagine that they would have done anything in their power to stop this happening. The news that Merckx had received an offer to sell the race does not surprise me, either. Knowing his temperament, however, it would have been difficult for him to have taken it up. It reminded me of what I had seen happen in the team during the Tour of Spain in 1968. We were riding that race not with Merckx but with Vittorio Adorni as team leader. Adorni was said to be Gimondi's arch rival, but I warned my teammates that a deal might go down between the Italians. And the way I see it, that is what happened. In one of the mountain stages, Adorni was suddenly faced with a strange collapse and Gimondi went on to win the Vuelta."

Van den Bossche also finds it remarkable that Merckx was presented with a fait accompli. "Merckx was informed of it very late in the day, just before the 17th stage was about to start," he says. "So any defense came too late. I am absolutely convinced that someone wanted Merckx out of the Giro, no matter what it took."

Merckx also has his thoughts on the affair. "Someone was making a mockery of the procedures," he says. "The second analysis was carried out without anyone being there to represent me. When we brought up this point later, we were told that someone had tried to reach us by telephone at our hotel but they had been unable to get through. What a load of rubbish that is! Besides, give me one good reason why I should have used a banned substance that day. It was a nothing sort of stage, and I knew that as the race leader I would have to report to the control. I would have had to be totally stupid to have taken something, wouldn't I?"

Even more incriminating is the offer Merckx received two days earlier from the Salvarani team. One of Gimondi's non-Italian teammates went to look for Merckx in his hotel room and came straight out and said that he would "be given a suitcase full of money" if he were to lose the Giro.

"My answer left him in no doubt", says Merckx. "I told him I wasn't interested. 'Whatever you do, don't tell me how much money is in the suitcase. Then I won't regret my decision later on,' I added to the messenger. That wasn't the only time I got an offer to sell a race in Italy, either. Anything was possible there."

The fact an offer was made to Merckx to sell the Giro is no proof that he was later the victim of a dubious plot in which the use of a banned substance was pinned on him. It was an accusation for which no hard evidence was ever found. There is not much point, therefore, to name names just for the sake of those eager to know who

MOTHER MERCKX REACHES FOR A CIGARETTE

When Merckx heard in his hotel room in Abisola that he had been found positive and would have to leave the Giro, there was great despair. At first he thought it must be a joke, but when it became obvious that it was deadly serious, he could scarcely believe the news. "It can't be, it just cannot be," he said repeatedly and burst into tears. Photographs of the tearful Merckx found their way all around the world.

His mother was badly affected, too, when she heard the news. "I actually reached for a cigarette," she says. "My husband Jules, who was himself a smoker, had been trying to get me to try a cigarette for years, but I had always refused. But in the consternation surrounding the doping affair I lit one up, without even thinking about it. And I have smoked ever since..."

THE BONKING DOCTOR AND THE HOLY MASS

The most unlikely explanations were forwarded for Merckx's positive dope control. Imagination knew no bounds as one hypothetical situation after another were considered. Some of the scenarios that were dreamed up were the sort that would make detective-story writers lick their lips.

One rather prosaic explanation that was considered feasible was the following soap-opera type scenario: the doctor who was responsible for the doping control in the Giro could have been a bit of a ladies' man who had met a "looker" in the tour caravan, and on the day of the stage to Savona they had gone off to do some horizontal jogging. His stand-in had not understood some of the orders he had written out and after the 16th stage, instead of pouring the contents of the bottles straight down the wash basin as was normally the case, he had dutifully carried out the control. The prevailing view was that doping controls in Italy were probably pure charades in those days. If this story had in fact turned out to be true, Merckx would indeed have been found positive because he had taken something before the important time trial to San Marino, which would have been traceable two days later.

Another explanation, which was inspired more by reli-gion, is the story virtually lifted straight out of the Testaments about the switching of the drinking bottles. The 16th stage was ridden on a Sunday, and just before the start in Parma the riders were given the opportunity to attend a mass being held right next to the starting place. The Catholic Merckx wanted to attend the service and walked right into the ambush. He had left his bike outside with the bidon still in its holder without giving it a moment's thought. While the pink jersey wearer kneeled at prayer (and, wrote the journalist from the *Gazetta dello Sport* 'just at the moment of the ascent of the Holy Host to heaven', as if he had seen it all happen), a devilish person-age swiped his water bottle and replaced it with another one, containing the banned substance found later.

At the time, some of the Italian newspapers looked in Merckx's own camp for the guilty parties. *Stadio* com-mented that in Merckx's entourage, "there are quite a few people who are of a suspicious character when it comes to banned substances". And *La Gazetta dello Sport* did not rule out the possibility of treachery, either. The inter-national press, however, spoke as one in claiming Merckx's innocence: he was the victim of a prank or a plot, that much was clear. Hardly anyone believed he had used a banned substance of his own volition.

it was. "Just take this from me, though," says Merckx. "One man's breath is another man's death. At least that has something to do with it. It was a sordid affair, and I gave my answer to it in the Tour de France which followed."

After the incident, there was certainly little left to the imagination of the press and public when it came to thinking up a scenario to explain why Merckx's sample was positive (see insert). One thing for certain is that in those early days of doping controls, almost anything was possible. As though by way of a premonition, Merckx declared at the start of 1969: "I'm not particularly frightened of having a fall or some other sort of accident. If I do get injured and I'm unable to carry on carving out the sort of career I envision myself having, I'll get by. Such risks are part and parcel of cycling, anyway. I have to accept the dangers, in the same way as I accept getting beaten. What does sometimes get me into a panic, though, are those doping controls. Most of them are carried out in very questionable circumstances, to the extent that a rider who is already faced with prejudice against him is left open to all sorts of maneuvering, and all sorts of tampering, without having a proper chance to defend himself, to prove his innocence or to be taken in good faith."

Martin Van den Bossche supplies an example in support of that view. "At the time, much, if not everything, was possible with those doping controls. The procedures kept going wrong. I know a case of a rider who had to provide a urine sample after Milan-San Remo in his hotel room. The rider said he couldn't urinate. When the regulation time was up, the doctor told him he had no choice but to declare him positive. 'Oh, yes? We'll see about that,' said the rider, who went to the door, locked it and kept hold of the key. Then he went over to a window and opened it. 'If you don't put down on that official form, right now, that everything is in order, I'll throw you out of this window,' the rider calmly told him. At which point the doctor – hand shaking – put his signature to the form."

Van den Bossche adds to that bizarre story another piece of indirect evidence: "As a form of reprisal, they got the rider in question mixed up in a doping control during the Tour de France later that year, and he was thrown out of the race."

It would certainly be ironic if it was the same rider who offered Merckx that suitcase full of money during the 1969 Giro.

"It was just incredible what used to go on with those doping controls," continues Van den Bossche. "I once received a letter from the federation telling me I had been found positive in Liège-Bastogne-Liège and that I had to pay BF 10,000. I wrote back by registered letter, laconically stating that I could not have been positive as I hadn't taken anything. I have the impression that the federation used to send letters like that out all over the place, just to see how much money they could make from it."

■ THE STIGMA REMAINS

The uproar surrounding Merckx's suspension put the sport's father-figures under enormous pressure. The management committee of the FICP, the professional branch within the International Cycling Union, met in Brussels on June 14, and decided to lift the suspension, which was due to run until July 1. As a result, Merckx could start in the Tour, after all.

Merckx was not entirely happy with that, as he was not cleared of the charge, only reprieved. "The doubts and the stigma will always remain," he said.

After this pronouncement, in some places there was even talk of class justice. Even some of Merckx's colleagues spoke frankly of discrimination and of the use of two standards and two levels of importance. Within the professional ranks, they even talked of raising a petition to keep Merckx out of the Tour. In the Tour of Luxembourg, some riders wanted to organize a sit-down strike as a protest against the preferential treatment Merckx had received.

Those reactions hurt Merckx, who has a character that refuses to recognize the evil in the world. Once more his trust in mankind took a terrible knock, and he learned yet again how the world resembles a jungle.

"Eddy was devastated for days by it", says his wife, Claudine. "He could no longer see any future in what he was doing, and he wanted to quit racing altogether. The attitude of his directeur sportif, Giacotto, who doubted his integrity, was high on

▽ *Chairman Moyson of the Belgian Cycling Federation announces that Merckx's suspension has been lifted.*

Eddy's mind in particular. Why exactly had Giacotto refused to appoint a mediator for the voluntary examination Eddy wanted to undergo?"

"I still remember who was prepared to stand by and watch me fall, and who was not at the time", says Merckx. "Some really disappointed me as people. And that pronouncement from the federation bosses was neither one thing nor the other. Either I was guilty and should serve my suspension until July 1, or I was innocent and should be acquitted. The federation said that I was actually guilty, but because I'd had a so-called 'impeccable past,' the penalty was suspended."

Here we see once again the Merckx who cannot stand compromise, convenience and diplomacy. He likes a black-and-white world in which you either win or you lose, and not "I could have won if I hadn't done this, that or the other on the so-and-so kilometer." To him, you are loyal or you are not, and not "Normally, I would stand up for you, but not this time." You either trust someone wholeheartedly or you do not trust them in the slightest. Merckx has no time for explanations or motives that might explain condemnable behavior, nor for subtle distinctions that shed a different light on an issue. A person is what he does, not what he says.

POSITIVE ON TWO OTHER OCCASIONS

Apart from the previously discussed positive sample taken at Savona, there were two other occasions on which Merckx was found positive after races. On November 8, 1973, the news emerged that after the Tour of Lombardy on October 13, traces of norephedrine had been found in his urine. Once again Merckx was furious about how the whole affair had been handled and shouted his innocence from the rooftops. The team doctor, Angelo Cavalli, accepted all the blame. He admitted he must have prescribed Merckx a cough syrup, Mucantil, which contained the banned substance.

In the spring of 1977, Merckx was caught for the third time. During the Flèche Wallonne, ridden on April 7, he was accused of using the infamous Stimul. After the first analysis, Merckx did not immediately ask for a second opinion, but he did lodge an appeal — later dismissed — against the cycling federation's judgment, on the grounds of improper procedures and negligence. At the time, there was a torrent of suspensions: Freddy Maertens, Walter Godefroot, Walter Planckaert, Guy Sibille, Michel Pollentier and Karel Rottiers all fell into the trap in short time. Professor De Backere of Ghent University had been secretly working on an analysis method that was able to trace Stimul, and once he had perfected it, he came down very hard.

"I was always one for having controls, on the condition that they were operated properly and that there were no loop-holes in the system," says Merckx. "Tracking down dope users was to my benefit. When I turned professional, I soon found out just what went on. I usually kept well away from the stuff, witness the hundreds of controls I was put through and which were nearly all negative. When I turned pro, regular doping controls were not yet in existence. In 1967, there was still no control in the

Giro. You should try to put yourself in the position of a rider who, in principle, is against doping, but can't help noticing that his rivals are using stimulating products and are enjoying an unfair advantage. The temptation becomes very great and the weakest are the first to give in. Doping is like other problems of society, such as alcohol or drug abuse. You will always have poachers so you will always need gamekeepers, too. But it is up to the individual to make the judgment himself. Anyone who thinks he will end up better for using doping, alcohol or drugs, will never make it in the long run."

Merckx is skeptical about the effects that doping has. "It is not what cycling is about," he says, vehemently. "Cycling is first and foremost about training, living for your profession and suffering — those are the essential things. At one particular time, belief in doping was so great that young riders were only interested in the address of a "good" doctor, while they regarded professional commitment as being of secondary importance."

Merckx has always been very angry about the discrimination shown toward cycling when it comes to the fight against drugs in sport. "In my day, other sports had hardly any kind of doping control," he says. "Don't you think that was outrageous? For years we were treated like the black sheep of sport. In recent years, we have seen just what has been going on in other sports. I'm not trying to justify its use in cycling, it's just that I get annoyed when people give the impression that all it takes for a cyclist to carve out a career for himself is to take a stimulating substance. That is a slap in the face to all the riders who put their all into their job, day-in day-out. Besides, there isn't a substance in the world that can make a racehorse out of a donkey."

THE BLACK HOLE

Savona and Blois were huge blows to Merckx. The biggest blow he ever had to face, however, happened as soon as he retired. For a top sportsman, the moment of retirement is always an obstacle hard to negotiate. But in the case of Merckx, who had been totally fulfilled in his career for so many years, on May 18, 1978 a razor-sharp scalpel put an end to the dream he had been living out for 17 years. Suddenly, all that was left was a black hole. And yet, the omens were already there.

Nineteen-seventy-five was the year that it all changed for Merckx. (That much is clear from the graph in Chapter Twelve, where his returns are expressed in the number of wins he achieved against the number of races he rode.) In the table at the end of this book giving a summary of Merckx's career, it is noticeable that the years after 1975 were to be a shadow of previous ones. At the beginning of the 1976 season, he won his last really big race, Milan-San Remo, but from then on, things were never the same. To put it in perspective, however, Merckx finished 6th in the 1977 Tour, and any Belgian rider doing that today would be regarded as a world star in his native land.

△ *In spite of his fractured cheek bone, Merckx still gave it all he had in the 1975 Tour. He would regret it later.*

The early part of the 1975 season was as phenomenal as ever, with wins in Milan-San Remo, the Tour of Flanders, Liège-Bastogne-Liège and the Amstel Gold Race, as well as second place in Paris-Roubaix, third in the Flèche Wallonne, sixth in both Het Volk and Ghent-Wevelgem: 'On s'excuse du peu'. Had Merckx, nearly 30 by then, finally bitten off more than he could chew? Did gorging himself on this copious menu lower his resistance? In any event, after that early season Merckx was struck down by a very bad throat infection that kept him out of the Giro. "That was no ordinary throat infection," says Merckx.

"I had a high fever and could hardly swallow because of the abscesses in my throat. I could hardly stand up and was forced to sit out the Tour of Italy. After that came a hellish Tour de France in which, going against all common sense, I carried on riding. In the meantime, the after-effects of that throat infection had probably still not entirely gone away. In that Tour, in 1975, I signed my own death certificate."

In 1976, a mononucleosis did indeed come to light, which was bringing Merckx continually into a state of exhaustion. "That was not all," he says. "At the end of September 1976, I won a criterium in Bourges, but over the next few days I could hardly move as a result of problems with my back. I could barely sit upright, never mind ride around. For a full week, I had to lie flat. I even considered packing it in then. In Paris-Brussels, I had discovered that I could hardly get to the top of the Alsemberg. And then my back went. I couldn't have picked up an apple from the ground. I was a cripple. By getting plenty of rest I got over it, but the discomfort never totally went away again. The year after that I took a plank with me everywhere to put under my mattress in hotel beds. I still have trouble to this day with my back — it has made it impossible for me to jog, for example."

■ STILL A FEW GOOD DAYS

Merckx's inevitable decline continued to bite in. As is so often the case with top sportsmen, however, the athlete himself found it to be an unacceptable state of affairs. "I heard Merckx's father-in-law, Lucien Acou, declare to a number of his colleagues at the start of Liège-Bastogne-Liège in 1976, that 'the old Eddy would be back some day',"says Joris Jacobs. "According to Acou, Merckx would win his sixth Tour that July. I went up to him and said: 'Lucien, you do know, don't you, that it will all be over soon?' The only thing that is sure in life is deterioration and later, death. But for champions and their entourage it is so difficult for them to accept that fact. Merckx must have been well aware of the extent to which he had been overburdening his body over the previous 10 years. He was always there every summer and winter, and because of that blistering temperament of his, he always went flat out. Then, at the age of 32, the lights suddenly went out on him. It's not really so surprising, is it?"

△ *In the Tour of Flanders in 1977, Merckx lost his strength early on. First he was caught by Freddy Maertens and later by De Vlaeminck. Then, on the Varentberg, the lights went out completely. It was becoming more and more obvious that the end was drawing near.*

Merckx laughs. "When you are young, you have many good days and a few bad ones," he says. "When you get older it is the other way around. People rely on there being good moments, though, even if they are more rare. You hang on to them, but you don't let yourself be fooled by them, of course."

To minimize the effects all the wear and tear was having on him, Merckx began to look after himself a lot better than he had previously. "During the winter of 1977-78, I lived like a monk for the first time", he says. "I didn't drink a single glass of beer and I never ate too much, I probably looked after myself too much. The fact that I wasn't yet physically worn out is borne by the five six-day races I won."

Patrick Sercu, who rode alongside Merckx with Fiat in 1977, confirms that. "He still had strength to spare," he says. "And the will to win had remained intact. It was mental problems that eventually finished him off."

■ THE MENTAL UNDERMINING

From a mental point of view, problems had been piling up. His main anchor fell away in June 1974 when, right in the middle of the Giro, Jean van Buggenhout, his manager (about whom more is written in Chapter Eleven), died of a heart attack, aged 69. For 30 years, Van Buggenhout had been writing the script for Belgian cycling. Irrespective of how one should judge Van Buggenhout as a person, one thing is certain: he acted like a lightning rod for Merckx, keeping all the contractual, financial and administrative worries away from his champion. When Van Buggenhout was no longer there for him, Merckx had to take on all that rigmarole himself. Now, all of a sudden, he had to deal with riders' contracts, he was responsible for finding sponsors, and he suddenly had to face being buttonholed by race organizers every other minute. For a while, he was able to fall back on the same people and structures as before to keep things ticking over. When touchy subjects needed to be cleared up, however, they started to fall by the wayside. His inability to take the plunge and throw the truth in the faces of faithful companions, made it even more difficult for him. That is how he came to remain loyal to his sponsor, Molteni, in 1975, even though questions were increasingly being asked about how the salami producer conducted its business affairs. For several months the riders had to wait for their wages to be paid, and although it angered Merckx, out of a sense of shame, he looked on passively.

He was to encounter trouble over team sponsorship. "During the 1977 season, our sponsor, Fiat, had verbally promised me that they would continue their sponsorship into 1978," says Merckx. "And as far as I'm concerned, a verbal promise is sacred. It meant I was able to sign personal contracts with the majority of my teammates, the way I had always done. Then, at the beginning of October, Fiat went back on their earlier decision, leaving me to start looking for a new sponsor at the eleventh hour. It put me under great pressure because I had personally engaged my teammates and team personnel. After a search littered with obstacles, the razor-blade manufacturers Wilkinson Sword were ready to step in. The jerseys were got ready and the bikes were sprayed. Then, suddenly, in the middle of December, Wilkinson Sword pulled out too. That was a huge blow. I had to go out looking again. When, finally, a deal was reached with C&A stores, I caved in mentally. I was still stupid enough to want to dive straight into things, instead of taking a month out and training peacefully abroad. I felt totally drained. I had come down with flu and feeling very dispirited. I would go out and train for an hour and then I didn't want to do any more. The loss of the older generation from the team was another thing that I wasn't happy with. Riders like Huysmans, Van Schil, Spruyt and Mintjens were no longer around, and

◁ *Merckx during his last race, on March 18, 1978 at Kemzeke. "Mentally I was totally drained," he says.*

the mentality and the old atmosphere had gone, too. I no longer felt really at home in that team."

The desperation increased. At the last minute, Merckx pulled out of the Mediterranean Tour before resurfacing for the Tour du Haut-Var, but in the season's opener in Belgium, Het Volk, he was forced to abandon. He fell victim to a nervous breakdown that was continually increasing in strength. The more he worried about his predicament, the worse it became. On March 18 he did, however, start in the Circuit of the Waasland in Kemzeke. It was to be his last race. Over the next few weeks, he neither found rest in the Swiss resort of Crans-Montana nor solace in the training rides when he returned home. Merckx was bogged down in a quagmire of despression.

On Wednesday May 17, 1978, Merckx climbed, with difficulty, onto his saddle for a training ride. It was then that he made the decision to put a stop to it. A day later, during a press conference at the IPC in Brussels, he announced his retirement. It was one of the most painful moments of his life. On May 22, Merckx went to the Giro to pay a farewell visit. He was greeted by supporters carrying a banner which said: "Eddy, senza di te, il ciclismo è orfano." (Eddy, without you, cycling is an orphan).

△ *His farewell at the start of the Giro in 1978: 'Eddy, without you cycling is an orphan.'*

The following months were nothing short of a living hell for Merckx. He could not see any way of getting out of his depression and was sucked in to the whirlpool of despair and self-questioning. Without his bike, he stood naked before the world again. The doubter within him was being given free rein. It was now abundantly clear just how vulnerable and sensitive Merckx was if his weapon was taken away from him. His obsessiveness as a rider had been so great that he had never given any thought to life after his career. That was something to worry about later. But that "later" had suddenly arrived, and came like a blow from a sledgehammer. Merckx, as he will admit himself, was reeling and his depression hit home. Any prospect disappeared from his life, and there was no more meaning.

"His retirement was so different to how I imagined it would be," declared Claudine in September 1978. "The climate at home has changed completely. We have, as it were, stumbled into a vacuum, into a void. The tension and the hellish pace of life, unique to competition, has fallen away totally. I miss that, more than I could ever have feared. Yes indeed, it has been hard for me, too, to get used to."

◼ FILLING THE VOID

"Those first few weeks were horrible", Eddy endorses. "I didn't really know how I was going to fill my life. I was badly affected, mentally. After I retired, I would have been better to have kept away from cycling for a few months, but the people at C&A asked me to keep involved with the rest of the team. It would have been hard for me to leave them out in the cold. After all, they had pumped in millions of francs on the strength of my name. As a result of this obligation, I couldn't go looking for an alternative. Fortunately, I had my family to fall back on. A rider who quits his sport is the loneliest person in the world, because during his career he was hardly ever at home and he hardly had the time to make friends. Once it is over, he doesn't have many people he can rely on. That came as no surprise to me. As a top sportsman, it's almost impossible to make many friends. For years, you are cut off from normal life. It starts at school, even. You can't be both a world champion and get an economics degree. A rider who wants to make it, has to choose. He pays for that

Helping out RTBF commentator Théo Mathy, playing football or aimlessly driving around: the void was hard to bear.

choice later, when it is time for him to give up cycling, by finding himself in a black hole ..."

Merckx had a very hard time filling the void. Luckily, the recently retired Belgian soccer player, Paul Van Himst, was around, and he had encountered the same problems that Merckx was suffering now. "One day, by chance, I passed him in Sint-Brixius-Rode", says Van Himst. "Guillaume Michiels was busy washing a car. I asked him how Eddy was. 'Terrible,' said Guillaume. 'Absolutely terrible.' I promised him I would give Eddy a call. That I did, and a few days later I went to visit him with my wife. Eddy really was down in the dumps. I'm not exactly the best person in the world to cheer someone up with a few well-chosen words, but I did spur Eddy on to have a game of football and to play a little tennis. Through that, he at least had the feeling of being back in motion again, and his social contacts improved. We discovered right away that we were on the same wavelength, because our upbringing, our careers and our retirements had a lot in common. In the end, it was Merckx himself who pulled himself out of the misery he was in. And when he started his bicycle-manufacturing business at the start of 1980, he once again had a goal in life."

"Before it went too far, I had to do some serious thinking," says Merckx. "I'm a person who always has to be doing something, and there I was sitting at home whining and complaining. I received several offers to make something of my reputation in public relations and that sort of thing. But I wasn't interested. I didn't want to be used as a symbol or an object on display. I still have difficulty with that, going and standing on that pedestal. They wanted to drag me from one reception to another, simply to show me off and to be able to say: 'Look, there's Eddy Merckx.' Then I had to go and stand there to be looked at, to be weighed up. I still find all of that so stupid. When I retired, I thought: 'The life I'm now embarking on won't have many connections with the previous one.' That wasn't the case, though, and I'm still paying the price of fame. In the end, I was happy that I hadn't carried on riding until I was 40 because I still had the time to build up something else, something new. Now I'm gradually coming around to thinking about slowing down a little. That's to say, to finally do something I really want to and be completely free to make my own choice. That would be wonderful. To be able to follow races, especially involving youngsters, to help my son and to do a bit of messing around with his equipment; what more could I want?"

▽ *Making custom bikes: at long last there was once again a purpose in life.*

The Year of the World Hour Record

Team	Molteni
Directeur sportif	Giorgio Albani (Ita)
Teammates	Georges Barras (Bel), Joseph Bruyère (Bel), Jos De Schoenmaecker (Bel), Jos Huysmans (Bel), Willy In't Ven (Bel), Marc Lievens (Bel), Frans Mintjens (Bel), Georges Van Coningsloo (Bel), Martin Van den Bossche (Bel), Ludo Van der Linden (Bel), Victor Van Schil (Bel), Herman Vanspringel (Bel), Michel Van Vlierden (Bel).
Number of Races	127
Number of Victories	50
Major Stage Races	Tour de France 1st
	• Points classification 1st
	• Mountain classification 2nd
	• Stage victories 6
	Tour of Italy 1st
Major One-Day Races	World Championship 4th
	Belgian Championship 2nd
	Milan-San Remo 1st
	Tour of Flanders 7th
	Paris-Roubaix 7th
	Liège-Bastogne-Liège 1st
	Amstel Gold Race -
	Tour of Lombardy 1st
	Het Volk 1st
	Ghent-Wevelgem 3rd
	Flèche-Wallonne 1st
	Paris-Tours 116th
	Paris-Brussels -
Other victories	World Hour Record, Flèche Brabançonne, Scheldt G.P., Mendrisio G.P., Baracchi Trophy (with Roger Swerts), Montjuich Hill Climb, Super Prestige Pernod ...

△ *Merckx prepares himself for his attempt at the world hour record.*

"The season didn't get off to a very good start – I crashed in Paris-Nice. As a result of that, a piece of my vertebra was broken off. Fortunately that particular area is bedded into a muscle group, so the consequences of the break were limited. The early season was again excellent, with victories in Milan-San Remo, the Flèche-Wallonne and Liège-Bastogne-Liège. In the Giro, I had to deal with Fuente, who made my life a misery. And in the Tour, too, it was clear to me that although I could still climb with the best in the mountains, beating them was becoming more and more difficult. In the Tour de France, which I won for the fourth successive year, I was also discovering that people were getting increasingly fed up with my domination. And the organizers were making it clear they felt the same, too. So, the year after, I stayed out of the Tour.

"I had been thinking of making an attempt on the world hour record for a while, but I was having such problems with my back during 1970 and 1971 after my fall at Blois in 1969, I kept having to shelve any plans I had. In 1972, however, I was still fresh coming out of the Tour and my back was feeling a little better. After finishing a race in Rummen, I went to look for the journalist, Willem Van Wijnendaele. I told him that I had decided, that very second, that I wanted to have a crack at the hour record. I knew that in the mountains I was no longer the same rider I had once been, but I could still catch fire on the flat. My attempt at the record in Mexico was successful, but it cost me blood, sweat and tears. It is pointless to think about how many more kilometers I might have been able to do if it had not been for the crash in Blois, or about how I would have done if I'd had the equipment and bikes available that those making attempts recently have had. In Mexico, the only thing I knew was that one attempt at it was quite enough."

The Bear

*"People rarely have the courage to be
completely good or totally evil."*
(Machiavelli)

"I would like to see everyone do all right."
(Eddy Merckx)

△ *Daughter Sabrina pushes the head of her playmate
under. "I hardly had any time for my family,"
Merckx says.*

In order to be able to write this book, we sought the advice of many people who have known Merckx from close by. We asked every one of them what they regarded as his greatest weakness. Nearly all of them spontaneously answered: "He is too nice."

"Eddy can't say no", says his mother. "He is always worried that he might hurt someone or make them unhappy. He is neither spiteful nor vindictive. Unfortunately, his natural kind-heartedness and forgiving nature made him something of a willing victim. He was taken advantage of many times. At least, that's what he always used to say."

It seems that the fanatical rider who for years pitilessly tormented the opposition was, in ordinary life, a gentle, vulnerable man who easily fell prey to shrewd profiteers. This still troubles his son, Axel: "My father is too good for this world. Many profited from him, while others played up to him. The sanctimonious attitude of some people makes me furious. I know people who don't even bother to say hello to me if my father isn't by my side. But if he is, they go out of their way to be friendly."

◁ *A Cannibal on the bike, a gentle bear to family
and friends.*

■ 'WHEN HE IS MAD, HE GOES QUIET'

Merckx's mother says the same — her son, Eddy, is too noble-minded for this angry, unfair world. Is it going too far, then, to assert that the bike was the only weapon Merckx had to keep him going in this world? Could it be that Merckx compensated for his inborn gentleness with an unseen assertiveness in competitive situations. (see Chapter Eight). In normal life, he was lacking the guts or the decisiveness and the verbal capabilities to stick up for himself. He hated conflict, kept out of arguments, and did not want confrontation. "When he is mad, he goes quiet", says Axel Merckx. Fortunately he could get rid of his ire on the bike. The more unfairly anyone treated him, and the more they tried to profit from him, the faster he rode.

According to his mother, Merckx cannot understand that anyone would deliberately want to do bad things. "He does not comprehend that someone would willfully torment someone else," she says. "He would and could be the friend of everyone."

Paul Van Himst says Merckx is always ready to do favors for people. "He never does it with ulterior motives; it's always spontaneous," says Van Himst. "That's just the way he is. In that respect, he is too tolerant, actually. If people approach him or keep pressing him, he nearly always complies with their wishes. That can go against him in the end."

Too much tolerance can have a boomerang effect. Conflicts which are not cleared up can continue to fester inside. Merckx rarely said what he was feeling straightaway and afterward he was always sorry. "He sometimes lets himself be guided by his

▷ *The Good Samaritan offers some refreshment to the injured Vanspringel who had fallen heavily on the Tour stage to Gap in 1970.*

TAX EVASION AND COMMITTING FORGERY

At the beginning of 1980, Eddy Merckx bought a genuine old Brabant farmhouse dating from the 13th century on Birrebeekstraat in Sint-Brixius-Rode, parts of which had been restored by the previous owner, Freddy Liénard. The renowned master bicycle manufacturer, De Rosa, gave Merckx the idea of starting up his own cycle factory. Freddy Liénard wanted to help put the product on a commercial footing. The 'SA Cycles Eddy Merckx Rijwielen NV' was founded, and Liénard was installed as sales representative/manager. The assembly line was constructed in the former farm stables and Merckx set to work.

"I was gullible as far as Liénard was concerned," says Merckx. "At first, he showed no hint of being a sponger — far from it. In fact, he kept the vultures at bay. Afterward, it became apparent that he was a freeloader himself. I could hardly believe it, I had known him for 10 years, after all. When his deception came to the surface, I was still not convinced of his guilt and wanted to give him a second chance. Perhaps I'm too impressionable. Fortunately, however, my lawyer advised me against it."

On December 16, 1980, Merckx was charged with tax fraud: he was accused of committing forgery to facilitate tax evasion. He was not arrested because, according to the examining magistrate, the amount of the fraud was less than 10 million francs ($30,000). In any event, the helpless Merckx was suddenly beset by judicial and financial problems about which he had taken no account in the dim and distant past. "Yet again, Eddy had shown too much faith in someone," says his wife Claudine. "Sometimes he is too naïve and too unknowing."

Merckx tries to defend himself. "Making the switch from a hectic life as a cyclist to that of a company manager was no piece of cake," he says. "I was happy that Liénard was around with all his commercial experience to keep the business on the right tracks. During a transitional period like that, you need someone who you can trust, don't you?"

Merckx parted company with Liénard early in 1982, after his cycle factory had been saved thanks to the cash injection by the Swiss company, Promo Publi, which included the investment of Merckx's own private money. Merckx provided an employment opportunity for several of his former teammates, and it was this sense of responsibility he felt toward them that was one of the reasons he carried on.

feelings," says his mother. "And that makes him vulnerable."

Merckx is aware of that. "I'm always a little quick to trust people," he says. "When I do trust them it is with 100 percent commitment. Maybe my disposition is too good, too. I'm pleased when someone else does well. That might make me an easy target for devious types, but I can't change my character."

A certain naïveté, or call it frankness, is not foreign to Merckx. "I believe in a world in which you don't always have to be on your guard," he says. "My commonsense tells me that's probably foolish. I don't want to go through life continually having to be vigilant and constantly afraid of evil, though. I want to retain something of my youthfulness within me. If I can't, what's the point of it all?"

△ *Spontaneously doing people a favor without any ulterior motives. (Merckx gives a push to a rider during a charity race in Tokyo in the fight against cancer.)*

■ A MAN IN NEED FINDS OUT WHO HIS FRIENDS ARE

Merckx has, nevertheless, had enough lessons in life. It has already been explained that it was likely that the doping affair at Savona during the 1969 Giro was a plot. After his career had finished, Merckx was exploited through his gullibility by businessman Freddy Liénard, and as a result his bicycle factory teetered on the edge of the abyss (see insert above).

"During that period, virtually the whole world was ready to stand and watch him fall," says Claudine, her voice still carrying pent-up anger. "It was like the old song: 'A man in need finds out who his friends are.' From a personal point of view, I found that time to be an enormously sobering experience. My eyes were opened wide. Eddy, too, found it hard to take the way some people were happy to let him fall. Thanks to his mellow nature, he has since gotten over it, but there are certain things I can't forget. The whole business hasn't stopped Eddy being too ready to trust. It may be true that if he is threatened, something inside him is broken for good, but vindictiveness and revenge are not words you will find in his vocabulary. He would never be out to get Rik Van Looy, for example, who gave him such a hard time, or Freddy Maertens — even though he still doesn't understand why he led him up the garden path the way he did in the 1973 World Championship. Yet if he was to bump into either of them, he would probably shake them by the hand or have a word with them. He is simply not a hateful sort of person."

Roger Swerts got the better of Merckx — two years his junior — on many occasions while the two rode as amateurs in 1964. "I still remember the way I stole the 'Het Laatste Nieuws Trophy' — a series of races testing a rider's consistency — after a long battle. I won a Renault R8 car, and Merckx had to settle for an R4. We were fierce rivals in those days. My professional debut was with Mercier, but my first few years were anything but successful. At the end of 1967, I was given the push by team manager Antonin Magne, and I was out of a job. I went to Lucien Acou's café near the Gare du Midi in Brussels and there I met Claudine, who was soon to be marrying Merckx. She promised me she would raise the matter with Eddy. A few days later, he rang me up to tell me that I could come and ride for his team. It would have been just as easy for him to let me down because places were scarce, and there were plenty of interested parties."

The way Jos Huysmans, too, ended up in Merckx's team points at the conciliatory nature of the Cannibal. "After the doping affair at Savona during the Giro in 1969 (see Chapter Nine), the BRT reporter, Fred De Bruyne, interviewed me in Evergem," says Huysmans. "Was Merckx guilty or not, he asked. And could his reprieve be justified? I answered that I found it hard to believe that Merckx would do such a stupid thing, but that notwithstanding, the law ought to be the same for everyone. It didn't go unheard by Merckx, and for several races afterward he wouldn't speak to me. During the Belgian championship in Mettet, he came up and rode alongside me. 'So you're against me as well,' he said. To which I replied that I wasn't. 'If I could improve a little, I might even want to ride in your team,' I added, for form's sake. A week later, Merckx asked me to sign a contact. I jumped at the chance."

No Words, Only Deeds

Roger De Vlaeminck, too, is full of praise for Merckx's magnanimity, despite the fact that there had been a number of conflicts between the two of them. "In 1986,

THE RECONCILIATION WITH LUIS OCAÑA

From the 1970 Tour onward, a cold war waged between Merckx and Luis Ocaña, which over time became increasingly bitter. It was the monumental 'hammer blow' that was inflicted on Merckx during the stage to Marseille during the Tour in 1971 that particularly hurt. A deal had been struck between Ocaña and Cyrille Guimard that assured the Frenchman of taking the green jersey. In return for that, all the Spanish teams put everything they had in the service of Ocaña. As is known, Ocaña had to pull out of the Tour after a fall during the 14th stage on the descent of the Col de Menté. At the end of the stage to Marseille, a gaggle of Spaniards arrived outside the time limit, but for some reason they were not eliminated from the Tour.

On each of the two days after Ocaña's fall, Merckx went to visit the Spaniard in hospital, but it was purely a formality. It had been Tour organizer Felix Lévitan's idea anyway, as he could see in it a tasty morsel for the media to chew on. Moreover, it is hard to shake off the impression that Merckx is still convinced that Ocaña was a little too willing to stay down at the side of the road on the Col de Menté. Merckx does not say it in so many words, but in his mind it is clear that he thinks Ocaña was a spent force by that time and that over the upcoming Pyrenees stages the Spaniard would have had to surrender the yellow jersey.

Moving on, in 1972 and 1973, Merckx and Ocaña hardly allowed themselves a glance of each other. In the autumn of 1973, both men had ridden the Grand Prix des Nations, after which they found themselves on board the same plane heading for Geneva. "The next day we were due to ride in Lausanne," said Ocaña. "In the plane, I went over to Merckx and in French asked him: 'Are you going to sulk all your life?' Then we had a drink together. After we landed we continued to promote our reconciliation with yet more liquid refreshment, until it reached a point where we just about found each other the greatest friends in the western world."

The day after that came the race, A travers Lausanne consisting of an uphill time trial and road race. "I won them both," remembers Merckx, with a hand to his forehead. "And that evening, somewhere nearby, there was another short criterium, which I won in the pouring rain. For two full days after that, I hardly felt human at all."

When Ocaña set up a company dealing in Armagnac after he retired, his appeal to Merckx was not in vain. "Eddy introduced me to the Belgian drink distributors, Fourcroy," said Ocaña. "He helped me in every way possible. It just goes to show once again what a big heart he's got."

△ *After several years' war, a spontaneous reconciliation took place between Ocaña and Merckx in 1973.*

he gave me the chance to return to competition as a cyclo-cross rider," says De Vlaeminck. "As a private sponsor, he provided me with a car and all the equipment I needed. I remember riding my first event at Juilly, north of Paris, and Merckx was there with Paul Van Himst, without having let me know beforehand. That was typical of Merckx: no words, only deeds."

How could Merckx's all-consuming ambition be reconciled with his kindheartedness? One's immediate impression is that his feelings have had to play second fiddle to the steamrolling effect of his ambition, and usually that is how it was. But even he will admit that he let important victories slip through his fingers because he let his heart rule his head. "That world championship in 1973 at Montjuich is a perfect example," he says. "During the closing stages with Ocaña, Gimondi and Maertens, I was getting fed up of all the rubbish I was getting from Maertens: 'If you would, keep things calm please, because I'm dead.' He promised he would lead out the sprint for me if I did. Unfortunately, I fell for his plea, when it would have been better for me to have ignored it and attack, which seemed to be my best option, anyway. Or I could have stayed out in front and I would have been world champion. Alternatively, Gimondi and Ocaña could have ridden themselves into the ground trying to catch me, leaving Maertens in the driving seat, and he could have become world champion. But everyone knows how it did turn out." Gimondi took the world title and Merckx finished only fourth.

■ THE ACCIDENT AT GEMBLOUX

Sometimes Merckx's obligingness reached the extent that he had to be protected against himself. "It was during a training camp at Gembloux," says Merckx. "I was riding my bike up to a crossroads and could see a truck approaching from the right, so I stopped pedaling. A car driver alongside me, however, thought the coast was clear because I had carried on through in the first place, and he drove on to the crossroads. I shouted to him to stop, but all he did was smile – he had probably recognized me. You can guess what happened next. The truck rammed right into the car. A child passenger was so badly injured that a leg needed to be amputated. I was absolutely shattered by it. I felt terribly guilty, even though I had no real reason to be. That man asked for money from me later, and at first I was going to take him up on it. But my lawyer stopped me. 'It's an endless road you would be getting yourself on,' he said. And I'm afraid I have to admit he was right."

The worst case of Merckx's altruism ultimately working against him, occurred in the 1975 Tour de France. "The biggest mistake I ever made," says Merckx now, frankly. It was the Tour of the infamous stomach punch Merckx took on the Puy-de-Dôme. On the morning of July 15, before the start of the 15th stage from Valloire to Morzine-Avoriaz, he was knocked down by the Dane, Ole Ritter. Merckx crashed down onto his face. He discovered he had broken his cheek bone and a sinus was perforated too. Merckx rode another very gutsy stage, in which he

While riding for Peugeot in 1966 and 1967, Merckx was a teammate of Tom Simpson, whose tragic death in the 1967 Tour is probably remembered by everyone. Merckx often shared a room with the Briton, who he admired for his devotion to his craft, his ambition and his good manners. Simpson, nevertheless, would regularly make things awkward for Merckx, as in the 1967 Paris-Nice.

"After winning the stage to Chateau-Chinon, I took over as race leader," says Merckx. "On the stage over the Col de la Republique, however, Simpson went on the offensive and took my leader's jersey from me. In spite of my position on the classification, he still considered himself to be the team leader. Two days later, I was out in front on my own on the climb of Mont Faron, with Aimar, Guyot and Simpson chasing me. Totally against my wishes, but on the insistence of my directeur sportif, Gaston Plaud, I had to wait for Simpson. I then had to tow him over the next 25 kilometers, helping him win Paris-Nice."

Most riders would have wished Simpson the worst after the way he acted on the Col de la Republique, but Merckx did not let the resentment last long. Eddy was one of the few continental riders present at the funeral of Simpson at Harworth, England on Tuesday, July 18, 1967, following his heart-rending death on Mont Ventoux (as most of Simpson's colleagues were still riding that dramatic Tour).

"The whole business was blown out of all proportion," says Merckx. "I'm not saying I have any doubt about whether Simpson had used a banned substance. I admit there was a lot of misuse going on at that time. The reason was that there were still no systematic controls in force. The most unfair aspect of it all is that Simpson has been remembered ever since as the big dope user.

"I find that hard to take. Tom was a formidable fellow who taught me a great deal about training methods, race tactics and familiarization with the course. Most other riders played their cards close to their chests, especially when it came to a young rider who was proving to be one of their most serious rivals. Simpson was warm and communicative. In as far as I got to know him, I can say with my hand on my heart that he was certainly not the drug-injector or pill-taker he is made out to be. Far from it. I remember several occasions when he warned young riders against using banned substances. On the Ventoux, Tom was really the victim of his uncurbed ambition. He probably made a stupid mistake on the day. At the heart of the matter, though, is that over the previous weeks and months he had not been living for his profession in the way he had always done before. Simpson was concentrating on business more than is good for a rider, after buying property in Corsica at the start of the year and devoting a lot of energy into moving house. Yet he continued to kid himself that he could win the Tour. His ambition knew no bounds, and he ended up paying the price for it. Another reason is that it was a terrible mistake to put him back on his bike when he was still groggy. In those days, the Tour was still being ridden in national teams. If his usual team helpers had been there, it probably wouldn't have happened. The discovery of alcohol in his blood afterward should not be blown out of proportion either, as I know for a fact that he was no drinker. It been boiling hot all day, though, and under such circumstances it was more likely that the riders would drink a cool glass of white wine or a pint of beer. As a matter of interest, did you know that in July 1967, in Brussels alone, 10 people died as a result of the heatwave. One final word on the subject: what happened to Simpson was tragic, but it is imperative that it is not overdramatized."

▽ *Merckx riding in the 1970 Tour past the memorial to Tom Simpson, just at the moment that Tour organizer Jacques Goddet is laying a wreath.*

continually made things hot for the leader, Bernard Thévenet. Over the next few days, however, the broken cheek bone was to cause him a great deal of pain. He was also having difficulty taking in food. And yet against doctor's advice, Eddy still wanted to reach the end of the Tour, no matter what it took. "Eddy stayed in it for the team," says Jos Huysmans. "He knew we would lose a lot of money if he were to abandon."

"It was really stupid of me", Eddy reiterates. "If only I'd abandoned right away. If need be, I could have laid down the money for my teammates to make up for anything they might lose. If I had the chance of reliving my career, that would be one of the few things I definitely wouldn't do again. Anyway, the reason I lost that Tour was that after my punch in the stomach I was prescribed a medicine that thinned the blood and which, looking back on it, was unnecessary. That was what caused me to blow up in such monumental fashion during the stage to Pra-Loup."

Merckx overstepped certain limits during that Tour and it was to cost him dearly for the rest of his career. That season he had already stayed out of the Giro due to a severe throat infection. A mononucleosis (an illness brought about by fatigue) came to light the following year," which must have been in my body for some time prior to that," says Merckx now. "I was tired all the time and was suffering with hypoglycemia (a fall in the blood-sugar level). Without doubt, 1975 was the absolute turning point in my career."

△ *Merckx was desperate to reach the end of the Tour in 1975 whatever it took. "The most stupid thing I ever did in my career," Merckx now realizes.*

A HEART MADE OF GINGERBREAD

The more one penetrates through to Merckx's soul, the more marked the contradictions become. The Cannibal – the superman, the merciless executioner on the bike – appears to be a relatively easily upset man with a heart made of gingerbread. Within him, he combines both the strength and the gentleness of a bear. This once again shows how the image of a star can differ from reality. Several character witnesses make it clear how tender-hearted the seemingly unrelenting Merckx was.

"A few months after the twins, Michel and Micheline, were born, I took Eddy with me on a visit to a friend in the maternity hospital," says his mother. "I asked him what he thought of the new-born baby. 'It's lovely,' he said. 'A lot nicer than Michel and Micheline.' He was slightly jealous of the twins, because I obviously gave them quite a lot of my attention. On one occasion, when I was washing them, he said: 'You prefer them to me.' I patiently explained to him that babies can't do very much for themselves and that I had to change their diapers, feed them, and give them something to drink and wash them. From then on he helped me a lot."

Merckx seems to be touched or moved very easily. "Once two deaf-and-dumb people shoved a letter into my hand at the Ghent Sport Palace," says Cécile Heleven, one of Merckx's most loyal fans. "They were hoping that I could get them

Merckx's autograph. I passed on the message to Eddy, and immediately after the race he went over to them and gave them his racing gloves as a present. They were thrilled to bits. Still in Ghent, Merckx once did a lap of the track with a young handicapped boy on his back. And I'll never forget what he did for our young daughter, Ingrid, who had hurt her head just before the criterium in Bilzen. Eddy won the race, and straight after the presentation he turned around and presented Ingrid with the bouquet. They may only be minor examples, but they are typical of his attitude."

IN TEARS

Of the thousands of photos of Merckx that have appeared, one which has left a lasting impression is one of him lying helplessly in bed crying in a hotel room in Albissola. "I have never cried after a defeat," says Merckx. "Except when it was a clear case of massive injustice like the doping business in the Giro. That was such a hammer blow that my whole world collapsed around me."

Merckx admits that he has a soul made of wax. He can still remember how easy it was to cry when he was a child. "I nearly always welled up whenever my parents left me staying with an aunt or uncle," he laughs. "I cried my eyes out a lot then."

Here, too, the similarities between Merckx and his rough-diamond of a father are marked. During the winter of 1962-63, national champion in the debutant category, Eddy was sent on a training camp to Bled in Yugoslavia. It was the first time the youngster stayed somewhere other than his parental home for any length of time. Jules Merckx, the man who never let anything of his stormy private life show on

▽ *A broken man in room number 11: a photo that went around the world.*

the surface, could no longer hold it back, even during the first day Eddy was away. "After lunch the tears came rolling down his cheeks," says his wife. "When Eddy was little, Jules used to let him climb onto his knee and play games with him – pulling his ears, hiding his nose, that sort of thing. The thought of it had made him feel tender. Eventually, we all ended up sitting around the table crying, because we missed Eddy. I still remember one of our neighbors walking in and hesitantly saying: 'Oh my God, has there been a death in the family?' When Eddy returned home, he told us that while he was in Yugoslavia he had lain awake each night crying."

Whenever there is a report on suffering in the media, Merckx is always saddened by it. "If he sees war or poverty on television, he is either angry or affected by it," says his wife, Claudine. "It's not only due to his character but also his upbringing. As a child, he was always shown a great deal of warmth and security, particularly by his mother. My parents were harder. If I was hurting somewhere, they would tell me straight away that it was nothing, or that it was not bad. In similar situations, Eddy was more likely to be given a cuddle."

"I always have a crisis of conscience when I am confronted by suffering", says Merckx. "It always makes me realize how good we have it here. Ninety-nine percent of our problems are to do with luxury. I get really angry at people who complain about trivial things without being aware of what kind of heavenly circumstances they live in."

■ NO SERVANT OF MAMMON

Merckx claims that he is anything but a materialist. "I know the value of money," he says, "because I have seen at first hand how my parents had to scrimp and save for years on end to make ends meet. So I've never thrown money down the drain."

Some of Merckx's former colleagues said he was not exactly a big spender. Sercu and Gimondi were the same in that they were aware of their roots; they knew what they needed to do to achieve something, and they, too, were a little on the frugal side. That is not to say that Merckx thought about money day and night. "Throughout his career, Eddy had no idea about the financial side of things," says Claudine Merckx. "He never even asked about it. I don't remember him ever coming up to me at the end of a season and saying: 'How much have I earned this year?' He never paid much attention to it. No, money was never a motivation for him."

There are a number of examples that underline the last point. At the end of the 1968 season, Angelo Baracchi made Eddy a princely offer to ride in his Trophy race – a two-up time trial, but Merckx, who had already ridden 130 races that year, refused.

André D'Hont, director of the Ghent Sport Palace, testifies that Merckx never haggled over money. "He was the cheapest rider I ever worked with," says D'Hont. "He was worth more than the price I paid him. Yet even if he only came to tie his shoelaces, you were guaranteed a crowd of 3000. And you never had any cause to remind him of his responsibilities to the public. He was always the first rider ready, and you never needed to ask him to put more effort in. Great times, they were."

Had Merckx been a servant of Mammon, he would probably have sold races by the cartload. "One of the reasons the team stayed so tight around Merckx was because we knew he never sold races," says Jos Huysmans.

MERCKX RIDES IN THE ROCKS

On the eve of the 1993 edition of Liège-Bastogne-Liège, a life-sized stone statue of the Cannibal was unveiled on the slopes of the Stockeu, a familiar energy-sapping climb on the classic course. It appears to be riding out of the rocks. The people behind it were the owner of a restaurant from Coo and a cycling-loving public official from Brussels. Merckx himself was rather surprised by the idea of it at first, since monuments are usually only unveiled after the death of the person concerned. So he made it clear in no uncertain terms that he still belonged to the land of the living and that he would like to continue to do so for many years to come. The stone on the Merckx statue was sculpted by the artist Yves Marian.

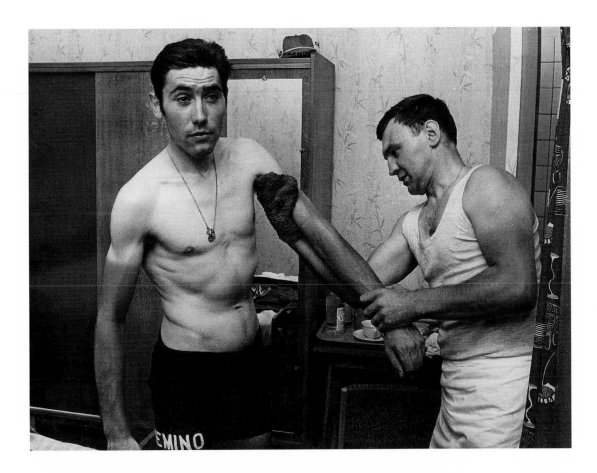

*◁ Trusty soigneur
Guillaume Michiels:
"Loyalty and good
performances were
generously rewarded
by Eddy."*

■ BORN TOO EARLY

Merckx seemed to regularly come up with a piece of generosity as well. "My
teammates were regularly paid extra if they had ridden well during a race," says
soigneur Guillaume Michiels. "And the personnel also got a bonus every now and
then. When Merckx won his first Milan-San Remo in 1966, his soigneur, Gust
Naessens, found an unexpected BF 20,000 (about $650) being slipped into his
hand. In those days, that was a fair-sized sum."

In the Tour, Merckx did not earn anything directly. The prize money was divided
between the team. "It is hard to make money," said Merckx in November 1972,
"but it's even harder not to spend it. After the Tour de France comes the Tour de
Pay-outs." On numerous occasions, Merckx was actually critical of the low prize
money in the sport. "When I won the Tour of Italy in 1974, my teammates earned
BF 28,000 (less than $1000) each. Scandalous!" he says.

In actual fact Merckx, was born too early, because he was not around to experience
the favorable economic climate of the 1980s. When he made his debut with Solo,
he was getting BF 12,500 per month, paid over ten months (about $6000). "Only
after my first Tour de France win in 1969 did I start to earn 'good' money," says
Merckx. "I mustn't grumble, though. Obviously, I realize I could have earned more
if I had been born 10 years later, but there's always something in life you could
regret. The worst thing is that my teammates – some of whom could easily have
been team leaders in their own right – did not get as much as they should have.
Just look at what a good domestique or no-more-than-reasonable rider has been

able to get the last few years. I also used to take as many teammates as I could with me to criteriums. I sometimes let organizers reduce the amounts on my contracts on condition that I was allowed to bring some of my teammates."

"Merckx's attitude to money was determined by his middle-class roots," says sports journalist Robert Janssens. "One of the laws of that social environment was that the first thing you worried about was your family. That was the cornerstone of life. Your wife and children had to be well looked after, and only when they were could you start thinking about yourself. I don't believe money was ever the principal motivation for Merckx; it was from a social viewpoint that he wanted to succeed. To put that in terms of the customs of his environment, that is to say that his family was safe and secure."

FAMILY TIES

The blood ties, that family solidarity and the responsibilities that go with it has always been an important element in Merckx's way of thinking. His constant concern for his mother is one component of that. "In 1991, I was having problems with one of my knees", says his mother. "I needed to have an operation on it, and Eddy made sure right away that I got the best doctor for the job. During the operation he rang three times. He had reserved a lovely room in the hospital in Antwerp, and he had it filled with beautiful flowers. I lay there for 17 days, and he came to visit me every single day. He showed exactly the same concern to his younger brother, Michel, when he was hospitalized following a car crash. When he rings me up he always says: 'It's your no-good son here.' He feels guilty because he can't get to visit me very often due to his being so busy."

△ *Eddy with his brother and sister: family ties are forever.*

MICHEL ALSO WANTED TO BE A CYCLIST

One day when Merckx was on the brink of turning professional, his mother heard a discussion taking place between Eddy and his brother Michel, four years his junior. "Michel told Eddy that he, too, wanted to become a cyclist," mother Merckx tells us. "Eddy told him that he had better forget it. Eddy's opposition to it was remarkable, and was probably because he had realized by then just how tough an occupation it was. 'Get the idea out of your head,' he said to Michel. 'You have a chance of continuing your studies.' Michel protested. 'But you gave up school, and I've got the same strong body as you.' To which Eddy answered: 'I love racing my bike, but for you its far too hard. Don't even start.' Eddy wanted Michel to have it better than he had, no matter what."

During his career, Merckx bought a building site on the Avenue des Goélands in Sint-Pieters-Woluwe, where he had a semi-detached house built. "Eddy really wanted us to go and live there," says his mother. "But when my husband died in 1983, it became far too big for me to live in on my own. I told him that for a house in that neighborhood he could easily rent it out for BF 30,000 to BF 40,000. But he insisted I stayed there. He said: 'Even if I could get a hundred thousand francs for it, you're staying here.'"

Merckx has tried to pass on the domestic values he was given to his own offspring. "Once we were married, Eddy didn't want me to go out to work any more," says his wife, Claudine, who taught business correspondence in English and Dutch at high school for a while. "He wanted someone to be responsible for the housework and for bringing up the children."

Indeed, Merckx hardly had enough time to devote to the children. "I had no family life," he says. "The worst time of all was during the criteriums after the Tour. Winters, too, were no better. After 10 months of hectic activity, I fooled myself into thinking that I could then spend two months with my family, but that was never the case."

For Claudine the preseason, with its training camps followed by a series of warm-up races, was the worst time. "Our daughter, Sabrina, was due to be born around the end of January 1970, but eventually didn't arrive until February 14," she says. "By then, Eddy's teammates had already left for the training camp. The manager of the Italian hotel where the team was staying would hang on the telephone every day asking if his idol was still planning to come and honor his establishment with his presence. In the end, it was decided to induce the birth with an infusion, but then it became clear that a caesarian was necessary. Eddy was furious when he heard that. "Did they need 14 days to decide that?" he said, thumping his hand against the wall. Sabrina was born at five minutes past midnight, and later that same day Eddy had to start in the Milan Six Days."

■ FATHER KNOWS BEST

Merckx probably feels slightly guilty that he left his children to their own fate a little too much, even though on the few occasions he saw them he tended to spoil them. "That may be true," says Claudine Merckx. "Nevertheless, he showed in the way he brought them up that he was a man of principles – strict and consistent."

"I certainly didn't want to make Sabrina and Axel spoiled kids," says Merckx. "That doesn't mean I gave them a spartan upbringing. I certainly didn't smack them very often (further questioning reveals that Axel never received a single clip around the ear, but that Sabrina who is more than two years older, received one now and then).

"In actual fact, Sabrina and I were brought up by my mother", says Axel, who was born on August 8, 1972. "I don't blame my father for that. On the contrary. He gave up part of his life for us. Our mom was always reminding us: 'Your dad isn't doing it for pleasure, he's doing it for us.' We enjoyed a good, solid upbringing. We were given a considerable amount of freedom, but as soon as we overstepped a certain boundary, we were brought back into line by both my father and mother. They let us have the opportunity to mark out a course for ourselves, but they were excellent guides. As a cyclist, I don't think I could imagine a better companion than my father."

It is nice to hear that in his care to instill certain virtues into his son, Merckx uses exactly the same terminology as his late father. That's why it was made clear to the cycling beginner, Axel, that he wasn't missing much by not going to the cinema (see Chapter 7). The principle that "father knows best" was inviolable, and in researching this book it was not brought into question by his children. It was only when Merckx senior began a sentence with: 'In my time...' that Axel would show any sign of mockery, by shrugging his shoulders. "When that happened, Mom would soon bring him back into line," says Axel, with a smile.

To what extent is Claudine Merckx complementary to Eddy Merckx? "First of

---

AXEL'S WOUNDED HEAD

There were times when Merckx had neither the time nor the mental space to devote to his family, especially during the season. "On the morning of the Tour of Flanders one year, I took Axel into the lobby of the hotel Eddy was staying in," says Claudine Merckx. "Axel had fallen and grazed his face, which was bleeding profusely. I rushed him up the stairs in search of Eddy's team doctor or soigneur. In the corridor upstairs, we bumped into Eddy who, as ever, was deep in concentration. When he saw what had happened to Axel he was slightly annoyed. 'Not this as well,' he said. A little later, we were standing at a pre-arranged point by the side of the course. As soon as he saw me, Eddy asked in sign language how Axel's head was."

A couple of years ago, we came across Merckx during an amateur race in the Basque city of San Sebastian, in which Axel was riding. Early on in the race Axel fell, injuring his leg in the process. Father Eddy was really wrapped up in it and continually expressed his concern. "When he's watching a race Axel is riding in, he often gets nervous," says Claudine. "He gets too involved in it. It's not really surprising, is it?"

▽ Daughter Sabrina and mother Claudine come along to watch daddy at work.

▷ *In order to make points clear to his cycling son, Axel, he used the same terminology his father had once used.*

'NO IS NO'

Eddy Merckx was a lenient father, but he was also a man of principle. 'You can go so far but no further,' was his motto. Fatherly authority was sacred. "Few words were necessary," says Axel Merckx. "A 'no' was a 'no.'"

Axel once went on a fortnight's skiing holiday with Wim Vervoort, but returned home early. When he was back home he was asked by another rider, Emmanuel Heynemans, to go training with him to the much milder Côte d'Azur. Father Eddy would not allow it. "I got a straight 'no' from him," says Axel. Merckx senior says: "He had to choose either one or the other. You shouldn't always serve youth hand and foot. I am an advocate of the school of hard knocks."

all, she has far more practical experience in the area of finance, administration and organization," says Merckx. "Above all, though, she was and still is much firmer than me. She is resolute and unshakable. Such an attitude does not suit everyone, but I must admit I was often happy when she solved problems in her forceful way."

The Disappointment of Montjuich

Team	Molteni
Directeurs sportif	Giorgio Albani (Ita), Robert Lelangue (Bel)
Teammates	Giancarlo Bellini (Ita), Joseph Bruyère (Bel), Jos De Schoenmaecker (Bel), Gianni Di Lorenzo (Ita), Jos Huysmans (Bel), Willy In't Ven (Bel), Eduoard Janssens (Bel), Marc Lievens (Bel), Frans Mintjens (Bel), Aldo Parecchini (Ita), Jos Spruyt (Bel), Roger Swerts (Bel), Martin Van den Bossche (Bel), Ludo Van der Linden (Bel), Victor Van Schil (Bel).
Number of Races	136
Number of Victories	51
Major Stage Races	Tour de France —
	Tour of Italy 1st
	Tour of Spain 1st
Major One-Day Races	World Championship 4th
	Belgian Championship 2nd
	Milan-San Remo abandoned
	Tour of Flanders 3rd
	Paris-Roubaix 1st
	Liège-Bastogne-Liège 1st
	Amstel Gold Race 1st
	Tour of Lombardy disqualified
	Het Volk 1st
	Ghent-Wevelgem 1st
	Flèche-Wallonne 2nd
	Paris-Tours 6th
	Paris-Brussels 1st
Other victories	G.P. Fourmies, Tour of Sardinia, G.P. des Nations, Montjuich Hill Climb, Super Prestige Pernod ...

△ *The first and only time he entered the Tour of Spain ended in overall victory.*

The reason for that is that Merckx — who on his bike gave the impression of being so decisive — was also a doubter who certainly needed to have self-assured people like his wife, Claudine Acou, or his manager, Jean Van Buggenhout, around. This will be discussed in the next Chapter. "For the first time since making my debut as a professional, I was not at the start for Milan-San Remo. I missed it because I had picked up a throat infection during Paris-Nice. By April, though, I had recovered and enjoyed victories in Ghent-Wevelgem, Paris-Roubaix and Liège-Bastogne-Liège. What made it a unique year was that I rode and won my only Tour of Spain, and also that I did not ride the Tour de France. Trying to equal Jacques Anquetil's record of winning the Tour five times did not interest me. I have always ridden according to my instinct rather than to a certain plan. Besides, I got a lot of resistance from Thévenet and Ocaña in that Vuelta. The nice thing about July was that for the first time since becoming a professional I had a chance of getting some rest. I even went with my family to the coast for a few days. I never really gave any thought to riding the trio: Vuelta-Giro-Tour.

"The world championship that year, held at Montjuich, was one of the major disappointments of my career. What really disappointed me was the part Freddy Maertens played in it. Had Maertens not hauled me in during the closing stages, I would have won. I remember that Maertens did the same in the world amateur championship in 1971 to Ludo Van der Linden, who had escaped with two foreign riders in the closing stages. Van der Linden was without doubt the fastest sprinter of the three, but Maertens dragged the main bunch up to the escapees. In that respect, then, he was on familiar territory at Montjuich."

The Doubter

"Doubt is homage to the truth."

(Ernest Renan)

"Being in Düren is nice, but endurance

is even nicer."

(Jules Merckx)

P icture the scene: Eddy Merckx leaning right over his handlebars, sitting in the saddle in his rather cramped style, his upper body almost horizontal. Above all, picture the look of determination on that face, that merciless look. This is the image of Merckx you see in books, in newspapers and on television. By extension, one imagines Merckx to be a totally reliable man; as someone who knows what he wants and who, should the need arise, ride through a wall to get it. That would be a mistaken impression, however, because hidden away behind the granite image was a rather fragile and hesitant person, who possessed neither the bravado nor the pretension to make others dance to his tune. "I may be a leader on the bike, but I'm not anywhere else," Merckx was already admitting during his career.

Waverers can be influenced and the same was true of Merckx. "Outside of racing, he found it difficult to solve problems to his own satisfaction," says his loyal helper Guillaume Michiels. "Whenever he was confronted by a complex problem, he would go and seek the advice of a number of people, before he would make a decision based on what he had been told by the last person he had asked."

Merckx freely admits that he is easily influenced. "But there are limits," he says, firmly. "I have certain principles that I consider sacred. If they are violated, it turns everything on its head, and I don't want to know any more. For example, if I'm set up to take part in something that smells a bit fishy, I pull out. I know that I can be manipulated to a degree, but anyone who thinks I'm a pushover has got the wrong idea."

THE DOUBT ON THE WAY TO MARSEILLE

On his bike, Merckx was not always as sure of what he had to do as it appeared to the public. Two days after the disastrous Tour stage to Orcières-Merlette in 1971, Merckx surprised the yellow jersey holder, Ocaña, with an early attack. "When we saw our lead was getting no bigger, I kept having to pep him up," teammate Jos Huysmans explained after the finish. "Two or three times he said we were fighting a losing battle. Each time I answered him: 'If we collapse into the grass as a result of our efforts, we'll probably find Ocaña is lying there, too. You don't know what might be happening to Ocaña behind us.'"

◁ *Behind the granite image of the rider was hidden a doubter (photo from 1977).*

A NEWLYWED ON NEW YEAR'S EVE

Merckx is aware that it is relatively easy to win him over and he is slightly embarrassed about that. "It is stronger than I am," he reveals. "On several occasions, I set off from my home to go to a meeting with my manager, Van Buggenhout, positive that I was not going to go along with his proposals. By the time I arrived home several hours later, Van Buggenhout had usually got his way. I remember that three or four weeks after my wedding, I dropped in on the Six Days of Charleroi. While there, Van Buggenhout sounded me out about whether I was prepared to take part in the Six Days of Cologne. As I'd only just got married, and as that particular event was always held around the turn of the year, I said there was no question of it. Van Buggenhout kept plugging away at me, though, telling me it was well paid and a young married man could use the money, and that it was good for my image, and that I ought to stay a bit active during the winter, and so on and so on. I grumbled against it a little, but within half an hour my signature was there on the contract. New Year's Eve was, therefore, not spent at home but on the track at Cologne. I received a very warm welcome back that evening, I can tell you."

Merckx allows himself to be talked into things by anyone. In 1970, after his second Tour victory, he rode a relatively large number of criteriums in France, and it did not

▽ *Never dare to say 'no', but every now and then say 'yes' with conviction. (Eddy Merckx and Claudine Acou get married on December 5, 1967)*

go down too well with Belgian race organizers. "I allowed the French to influence me," was his excuse at the time. "They had told me that cycling was in decline in France and that I was morally obliged to do something about it, at the very least by riding in French criteriums. I was swayed by their arguments."

He admits that he rode more criteriums than was good for either him or his wallet. "I was well aware that they all wanted me on their posters to advertise their event," he says. "If I refused, though, the organizers went mad at me. In the end, I decided that my teammates and I would be financially better off for riding them, so I usually jumped at the chance. I was wrong to do that. Looking back on it, I see it as playing a part, in the long term, in shortening my career. So ultimately, it led me to lose out financially."

Another example of Merckx's compliancy was when he was suffering with bronchitis at the start of the 1974 season. He knew that it was as a result of him appearing in a number of six-day races. "The changeover from riding in the heated sport halls to going out on the road messed me up," he says. You would assume that Merckx would not want to make the same mistake again, but a year later, just before the road season got underway, he rode the Six Days of Antwerp again. Why? "The track managers kept nagging on at me until I said yes," was his excuse.

■ JEAN VAN BUGGEHOUT, THE ROARING LION

It goes without saying that Merckx needed strong characters around him to keep the wheeler-dealers, the wolves and the leeches at bay. This was something the obliging champion with his big heart did not seem to be able to do himself. This is where manager Jean Van Buggenhout stepped in. This man was a pivotal figure in the cycling establishment through the 1960s and in the early 70s. He operated as an intermediary between riders, organizers and federation bodies, and he ruled with a rod of iron. "He was tough and he was smart, facets that were missing in Merckx," says Guillaume Michiels. "By acting as he did, Van Buggenhout made Merckx less vulnerable to the outside world."

"Van Buggenhout also protected Merckx against himself," is the opinion of sports journalist Robert Desmet. "Eddy had a shocking temper, but Van Buggenhout kept it under control. That's why Merckx didn't make his Tour debut until he was into his fifth season as a pro."

"I'm enough of a doubter as it is," said Merckx at that time. "I need someone who is authoritarian, like Van Buggenhout. Not being firm enough has been my biggest shortcoming. I never dared to solve problems forcefully. I mean outside of racing, of course."

Merckx emphasizes that he was not like putty in Van Buggenhout's hands. "In fact,

THE TIME TRIAL IN ALBI

The impressionable Merckx even allowed himself to be needled by Guillaume Driessens, a man in whom he by no means had the most complete trust. In the 1971 Tour, three days after ceding the yellow jersey to Luis Ocaña after that eventful stage to Orcières-Merlette, a crucial time trial in Albi was on the schedule. Shortly after Merckx had done what was required of him, Ocaña came riding onto the motor-racing circuit where the time trial was to finish. At that precise moment, the Spaniard was passed by a car belonging to one of the television companies. Driessens, who was standing next to the still-sweating Merckx, immediately saw an opportunity to rant and rave.

"Look at that car," fumed Lomme. "It's scandalous. You can't win a Tour like that. You'll have to lodge a complaint to Lévitan, we can't have this." Merckx, still hot from his efforts was swept along with Driessens anger and, uncharacteristically, started to make an enormous fuss about the way Ocaña had been towed in by the cars. "The press were standing nearby and listened eagerly, of course," Merckx remembers. "Looking back on it, there was nothing you could have accused Ocaña of and I apologized to him. I had let Driessens get me into a lather."

△ *Merckx lets fly at Tour organizer Felix Lévitan after the time trial at Albi. His mechanic Marcel Ryckaert listens in.*

I did sometimes dare to go against him," he says. "At the end of my debut season with Solo and the unhappy experience of riding alongside Van Looy, I wanted to leave the team. Van Buggenhout was against it, but I got my own way and signed for Peugeot. Two years later, Van Buggenhout wanted me to stay with Peugeot but I was determined to sign for Faema, and that's what I did. Jean may have been as hard as nails, but he had a heart that beat for cycling. He certainly never lost out personally from his dealings, but I remain convinced that his main aim was to make cycling a better and more attractive sport. He regularly hauled his stars over the coals – me included – if they didn't give the public what he thought they should be giving them. During the six-day events, for example, he often came to speak to us at four in the morning to say: 'Stick another pursuit in the program, will you, before the crowd goes home?' In the Six Days of Brussels, he once came in shouting to me to get out of the kitchen. I felt I had been riding well that evening and wanted something to eat. He came storming in like a madman. 'What do you think you're up to?' he screamed. 'You, from Brussels, letting your own people down.' With that, I had no option but to go straight back out onto the boards.

▷ *The rock for Merckx at times of great doubt was Jean Van Buggenhout. Like a lightning rod, Van Buggenhout kept Merckx away from the worries outside racing (photo from the Tour in 1969).*

"He certainly didn't treat us with kid gloves. If I was somewhere at the back of the main bunch during a criterium, he soon let me know about it. I was slightly afraid of him. Sometimes he was like a roaring lion. He had an enormous amount of power in those days, too. There was the power he gained from his money, from his contacts, and from the sponsors. He was the big man behind nearly all the criteriums. You couldn't get away from him. Walter Godefroot used to ignore Van Buggenhout, but he lost out on a great many contracts as a result. On a sporting level, though, I had a free hand. In races, I was the boss. Van Buggenhout never told me what my tactics for a race should be. Each year, we would hold discussions to put the team together. However, he did force a figure like Guillaume Driessens on me, and it was because of Van Buggenhout that my professional debut was with Solo, alongside Van Looy. Was Van Buggenhout a blessing or a curse for me, then? If I were to draw up a list of pros and cons, I think the pros would outweigh the cons. Yet Van Buggenhout was never a friend or a comforting figure to whom I could take my problems. He was more like a guide who marked out the beacons of my career. He probably made me ride too many races, but in those days it was only through the quantity of races that you could earn enough to pay the rent. The monthly wages were not as high as they became in the 80s and 90s."

STANDING ON YOUR OWN TWO FEET

Claudine Merckx is more balanced in her judgment of Van Buggenhout. "He made Eddy ride too much, especially during the winter," she says. "I knew what they were like, those six-day races, because my father had ridden so many. The concentration, the stress, the smoke, the living during the nighttime rather than during the day, it eats away at you. I often pointed out to Eddy that he should take more rest and wind right down, but he didn't want to shirk his responsibilities. He was the same with criterium organizers. Eddy covered thousands and thousands of miles in his car during the weeks following the Tour. I know it was mainly Guillaume Michiels who drove, but it still must have been really debilitating. Van Buggenhout, who was a qualified accountant, was an intelligent man who solved many of Eddy's problems for him. His death in 1974 left a void, as I think he would have been a good guiding hand for Eddy after he retired. He would have tried to find alternatives for him, and he would have been able to provide answers for him more quickly. As it turned out, after Eddy's retirement, we were left to our own devices to climb out of the hole we found ourselves in."

This ties in with what Johan De Muynck points out as being one of the biggest problems Merckx had to face. "From his earliest days in the sport, he had someone around to do everything for him," he says. "There was always someone to make all his major decisions for him. In the first place, this was Jean Van Buggenhout. It may have been convenient for Merckx, but he had to give up a good deal of his independence for it. Only later, did he develop sufficient maturity to be able to make decisions for himself. For years, he had nothing in life to worry about other than

GEMINIANI'S OFFER

Jean Van Buggenhout's angry outbursts were legendary. "Before the world championship in 1965, Raphäel Geminiani made me an offer to go and ride for the Ford team the following season, alongside Jacques Anquetil," says Merckx. "Bernard Vandekerckhove received a similar offer. Bernard jumped at the chance and signed right away. Fearing Van Buggenhout's reaction, however, I kidded Geminiani that before I signed I would have to get my father's permission, because I was not yet 21. Van Buggenhout had heard the alarm bells ringing somewhere and stormed into my room like a raging bull. 'You ugly monkey, you've gone and bloody well signed for 'Gem', haven't you?' And then followed with a tirade of abuse like you've never heard before. I virtually had to go and stand on my head before he would believe that it wasn't me who had signed, but Vandekerckhove."

racing. Outside his racing, he was never required to be resourceful or to stand up for himself. In 1974, when Van Buggenhout was suddenly no longer there, Merckx had a big gap to fill. Suddenly, he had to take on alien activities like finance, administration, sponsorship and contracts. His inexperience in the field was to surface with distressing consequences. That, too, played its part in drastically cutting short his career."

With her unswerving character and logical mind, Claudine provided welcome support to Eddy, a man who would only occasionally say what he thought if things did not suit him. "In that respect, I'm just the opposite of him", says Claudine. "I impulsively say what I think about anyone or anything, and, as a result, things are always kept crystal clear. Eddy pushes difficult pronouncements and decisions to one side, but inside that inability to settle things lingers. A role-sharing situation spontaneously developed between us in which Eddy ultimately felt it better that I make the decisions – formally at least. He probably resents firm people slightly. But isn't it true that sometimes, we don't like to see a character trait in others that we would like to possess ourselves?"

▽ *Wife Claudine often solved official problems while Eddy weighed up the pros and cons.*

◁ *Herman Vanspringel on his non-selection for the Tour in 1972.: "Merckx always behaved in a proper way, but he tended to seek to avoid conflict."*

HERMAN VANSPRINGEL'S DISAPPOINTMENT

The alliance between Vanspringel and Merckx in 1971 had been anything but planned or deliberately carried through. The two of them became teammates more through circumstance than of their own free will. "I had been riding for Mann-Grundig for several years," says Vanspringel. "At the end of the 1970 season, though, it was not entirely certain whether they were going to continue their sponsorship of the team. I continued to believe that they would, but then had the door slammed in my face. At a very late stage, I found myself having to look for a new team. I contacted Molteni's management myself, only to receive a hell of a shock when I found out that Merckx had already signed for them. His manager, Van Buggenhout, assured me, though, that this would not be a problem. Merckx himself saw no undue difficulties in it either, and I was assured I would regularly be allowed to take my own chances. The marriage didn't turn out to be such a happy one, though. I may have been no Merckx, but I thought I was too good a rider to suddenly go and ride in the service of someone else."

In 1971, the working relationship was still running smoothly, but in the next year things took a downturn.

Three days before the start of the Tour de France, Vanspringel was told bluntly that his services would not be required for *la grande boucle*. "I was knocked right off my feet," says Vanspringel, still dismayed. "I had just been preparing for the Tour in Switzerland, at my own expense. The official version was that Molteni were unhappy that I would be going to ride for another team, Rokado, the following season. They were afraid that because of that, I wouldn't be putting my all in for Merckx in the Tour. That was absolute rubbish, of course. Rokado was a brand new team, so who exactly was it I was supposed to have been riding for in that Tour? I even rang Eddy up about it, but to my great disappointment he refused to commit himself. "There's nothing I can do about it," was all he said. I really felt I had been badly let down. Merckx did nothing for me at that time, probably because if he had, he would have been bringing problems down on himself, either with the rest of the team or with Van Buggenhout. He hated conflicts. Eddy has always acted in the proper manner in every respect, and he never did the dirty on anybody. But I've never really got over his non-commitment before that Tour. I couldn't believe it of Eddy."

A REAL WORRIER

The inability to make a decision originates in the puzzling mind of Merckx: he has always been a patent worrier. He regularly complained that he was hypersensitive and that he changed his mind too often. When he retired, he was asked if he had retained this over-sensitivity right to the end of his career. Merckx answered: "Yes." "Wasn't that one of your weak points?" he was asked by Het Nieuwsblad. To which he answered: "Yes." To the questions: "Do you worry about everything more than is really necessary?" and "Are you a worrier?" the reply came: "Yes."

One way Merckx had of airing his ever-nagging doubts was complaining loudly about

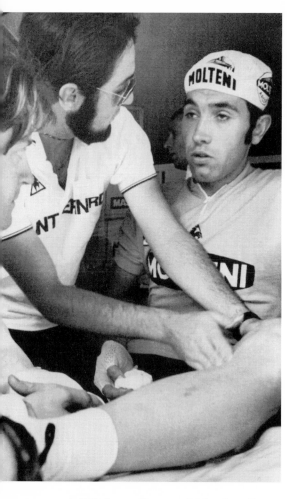

△ *"Merckx was always complaining about all sorts of minor irritations," many of his opponents felt.*

all manner of problems. "He was the same as a youngster," testifies Patrick Sercu, who rode with Merckx on the track many times in the junior categories. "There was always anxiety hanging over him. At the start of a race, he would often have a good moan. Once he was on his bike, though, he underwent a metamorphosis. You might even go as far as to claim that Merckx was fated to live out his life on his bike. When he was not cycling, he always put off decision making, but when he was, the transformation was remarkable."

Merckx's complaining started to get on the nerves of some of his rivals. "He moaned all the time about all sorts of minor ailments," says Bernard Thévenet. "Even though he kept on winning. All that grumbling began to come over as rather unwarranted in the end. It was almost degrading for us. Just imagine how total his dominance would have been if it hadn't been for all those maladies!"

"My incessant complaining had more to do with the screaming uncertainty within me," says Merckx. "I was anxious and nervous and too focused, because I was never totally sure what I was capable of."

Here, too, his upbringing rears its head. Merckx was taught to remain humble, because 'being in Düren is nice, but enduerance is even nicer,' his father had repeatedly told him. It is a reflex that one often comes across with people who lived through the war: hold on to what you have got and never crow too soon about victory, because nothing is completely certain.

■ A PERMANENT EXAMINATION

The more Merckx won, the more he questioned whether he could confirm his success. It started as early as 1964, when he won the world amateur championship. Many people finding themselves in such a position would at once start dreaming of a marvelous professional career. "After Sallanches, his doubts only became greater," says Claudine Merckx. "'All the time he used to say: 'There have been so many world amateur champions who have never made it as professionals.' Before the start of every season he came out with the same old song: 'Will I be able to do what I did last year? Will I be able to ride as well?' He used to have a terrible time with it. He really did, you know."

"But there's nothing wrong in that at all," claims Merckx. "Cycling is a tremendously hard sport. You have to prove yourself from scratch every day. Victory in a classic or a major stage race is not like an exam certificate that you can fall back on for the rest of your life. In top-class sport, even though they don't give out certificates, you are always being examined. I never had the feeling that I had made it, not even after I had won the Tour. In that sense, I've always kept my feet on the ground. Every year, I would wonder: 'Can I still do it?' Add to that the fact that fate may hit home at any time. In 1969, I was very lucky in Blois. My career or even my life might have finished there and then."

One of the effects of Merckx's uncertainty was his great nervousness. Anyone living with the feeling that something terrible could happen to him at any moment can never be at ease. Merckx was troubled by this feeling not only during the daytime, but at night, too. "Eddy was a very bad sleeper," says Jos Huysmans. "First of all, he had trouble getting to sleep to begin with. In many hotels, they left out earplugs and a sleeping mask. During the night he regularly lay awake. It must never have been tranquil in his head. For a start, there was the enormous external pressure on Merckx, but it must be said that he also put himself under pressure. It was always a mystery to me where he kept getting his energy from and how he was able to convert it."

Eddy's wife, Claudine, spills the beans about one of his less-publicized habits: "He used to lie in bed worrying and tossing and turning all night," she says. "He regularly woke up in the middle of the night and slipped out to the garage to fiddle about with his bike. Thankfully, as he's grown older, his sleeping habits have improved."

"That's right, and it's yet another reason to be jealous of my wife," laughs Merckx. "She can fall asleep wherever she is sitting, but I've never been able to. I've sat next to Guillaume Michiels in the passenger seat of the car over thousands of kilometers during the crazy round of criteriums after the Tour, and not once did I ever fall asleep, even when I was absolutely exhausted. It was a massive handicap. I would have been able to recuperate a lot better if I had been a good sleeper, but there were so many thoughts running through my head when I slid between the sheets. Sercu and Bruyère

'I FELT LIKE A CAT ON HOT BRICKS'

Not only was Merckx on edge at night-time, during the daytime he was also did a lot of worrying, too. In competitive racing, his concentration was so intense that he sometimes made mistakes. In the final time trial on the last day of his first Tour de France — which he was to finish as the victor — Merckx rode straight on for 200 meters instead of turning left, almost causing him to fall. And as he was riding into the velodrome at Vincennes, he was nearly sent in the wrong direction. "I was like a cat on hot bricks," Merckx can still vividly remember. "When you are in a state like that, you are looking out for every kind of problem, but at the same time you forget about important things like steering your bike."

▽ Tension and worries about his back pain turned him into an equipment fanatic.

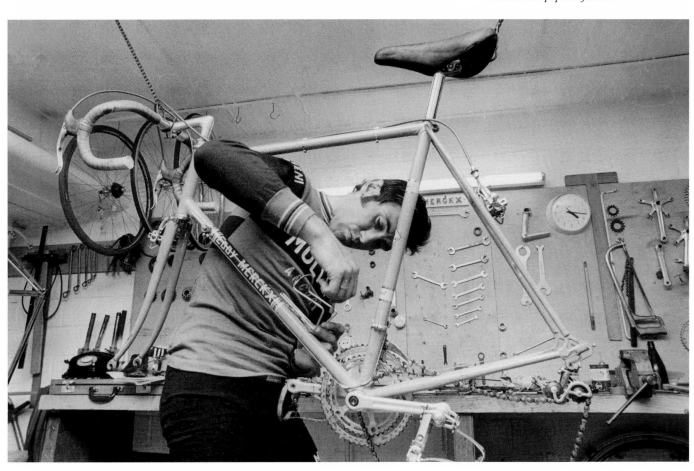

▷ *Claudine can fall asleep anywhere at any time, while Eddy on the other hand once needed a sleeping mask and earplugs.*

GOING HOMEOPATHIC

When it came to medical matters, too, Merckx was suspicious and unsure. The world of doctors was strange and inaccessible to him, and he had one or two nasty experiences with them. In the Tour in 1975, after being punched in the kidneys on the Puy-de-Dôme, he was administered a blood-thinning medication that he insists was responsible for the amazing slump he experienced during the crucial stage to Pra-Loup. And in 1973, the team doctor had prescribed him Mucantil — a cough syrup containing norephedrine — and he failed a dope control after the Tour of Lombardy as a result.

"I have always had a healthy mistrust of medicines," says Merckx. "The conventional medical supervision you received in cycling scared me off a little. When things were starting to go seriously downhill for me in 1977, I didn't want to take any more medicines at all, so I went looking for alternatives. After my unexpectedly poor performance in the Tour of Switzerland, I allowed myself to be treated by a homeopath. The results were staggering. I flew. During training rides with the team I could attack whenever I wanted to. It gave me a genuine euphoric feel. I believed in his new remedy immediately, and clung on to it psychologically. That was the kind of normal reaction you would expect when you are feeling upset. When it comes down to it, though, there is no remedy on earth that can keep the natural deterioration process at bay."

were just the same. It was frightening, really. Mentally, I could never switch off. During stage races, I would run through the following day's stage time and time again. A hundred times I would pick out a bike, a hundred times I would make the start and a hundred times I would attack – each time at a different place. It would eventually drive me mad. When I was sharing a room with Jos Huysmans, I used to go completely crazy, because Jos would only take about three seconds to be in dreamland. And when I did finally get to sleep, I often dreamed about racing. It was a very bad omen if I won the dream race, because that meant it would usually go wrong the following day. When I was having tax problems, I had a lot to put up with at night. I literally couldn't close my eyes, while Claudine would be lying peacefully next to me, asleep. It must be heavenly to be able to put all your troubles aside like that."

Not a Single Classic Victory

Team	Molteni
Directeurs sportifs	Giorgio Albani (Ita), Robert Lelangue (Bel)
Teammates	Jean-Pierre Berckmans, Joseph Bruyére, Christian De Buysschere, Ludo Delcroix, Jos De Schoenmaecker, Jos Huysmans, Edward Janssens, Marc Lievens, Jacques Martin, Frans Mintjens, Roger Rosiers, Karel Rottiers, Jean-Paul Spilleers, Jos Spruyt, Etienne Van Braeckel, Victor Van Schil (all Belgium).
Number of Races	151
Number of Victories	38

Major Stage Races		
Tour de France		1st
• Points classification		2nd
• Mountain classification		2nd
• Stage victories		8
Tour of Italy		1st

Major One-Day Races		
World Championship		1st
Belgian Championship		-
Milan-San Remo		-
Tour of Flanders		4th
Paris-Roubaix		4th
Liège-Bastogne-Liège		-
Amstel Gold Race		-
Tour of Lombardy		2nd
Het Volk		-
Ghent-Wevelgem		2nd
Flèche-Wallonne		-
Paris-Tours		abandoned
Paris-Brussels		-

Other victories	Tour of Switzerland, Montjuich Hill Climb, Critérium International, Super Prestige Pernod ...

△ *His last overall victory in the Giro, ahead of a young Baronchelli (r) and world champion Gimondi.*

"Apart from my debut year, 1965, I had won at least one-classic every year. When it came to one day races in 1974, however, I had to settle for the world championship in Montreal. Winning my third professional world title did give me immense pleasure, though. Illness caused my early season to be a total washout. After the Six Days of Antwerp, I caught bronchitis and did not take care of it properly. I made my re-entry into competition too soon, because I was determined to win the Tour of Flanders and Paris-Roubaix. My riding was back to normal in the Giro, but during the Tour of Switzerland, which came after it, an enormous cyst appeared on my backside. It forced me to miss the Belgian championship in Bornem, and even at the start of the Tour my suffering was not yet fully over. After the prologue in Brest, the lining of my racing shorts was soaked in blood. It was to stay like that for the duration of the Tour — on some days it was worse than others — without my rivals knowing anything about it. It was when climbing that I had the most problems with it. That sort of problem gets to you mentally, because you fear that it might get worse at any moment.

"Bad luck dogged me in the late season, too. Flu caused me to miss Paris-Brussels, and in the Tour of Lombardy, I was beaten by Roger De Vlaeminck. At the beginning of November, I fell during a track meeting in Madrid and tore ligaments around my knee, meaning I had to wear a plaster on my right leg for six weeks. In short, partly thanks to my bad luck, 1974 proved that I was only human. The first signs of wear and tear were beginning to show."

CHAPTER TWELVE

The Cannibal

"Ambition springs forth perhaps more
from a fear of being beaten oneself than
from a desire to beat others."
(Beauchêne)

"The day I no longer turn up at the start
of a race to try and win it is the day
I shall no longer dare to look at myself
in the mirror."
(Eddy Merckx)

VANSPRINGEL AND THE EXTRA HEAT IN MENDRISIO

Herman Vanspringel witnessed Merckx's burning ambition at very close hand. "Eddy took it a long way indeed," says Vanspringel. "At times, too far. I remember a race from 1971 at Mendrisio on the same course where Merckx had previously won the world championship. I was out on my own at the front. To my utter amazement, I was suddenly hauled in by Merckx — a teammate of mine, remember. And at the end of the race I was absolutely livid because he beat me in the sprint. 'Aren't I allowed to win anything, then?' I shouted to Merckx. He answered that the organizers wanted to see him win. And I suppose you couldn't argue with that — it's just that in those days every organizer wanted Merckx to win."

Merckx may have been a doubter and he may have been kindhearted, but he did possess one trait that overshadowed all his other attributes: he had a colossal will to win. In the final chapter, we will discuss what it was that fed it and where it had its origins. His ambition and pride were of a caliber never seen before. "If he went 10 days without winning a race, he would be in a terrible state," says Guillaume Michiels.

His former rivals dig deep in their search for an appropriate word to describe Merckx's burning desire to perform well. Unworldly some call it, others say phenomenal, demented, crazy. Words alone fail to express it. De Vlaeminck talks of it as a sickness, or an addiction, "which I suffered too," he adds. "Although I must admit I was sometimes shocked by his determination," says De Vlaeminck. "One minute you were sitting with him drinking a friendly cup of coffee and two hours later, in a race, he no longer wanted to know you and he was showing you a clean pair of heels. In my opinion, it was stronger than he was."

◁ *The immense urge to win etched on his lips and carved right across his body. (Merckx on his way to his seventh and last win in Milan-San Remo)*

THE BUZZ OF BEING IN FRONT

The 1967 French winner of the Tour, Roger Pingeon, described it perfectly when he said Merckx was addicted to the buzz of being in front. This ties in with what Merckx himself says of his earlier feverishness. He himself claims it was never his intention to ride others into destruction, but simply to win himself. The result of both ambitions is probably the same, but the basis for them is totally different – one testifies to a negative attitude, the other to a positive one. The debris behind him and his rivals' teeth gnashing and wailing were only secondary effects which he was not really striving for, but which he found impossible to avoid. After his victory marches, he certainly hardly ever resorted to misplaced forms of megalomania or made humiliating references to the impotence of his rivals. He only ever twisted the knife into the wound of the umpteenth defeat he had inflicted on others when he was ostentatiously challenged or a wrong had been done to him.

▽ *The buzz Merckx got from being in front made his rivals wince: De Vlaeminck, Dierickx and Verbeeck suffer like silent witnesses during Liège-Bastogne-Liège in 1975.*

RIDING HORSEBACK AND TABLE TENNIS

As a child, Merckx displayed an unusual will to win. "In our neighborhood, we often used to play games where a few of us could join in, such as riding horseback or dominoes," he says. "If I were doing badly, I fiddled angrily with the paternoster beads I always kept in my pocket, especially when it was my turn to throw the dice. We used to play for stakes of around 10 cents. I thought it was terrible if I lost money. If I could finish with two francs more in my pocket than I started with, I felt as rich as the king. Across the road from where we used to live was the Cheval Blanc Inn, where I often used to go to play table tennis. I always played to win and I remember never being left untouched by defeat."

That ability to focus, combined with the exceptional physical gifts nature had endowed on him, formed an explosive mixture on the bike. Guillaume Michiels gives an early example of it: "It was in the winter of 1961, when Merckx was only 16 years old. Emile Daems, Willy Vannitsen and me, and a couple of other professionals, would go on our Sunday training rides to Genval. We let Eddy come with us sometimes. One day, at the foot of the cobbled climb, someone in the group shouted: 'First one to the top!' To the right of the cobbles there was an asphalt cycle path, on which Daems went flat out. Eddy got up out of his saddle in the middle of the cobbled section and Daems had to push as hard as he could or he would have had to let Eddy go. That temperament of his was already there, even then."

▽ *The gawkish lad with melancholy eyes was to grow into the Cannibal of cycling. (Merckx after his overall victory in the Tour of Limburg on May 17, 1963)*

A SCRAWNY, GAWKISH LAD

Sports journalist Joris Jacobs first came across Merckx during the 1963 Tour of Limburg. Merckx won two stages and the final classification. "What first struck me was the contradiction in his build," says Jacobs. "At the starting line I saw a scrawny, gawkish lad with dark, melancholy eyes. Once on the bike, however, that timid-looking figure became irrepressible. I can still remember a race in Old Turnhout in which he attacked after about 10 kilometers, and for the next 20 kilometers he stayed one hundred to two hundred meters in front of the chasing pack. 'What came over you?' I asked him at the finish. 'I had a little back pain before the race and I wanted to test it out,' he laconically said. When he turned professional in 1965, I wrote in Het Nieuwsblad: "Merckx will win everything there is that is worth winning." I was sticking my neck out writing such a thing because in his amateur days Merckx had never shown much as a climber. But he had it in him, you could see that. In the Giro in 1967, I had a heated discussion with Guillaume Driessens on a quiet terrace bar. When I said that I thought Merckx would become three times as big a rider as Van Looy, Driessens could only scoff."

AS LONG AS THE BLOOD FLOWS

"The most remarkable thing about Merckx was perhaps not so much that he always wanted to win, but that he never accepted defeat as long as there was a glimmer of hope," says Bernard Thévenet, who inflicted a real beating to Merckx in the 1975 Tour. "Merckx never gave up. Even when everybody else was convinced that he was beaten once and for all, he kept persevering. Because of his ability to focus on the job in hand, he sometimes did manage to pull victory from the jaws of defeat, as in the 1972 and 1974 Giros when he forced José-Manuel Fuente — in a class of his own as a climber — to his knees with surprise attacks. I discovered his persistence myself in the 1975 Tour. In the Pyrenees and on the Puy-de-Dôme, I had reduced his lead over me to one minute. In the first Alpine stage to Pra-Loup, Merckx attacked on the Col d'Allos. He opened a gap of 50 meters straight away. I tried to limit the damage but I blew up 500 meters from the top. Merckx was in difficulties, too, but on the descent he built up a lead of around a minute. I could see my chance of overall victory disappearing and I became very nervous. During the final climb to Pra-Loup, however, I heard from the spectators lining the road that I was slowly but surely winning back ground from Merckx, who was suffering an almighty collapse. Two kilometers from the top, I could see him up ahead of me. I got up to his back wheel, and in a place where the asphalt had melted in the middle of the road I went through as forcefully as I could. And the molten asphalt prevented Merckx from taking my wheel

right away. At the foot of Pra-Loup, I had been a minute behind, but at the top I was two minutes ahead. It was a crushing blow for Merckx. Nevertheless, he kept attacking over the next few days like a man possessed. Did you know that on the final day of the Tour, he even attacked on the Champs-Elysees?"

Merckx's reaction is short but to the point: "'As long as the blood flows, there is hope,' I always say. While there was still a theoretical chance of winning, I felt it was my duty to give it all I had right until the finish."
He also takes the opportunity to reflect a little on that year's Tour. "That Bernard Thévenet," he says. "In that Tour virtually the whole peloton was on his side. He probably still lights a candle to Moser every now and then for bringing him back to the leaders on the descent of the Madeleine on the 15th stage to Morzine-Avoriaz. Thévenet was going to be France's new hero, and I was certainly to be stopped from winning the Tour for the sixth time and breaking Jacques Anquetil's sacred record. The whole mood was charged against me. The race organizers had had enough of my domination, too, because they feared it was affecting the allure of their race. That was the reason I didn't ride it in 1973, actually. In 1975 the fates finally conspired against me. First of all there was that punch in the stomach on the Puy-de-Dôme, and after that there was the crash in Valloire at the start of the 15th stage in which I fractured a cheek bone."

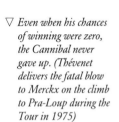

▽ *Even when his chances of winning were zero, the Cannibal never gave up. (Thévenet delivers the fatal blow to Merckx on the climb to Pra-Loup during the Tour in 1975)*

It was also remarkable the way Merckx gave full vent to his will to win no matter what the race, be it road or track, important or insignificant. "I once rode an evening criterium with him at Saint-Cyprien," ays Luis Ocaña. "It was the sort of race no one bothered to stop up for. As always, though, Merckx went at it like a man possessed. And as we were out for each other's blood at the time, I was not going to play second fiddle to him. Before the end of the race, we had both lapped the entire peloton."

According to Merckx, he had acted this way because during another criterium that afternoon, a certain Frigo had stayed on his wheel the whole race. "This Frigo was also riding at Saint-Cyprien and started playing the same game there, too," says Merckx. "So I let him know with my pedals just what I thought about it all."

■ THE RED RAG AND THE BULL

Merckx usually became extremely agitated if he felt himself being challenged. "In its preview of the 1969 Tour of Flanders, *Het Nieuwsblad* remarked somewhat scornfully that Merckx seemed to lack a necessary something for winning this

particular classic," says Guillaume Michiels. "I was there when Eddy read that. 'We shall see,' he said. 'As long as the weather's right.' By which he meant: as long as the weather's bad. And bad it was. It absolutely pelted down that day and it was bitterly cold. The rest is history. Merckx took off on his own 70 kilometers from the finish and that was the last the others saw of him. Second-placed man, Felice Gimondi, finished over five minutes adrift."

André D'Hont, manager of the Ghent Sport Palace, remembers as if it was yesterday a national championship Madison race that Merckx and Sercu won by nine laps,. That was on October 15, 1967 when Sercu and

△ *When it was suggested in one of the newspapers before the 1969 Tour of Flanders that "Merckx is lacking a necessary something to win this classic," it was just the challenge he needed. His answer was loud and clear: in apocalyptic weather conditions he pulverized the rest of the field.*

Merckx completed the 100 kilometers at an average speed of almost 50 kph and broke three records in doing so. "It brought the house down," says D'Hont, savoring the memory. If Merckx is asked why he didn't think two or three laps lead was enough, he says: "The crowd kept shouting 'three, four, five, six...' And it was reported in the papers that our opponents planned to form a coalition against us. I found that rather challenging."

To that, D'Hont adds this anecdote: "During one six-day event, Sercu and Merckx, who were teammates, had both won their derny races, but Sercu's time was slightly better than Merckx's. Eddy was extremely put out about that and he made it very clear to his pacemaker, Maurice De Boever."

If Merckx had not been directly or consciously challenged, then he found his own reason to come up with the goods. "One morning, near the end of the season, Eddy opened his newspaper," says Guillaume Michiels, "and in it he read that Roger De Vlaeminck had won a race the previous day. 'He'll soon have won more races than me this season,' said Eddy, and he immediately got out the federation diary to see if there was a race being held anywhere that day. As it transpired, there was. So we drove there as fast as the car would take us. Need I add that Eddy won the race?"

It is with great relish that Merckx talks about how he thrashed Luis Ocaña in the evening criterium at Sint-Pieters-Woluwe in 1973. "That year I had stayed away from the Tour, and it was won by Ocaña," he says. "Sint-Pieters-Woluwe gave me the opportunity to see which one out of the two of us was the best.

"That was an enormous motivation to me. That morning, I went on a ferocious training ride with Joseph Bruyére. I arrived at the start as late as I possibly could so that neither Ocaña nor anyone else could put me under pressure, and to allow me to remain as calm as I could. 'Not too quick, eh?' was all Ocaña had time to say to me before the start. 'Definitely not,' I replied. 'I'm still having trouble with my back.' No sooner had the start signal been given than Bruyére and I turned on the heat. You should have seen it. The field was scattered all the way down the circuit. Ocaña gave up and I won."

■ THE TOUR DEBUT IN 1969

One of the greatest challenges Merckx ever had to face was his first Tour de France in 1969. For two years, the Belgian public and media had been screaming at him to ride the Tour, but in both 1967 and 1968 Merckx had resisted the pressure. As it transpired, he had probably envisioned his Tour debut being made in different circumstances. The doping affair in the Giro and his subsequent suspension was something he regarded as a grave injustice, which kept on tormenting him. "The week after Savona, Eddy thought about packing the sport in," says Guillaume Michiels. "But within a short time, the old fire had returned. Every day he trained, doggedly sticking behind my motorbike, continually urging me to go faster. After one of these rides he said to me: 'The first day I feel good in the Tour and there is a tough stage scheduled, I'll put 10 minutes into everyone else.' I was not used to such a decisive statement from him and afterward I often teased him about it. And the reason I do is that his 'raid' on the stage to Mourenx-Ville-Nouvelle only brought him a victory margin of eight-and-a-half minutes over the second-placed rider."

The solo ride Merckx treated everyone to must go down as one of the most brilliant escapades of his whole career. At the start of the 17th stage to Luchon, Merckx – in yellow – had a comfortable lead in the overall classification. There was nothing to

---

WHEN AXEL BEGAN WINNING

When Axel started racing in the debutant category, his father accompanied him on his training rides every now and then. "Whenever he saw a climb, he got into position and sprinted to be the first to the top, and I had to concede defeat every time," laughs Axel. "But once I got stronger and began winning races myself, I stopped playing that little game."

△ *In his first Tour de France, Merckx wiped the floor with anyone and everyone. The Savona affair needed to be avenged. (Merckx leads here from Raymond Poulidor)*

suggest that he would risk going on the offensive over the Tour's most grueling stage, taking in the climbs of the Peyresourde, Aspin, Tourmalet and Aubisque. "To this day, I can't believe that it was a planned assault," says 'privileged' witness Roger Pingeon. "During the first of the day's climbs, his teammates were out in front, as usual. At the top of the Tourmalet, the race favorites were still together. There, Merckx, true to form, went to the front in order to minimize risks on the descent. Once again, he shot down the descent like a stone and a small gap opened. It gradually grew bigger: first 10 meters, then 20, and then 50. I looked at Raymond Poulidor, and he shrugged his shoulders as if to signify that Merckx had no reason to continue his break. There were still another 130 kilometers to go."

The state of play 100 kilometers down the road, however, scarcely seemed feasible: in Mourenx-Ville-Nouvelle Merckx's lead had grown to more than eight minutes over a group of six that included Pingeon and Poulidor; 15 minutes over Jan Janssen and Felice Gimondi and more than half-an-hour over a dazed group of 61 riders.

What inspired Merckx to such an act of highway robbery? It was not only thoughts of Savona racing through his head. In Chapter Three we discussed his brush with Martin Van den Bossche, who had signed a contract with Molteni the previous day, and this had made Merckx livid. On that subject, Merckx said that at the top of the Tourmalet all sense of reason went out of his pedaling.

▽ *When it came to boozing, Merckx lived up to his nickname, too. Jacques Anquetil, here with Merckx during a track meeting after the Tour in 1969, was to discover this during a night out in Châteaulin.*

■ UNDER THE TABLE

People often talk of the transformation Merckx underwent once he was sitting on his saddle. That is not to say his urge to affirm was not present around the clock, however, and it manifested itself wherever possible. "Eddy was determined to win in everything he took part in," says Roger Swerts. "I know that soon after the birth of his son, Axel, our whole team went for a drink after the criterium in Bilzen in De Drijtap

THE BATTLE OF CHÂTEAULIN

An anecdote told by Roger Pingeon and later confirmed by Jeanine Anquetil testifies to the fact that Merckx never avoided a confrontation. "After the criterium at Châteaulin in September 1969, we were invited to a banquet by the race organizers," says Pingeon. "Beforehand, there was a reception, but before it had started Jacques Anquetil took me to one side and said: 'Let's see if the young lad can take a punch.' Maître Jacques — who enjoyed quite a reputation thanks to his ability to drink vast quantities of alcohol without batting an eyelid — needled Merckx continually and let the champagne flow freely. "Come on Eddy, have another glass," Anquetil kept insisting. The meal that followed was washed down with red and white wine. Part of the group, with Anquetil to the fore, made their way to the dance tent at around 11 o'clock. Once there, Anquetil continued knocking back the whiskies. Between him and Merckx, a real drinking contest developed. Anquetil could see that in Merckx he had a tenacious rival and finally moved on to doubles. But Merckx still didn't falter, while Jacques gradually started to speak with a slur. At a certain point, a photographer came into the dance hall. This chap was careless enough to start taking snaps of the high-spirited group of stars. When Anquetil realized what was happening, he grabbed the camera out of the hands of the surprised photographer and threw it angrily at the wall, smashing it to pieces. This, of course, shattered the happy atmosphere, and we slunk off - Anquetil looking suspiciously as though he was having to use his wife, Jeanine, to hold him upright. He was so inebriated that Jeanine wisely took him back to his hotel. Merckx was still standing straight and suggested we go and have something to eat. The group of us: Jan Janssen, Lucien Aimar and yours truly had to hang on to each other with great difficulty, but out of a misplaced sense of pride and with feet scraping along the ground, we followed Merckx. In the all night restaurant Merckx ordered - and I'll never forget this - first of all onion soup, which he gave a regal covering of grated cheese, and after that some breast of chicken, and he finished off with an impressive steak which he tucked away with great relish. The rest of us were hanging half-dead over our seats and could hardly believe our eyes. This just goes to show what sort of constitution the man had."

café, near Maurice Nelis's. Merckx drank us all under the table.
He even turned that into a race, too."

Whenever Merckx takes part in an activity in which there is
an element of competition, that same fire comes to the
surface. "When we used to play cards, you saw the same
Merckx as you would see in the closing stages of a classic, determined to the last,"
says Jos Huysmans. "Even during soccer matches in winter, he always wanted to win."

On one such occasion, in a post-Tour soccer game between Belgian and Italian
professionals, Martin Van den Bossche used Merckx's fanatical will-to win to tease
him. The Belgians were leading 2-1 near the end of the match. "Van den Bossche
came over to tell me that he was going to commit a foul in the penalty area just to
annoy Merckx" says Ronald Dewitte, who was keeping goal for the Belgians. "And
much to Merckx's fury that's what he did. As it happened, I somehow managed to
save the resulting penalty, but Merckx had got really worked up at the thought of us
letting victory slip away."

Something else Merckx found irritating were victories that dropped into his lap. The
taste of victory was only sweet if it had been hard fought for. "Easy victories were not

△ *Merckx had an unbridled urge to do well in
everything he did. "Even in football matches
during the winter, winning was the main
priority," remembers Jos Huysmans.
On this team photograph we can spot,
from left to right (back row) Roger Swerts,
Eddy Merckx, Jos De Schoenmaecker, Ludo
Van der Linden, Willy In't Ven, Joseph Bruyère,
(front row) Herman Vanspringel, Marc Lievens,
Frans Mintjens, Jos Huysmans, Vic Van Schil
and Jos Spruyt.*

△ *The taste of victory was only sweet if it had been hard fought for. "Easy victories don't satisfy you," says Merckx.*

satisfying," says Merckx. "I also used to hate it when opponents were too quick in conceding defeat."

"He's still the same," says his wife, Claudine. "When he's playing cards, tennis or racing his bike against someone who is no match at all for him, he soon wants it over and done with. If, on the other hand, someone is too good for him, he will not accept the other person holding back. Once Eddy went playing tennis with Sabrina and her husband (ex-professional tennis player Eduardo Masso) and a tennis coach. They played doubles, with Sabrina and the coach playing against Eduardo and Eddy. At one point, Eddy was under the impression that the coach was not playing all out and that he wanted to save him from embarrassment. He found that really humiliating. Axel, too, brought a blush of shame to his cheeks. When Axel was 12 or 13, and was still playing soccer with the Anderlecht junior team, Eddy regularly went jogging with a neighbor. Axel pestered him time and time again to let him go with him, but at first Eddy didn't know, because he didn't want to have to reduce the tempo to the 'snail's pace' of his son. Axel kept on at him until finally he assented. And when he did join them, he left his father trailing by minutes. Eddy, of course, thought it was terrible."

THE BATTLE WITH JOSÉ-MANUEL FUENTE

Merckx's ambition may have been unmatched, but that did not mean he would use anything he could to reach his goal. His ethical sense of values and his gentle nature told him that the end did not justify all the means. "I never manipulated the press to get a rival's back up, for example," he says. "Psychological warfare was wasted on me. I didn't want to lord it over my rivals on a human level but on an athletic one. In order to achieve my goal, I left nothing to chance. Before a race, I needed to know everything about the course and the weather forecast. I found out my opponents' weak points and about the make-up of their teams. In the race itself, I was always ready to make the most of the circumstances. If the weather turned, if there were echelons, or if an unannounced obstacle appeared: I always set a trap. In that way, I twice made Fuente eat dirt in the Giro. I had to force him onto his knees tactically. A good example was the 14th stage in the 1974 Giro from Pietra Ligure to San Remo. Fuente had claimed earlier that he was going to put minutes into me in the mountains. The stage to San Remo was not particularly tough, but the weather was poor. In the closing stages, the young Gibi Baronchelli made his move, and although I was able to limit the damage Fuente lost several minutes."

This is reminiscent of the way the 1971 Tour took shape, in which the climber, Luis Ocaña, got the measure of Merckx. The Spaniard had already given Merckx a warning in the closing stages of the eighth stage with its finish on the Puy-de-Dôme. Two days later, Merckx lost the yellow jersey on the stage over the Cucheron and the Porte to Grenoble. The real hammerblow came the following day when Ocaña launched an attack that gained him almost six minutes on Lucien Van Impe and almost eight

◁ *The battle with José-Manuel Fuente on the Col de Jaffrau during the Giro in 1972: climbing was no longer the playful activity it once seemed to be.*

minutes on Merckx. The Cannibal dropped down to fifth overall, 9:46 down on leader Ocaña. It looked as if the outcome of the Tour had been decided.

"During the night of that disastrous stage to Orcières-Merlette when I lost nine minutes to Ocaña, I devised a plan," says Merckx. "On the following stage, after the rest day in Orcières, I would attack right from the start. I saw Ocaña before the start of the stage, basking in the glory of his yellow jersey and jovially talking to several journalists. 'Just you wait,' I thought. I was also pretty incensed by the decision of the race commissaire to allow a number of riders to start the stage, even though they had arrived in Orcières outside the time limit. That would play into Ocaña's hands on the stage to Marseille, as it meant he could rely on the help of more teammates. In Orcières, only 38 riders had reached the finish within the time limit. As it turned out, with Rinis Wagtmans riding like a kamikaze pilot out ahead of me and Jos Huysmans as a second teammate alongside me in a group of 14 riders, I shot down from the start in Orcières like a stone. That attack would have definitely paid greater dividends if the team management – in this case Giorgio Albani – had not made an incredible tactical blunder. Back in the main bunch Joseph Bruyère had punctured, and Albani ordered four of my teammates (Swerts, Mintjens, Stevens and Spruyt) to wait for him instead of using them to do the spadework at the front of the peloton."

The 1971 Tour de France did not only burn deep memories into the head of Eddy Merckx, the other leading player that eventful Tour, Luis Ocaña, could practically recall events on a minute-by-minute basis. The glasses through which he saw them, however, are a totally different pair to Merckx's, of course. The plucky Spaniard was a typical stage racer who fearlessly tried to challenge Merckx's proud fortress of invincibility.

"At the start of the Tour de France in 1969, I was bursting with ambition," said Ocaña. "After all, I had finished second in the Tour of Spain that year. Lack of unity within my Fagor team had cost me the victory in that race. Just before the start of the Tour, I did win the Midi Libre, though. I was really geared up to take Merckx on, but during the first mountain stage I had a heavy fall on the descent of the Grand Ballon. I was pushed to the finishing line by several of my teammates, but I was feeling more dead than alive. Two days later, I was forced to give up and my first chance had gone."

A year later, in 1970, the proud Ocaña was ready to have another go, this time with even more passion. "I had won the Vuelta," he said. "And I detested the mentality of the peloton which I felt all too readily submitted to the dictates of Merckx. Their resignation made me sick, because I knew you could take Merckx in the Tour: I was certain I could get the better of him in the high mountains. Unfortunately, in that Tour I was as sick as a dog due to problems with my liver.

"1971 would have to be when it happened, then. And it would have if it had not been for that crash on the Col de Menté. I had already put him through the mill in the Dauphiné Libéré, when I shook him off climbing the Granier, but I couldn't finish the job off on the next climb, the Forclaz, because it started to rain. In wet weather, my chances were cut in half. It had proved, though, that if you got Merckx on one of his lesser days, you could really hit him hard on the steepest climbs. And that much was proved in that Tour when he lost nine minutes on the way to Orcières-Merlette. It was a real psychological breakthrough, and suddenly the peloton began to realize that the almighty Merckx was not invincible. The demigod suddenly took on human traits again. The way Merckx performed two days after his defeat in Orcières-Merlette once again confirmed his burning ambition. Why had he got it into his head to unleash such a crazy attack? I'm sure Merckx ate, slept and drank racing (as Merckx admits in Chapter Eleven). The battle lines had obviously been well drawn as Merckx called in the help of one or two colleagues who he wanted to accompany him on his adventure. It actually began with a breach of the regulations and the stage was neutralized for 500 meters following the official start, with organizer Felix Lévitan riding ahead of the bunch waving the red flag. The attack launched by Merckx and his

cohorts had started before the flag was lowered and I was extremely put out by this flagrant rule infringement. In the end, though, the time difference at the stage finish, Marseille, was only 2 minutes and 12 seconds, a relatively small return for Merckx on all the effort he had had to put in over the full 251 kilometers of the stage. The effort had taken nothing whatsoever out of me as three days later, in the Albi time trial over 16 kilometers, I lost a mere 11 seconds to Merckx in spite of problems I had with my chain."

During that time trial, Ocaña had something else to think about. "As the yellow jersey holder I expected to be followed by a fleet of cars and bikes," he says. "But to my consternation the interest in me was very slight, and they all swarmed around Merckx, as usual. That is a trivial detail you might say, but don't underestimate the effect it can have. Each motor bike takes its turn to ride alongside you, and when you add it all up it makes a few seconds difference. But anyway, I didn't let that worry me greatly. I was seething, though, when I heard that Merckx had claimed I was getting too great an advantage from all the cars and motorbikes riding alongside and sometimes in front of me (see Merckx's version in Chapter Eleven). His comments were rather uncharacteristic of him, and they were probably inspired by the new situation he found himself in — for once having to close a gap on a rider in yellow who would not yield an inch. That was something he wasn't used to, and it was making him hypernervous. I was sure I could keep my lead in the Pyrenees, especially as the mood in the peloton was turning right against Merckx. They were not at all happy with his attack on the stage to Marseille. Merckx put the cat among the pigeons from the word go in virtually every stage after that, and when he did the peloton automatically grouped around me to counter the superman. Let's just call it mass psychology, and it played on Merckx's nerves even more. Everywhere he looked he could see my evil hand and our relationship soon deteriorated so much that it certainly went beyond pure sporting rivalry. We really started to disapprove of each other."

Then came the first Pyrenees stage, from Revel to Luchon, which was to end in such a dramatic fashion for Ocaña. "Merckx was extremely uncomfortable again," says Ocaña. "During the descent of the Portet d'Aspet, he took insane risks: we were even passing motorbikes. Yet still he couldn't shake me off. It was the same on the climb of the Col de Mente too, but during the descent there was a thunderstorm and that's when the drama unfolded. I slipped and went down and Zoetemelk landed right on top of me. Although I didn't break anything, a number of vertebrae were displaced."

Ocaña once more failed to win the Tour the following year. "Three times in a row I had failed, and I was pretty fed up about it," he says. "1972 was, at long last, going to be the year. I had won the Dauphiné Libéré and the Spanish championship and was in peak condition. Everything was going to plan until the stage to Pau. I attacked on the Aubisque, but Merckx came back at me. On the descent, I punctured and had to fight my way back alone, until I joined Zoetemelk, Thévenet and Santy. As we came out of a bend, though, our path was blocked by a line of cars. I had the choice of either hitting the cars or riding straight into the rocks. The way I got round it was to go down myself. Santy was less lucky and was seriously injured. In Pau, I actually only had a minute's deficit, but to my fury I could not find a single soigneur from our team. I had to go looking for our hotel on my own, sweating and exhausted. Probably as a result of that, I picked up a lung infection, which was to ruin any chance I had. As it turned out, I had to wait until 1973, and the absence of Merckx, to win the Tour."

◁ In the 1972 Tour, Luis Ocana wanted to avenge the blow he had been dealt by fate the year before. "I was in top condition, but I was dogged by bad luck once again," says the Spaniard, who here, like Poulidor, Agostinho, Martinez and Van Impe, is creaking under the pressure of Merckx's tempo.

At the stage finish in Marseille, after an insane escape that had lasted 250 kilometers, Merckx had to content himself with a gain of 2 minutes, 12 seconds. It did not look as though the effort had been worth it. In the chasing group, Ocaña had been able to rely on a good deal of support, not least from Cyrille Guimard and his teammates. In exchange, Guimard was given a clear run to the green jersey.

"That Green Jersey of his is still hanging somewhere up in the trees of Les Landes," says Merckx, with unprecedented ferocity. "On paper, the stage from Mont-de-Marsan (which not without significance was the place where Ocaña, who had been forced out of the Tour after his fall on the Col de Mente, was then living) to Bordeaux held no danger. When it transpired that we had to contend with a sidewind, though, I immediately summoned up a couple of teammates. Echelons formed and Guimard missed the right bus. I won the stage and took the green jersey. Anyway, the point is, setting out your tactics in cycling is very difficult. In soccer you have 11 playing against 11, and to a certain degree you can work out a plan. In cycling, though, you are riding with a handful of teammates against a hundred and fifty others. There are too many factors you have to take into account that you have no control over. The most important factor you can keep in your own hands is yourself. I always placed the greatest emphasis on that."

△ *Merckx was humble enough not to act like a megalomaniac, in spite of his obvious dominance. When Guimard was being driven to despair by the Cannibal in the 1972 Tour, Merckx offered the Frenchman a consoling hand.*

'WHAT GEAR RATIO ARE WE USING TOMORROW?'

Merckx did indeed have all the time in the world for his sport, and he was constantly preoccupied with it. "He was fixated with his job to an incredible degree," says sports journalist Joris Jacobs. "I remember an incident in the hotel the Belgian team were staying in before the Olympic road race in Tokyo in 1964. Walter Godefroot, Roger Swerts and Jos Boons were hanging around in the lobby with some of the team personnel, chatting about this and that. The timid Merckx, who kept himself pretty much to himself, suddenly went over to the chatting bunch. 'What gear ratio are we using tomorrow?' he blurted out. It was just as if someone had poured cold water over them. Apart from Merckx, none of them had given this problem one second's thought. Merckx had a very high opinion of his job and also of his rivals. He has hardly ever uttered an improper word about any of them. I remember a minor-ranking race in Switzerland that was ridden in the most appalling weather. It absolutely bucketed down and it was freezing cold. A leading group of about 10 riders were minutes ahead of the rest of the field containing the big names, which eventually gave up the chase. No one's heart was really in it any more. Merckx said to Godefroot and Vanspringel, however: 'I'm sorry, but I can't bring myself to abandon here. I'm going to carry on to the end.' He had certain ethical views on his profession. He felt that you should always fulfill your obligations."

The colossal appetite for success Merckx possessed provoked a reaction eventually. Unlike other top riders, he never seemed prepared to reach any sort of compromise.

The notion of give and take, on which much social balance is built – not only by everyone in riding circles but also by society in general – was wasted on him. He took no pleasure from sharing the cake, even though he was getting by far the biggest slice. Merckx wanted nothing to do with diplomacy. His viewpoint was simple: when you appear at the start of a race, you must want to win it. You do not go there to make up the numbers, and you certainly do not hand out any presents to stay friends with someone.

■ RACING TO WIN

That attitude did not always go down well with others. It was not only his continual dominance that rankled, but also the manner in which he dominated. Often it was perceived as humiliation. It seemed as if Merckx not only drew pleasure from beating his rivals, he wanted to crush them at the same time. Paris-Luxemburg in 1969 is a good example of that. That year, Felice Gimondi was taking part in this stage race that was regarded as preparation for the world championships. The Italian was

▽ *Gimondi in the rainbow jersey, alongside his 'bête noire' during the Tour of Italy in 1974.*

THE BÊTE NOIRE

Eddy Merckx, born June 17, 1945, and Felice Gimondi, born September 29,1942, both turned professional in 1965 and both retired in 1978. Gimondi, three years Merckx's senior, carved out his career in a totally different way. Through late withdrawals by several of his team-mates, he made his Tour debut in his first season as a professional and he won, too. While Merckx was slowly finding his feet, only riding his first Tour in 1969, Gimondi was making a real name for himself by winning Paris-Roubaix, the Tour of Lombardy and Paris-Brussels, as well as the Tour of Italy in 1967, and the Tour of Spain in 1968. Then along came Merckx, and Gimondi was forced to take a back seat. When Merckx won the Tour in 1969 and 1972, Gimondi finished 4th and 6th respectively. In the Giros, Merckx won in 1968, 1970 and from 1972 to 1974, Gimondi finished 3rd, 2nd and 8th, 2nd and 3rd respectively. In 1969, Gimondi won the Giro for the second time after Merckx had been disqualified for taking a banned substance. The persistent Italian then won the event for the third time in 1976. How his honors list would have looked had it not been for Merckx is impossible to speculate. This question, which could also be posed when discussing Godefroot, De Vlaeminck, Vanspringel, Verbeeck, Zoetemelk, Poulidor, Ocaña and many others, is irrelevant anyway. It would be just as easy to ask how the world of science would have looked without Einstein or what would have happened to the Soviet Union had it not been for Michail Gorbachev. Although Gimondi did, however, let slip in 1970 that: "If Merckx had been born 10 years later, think how much happier I would have been. He possesses every conceivable quality a complete rider needs. What are his shortcomings? I don't know, but I'd like to find out, so that I could play on them."

extremely angry at not being selected for the world's and wanted to show the selectors the error of their ways in Paris-Luxemburg. Merckx, however, took no notice of Gimondi's whining and, in spite of the relative unimportance of the race, he went at it like a madman once again and won by a considerable margin. "Merckx always wants to steal the show," was how it was reported at the time. "He should have let Gimondi win. He is going to kill off commercial interest in the sport completely."

When reminded of this episode, Merckx's reaction is as laconic as it is straightforward: "The day I arrive at the start of a race not trying to win it is the day I shall no longer be able to look myself in the mirror," he said. "I do not claim to ride to the limits of my strength every time. It's just that to not seize the chance when it appears is something I find immoral."

For the umpteenth and not the last time, Gimondi was faced by Merckx's indomitability during the 1969 Tour de France. During the closing stages of the 11th stage, Merckx and Gimondi were out alone at the front. At the finish in Digne, Merckx beat Gimondi in the sprint. "Merckx had promised me the stage victory on the way," claimed a disgruntled Gimondi afterward. Merckx denied that any such arrangement had been made. "I rode the final 10 kilometers at the front to put time into Pingeon. And as I had done all the work, I deserved the stage win," he said, with conviction.

LET 'POUPOU' WIN FOR ONCE

Eventually it was not only his opponents, but a section of the public who became fed up by Merckx's dominance. During his second Tour de France, Merckx was jeered by French spectators on a number of occasions. "I win too often," he conceded at the time. "I get letters begging me to let Poulidor win for once."

To that, he now adds: "I never gave in to appeals like that. Just the opposite, they made me ride even harder."

There is an endless supply of examples that demonstrate Merckx's relentlessness. While already certain of overall victory in the 1973 Tour of Italy, Merckx did Roger De Vlaeminck out of the points jersey on the penultimate stage. His dominance in the Tour of Italy and his refusal to share any of the cake with the Italian teams are probably what lie behind the doping affair at Savona in 1969, although that cannot be directly proved. Not only were begging letters sent to him to let others win, but there were also threatening letters. Certain elements in the peloton called for strike action because Merckx threatened to starve the other big names of their victories. The background to it was financial. All the criterium organizers wanted to see Merckx at the start of their events, but he took the blame when he and his teammates walked off with the lion's share of the prize money. "That was a load of rubbish," says Walter Godefroot, however. "Merckx brought bigger crowds to the criteriums, and in the long run we were all better off because of it."

"Merckx's dominance had major effects at another level," claims Johan De Muynck. "Probably blinded by his personal ambition, he was not aware of the stranglehold he had on professional cycling at the time. As a result of his dominance, a great deal of talent that came after him was lost to the sport. And why did that happen? Because he ruled so supreme as an individual, strong collective blocks were formed in which even promising youngsters were brought into the firing line. These young professionals were not given the time or the chance to develop slowly because they were being asked right away to join in the crusade against Merckx."

GREEN FOR GODEFROOT AND SERCU

Nevertheless, there was the odd occasion when Merckx turned down the heat on his rivals a little. In the 1970 Tour de France, Walter Godefroot won the green jersey because Merckx distanced himself from it. "There was a discussion beforehand between our team managers, Pezzi and Driessens," says Godefroot. "It was put to Driessens that Merckx surely wasn't going to set out to win everything, was he? And it was spelled out for him that he would face all-out war with me if he really wanted to give me a hard time."

Merckx admitted at the time that he was not out to take the green, it was just that everything was in a mess inside. "I let myself be influenced by people who claim that it is bad for the sport that I keep on winning everything," he said. When asked if it was anything to do with sport, Merckx answered: "No, not really."

In the same detached manner, Merckx let Sercu win the green jersey in the 1974 Tour. Merckx felt he had become too big a name for it, and that all the sponsors, the organizers and the public were interested in was him. Once on the bike, he could barely suppress his racing fever, but he regularly had crises of conscience during his period of dominance. "I remember us once talking about it," says his former lieutenant, Jos Huysmans. "Eddy wondered whether it might be better if he let others win more often. I answered him by saying that he could not expect to get any presents from the others when he was on the way down."

■ VORACIOUSNESS TAKES ITS TOLL

It took some time, but Merckx eventually paid the price for his voracious appetite. Not only had he ridden a ridiculously high number of races, but they had nearly all been right to the limits of his strength. Furthermore, his pulling power was so great that when he was sick or injured, he was always inclined to return to competitive action too quickly. "Throughout my career, I tended to start again too soon," he says. "You think you'll be all right, that there are no limits, and that everything will turn out all right if you put your mind to it. Looking back on it, that was wrong."

Merckx the cyclist did not have total control of himself. His commonsense often told him what he should leave well alone, but there were many times when his temperament drew him toward new adventures. As long as his body could carry out what he wanted it do, there was nothing to worry about. On April 25, 1971 came a first twist in that scenario. In Liège-Bastogne-Liège, Georges Pintens put a question mark against the myth of Merckx's invincibility. After an amazing spurt, Merckx had caught up to Jos Spruyt and Yves Hézard and immediately left them for dead. Suddenly, however, his engine started to splutter. The frail-looking Georges Pintens got a reaction going, and five kilometers before the finish the unthinkable happened – Pintens made up five minutes and, to everyone's amazement, caught the Cannibal. In desperation, Merckx dug in and hung on to Pintens's wheel before beating him in the sprint. But the image of invincibility which hung around Merckx had been tarnished. "I know some journalists jumped three feet into the air that day," says Joris Jacobs, from *Het Nieuwsblad*. "Merckx's

△ *In his early years especially, Merckx was a force to be reckoned with in the final sprint. (Here he is seen beating speed merchants Jan Janssen and Ward Sels in the 1967 edition of Ghent-Wevelgem)*

△ *In the 1971 edition of Liège-Bastogne-Liège, the frail Georges Pintens put a question mark against the myth of Merckx's invincibility. After the race, the Cannibal did not look very happy at all.*

dominance was even beginning to bore some of the scribes."

"In that Liège-Bastogne-Liège, I had once again rushed into it too soon," remembers Merckx. "The previous week, I had been laid low with gastroenteritis, and I had been forced to miss the Flèche Wallonne as a result. For three whole days I went nowhere near my bike. But when I was over it, I could feel my juices flowing with excitement once again. I couldn't contain myself and we all saw what the consequences were."

Bernard Thévenet also refers to Merckx's gluttony for success. "As long as his body could keep up with his ambition, everything was all right," says the Frenchman. "But at times, certainly towards the end of his career, Merckx became too passionate and too irrational in his ambition. He would sometimes hunt for two hares at the same time and end empty handed. The 1975 Tour was a good example of that. When he realized that taking yellow was not going to be the cut-and-dried issue it had been before, as a form of insurance he eyed up Rik Van Linden's green jersey. The result of that was that Van Linden's Salvarani team became my natural allies, making Merckx's quest for the yellow jersey more difficult than it otherwise would have been. During the latter years of his career, he was unable to adjust his ability to focus to his declining capabilities. That ultimately made his departure all the more painful, even for someone of his caliber. He refused to accept that the end was drawing closer, and he kidded himself that the enormous hammer-blow he suffered on the stage to L'Alpe d'Huez was a one-off. He wanted to leave cycling by the main gates, leaving a lasting impression and image behind. Sadly, when it was time for him to go, he quietly slipped out through the back door."

△ *Doing anything to jump onto that famous back wheel. (De Vlaeminck has to dig his heels in behind Merckx in the 1973 edition of Paris-Roubaix)*

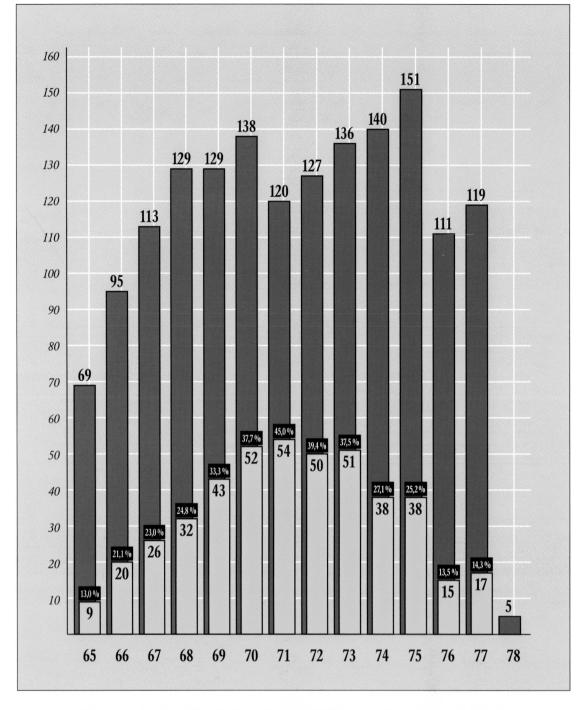

▷ It can clearly be seen on the graph how Merckx's returns increased from his first year as a professional until reaching a peak in 1971, when he won no less than 45 percent of the races he took part in. The years 1972 and 1973 are still phenomenally good, but after that the decline slowly sets in, until it spectacularly gathers pace in 1976. The graph also clearly illustrates that after 1975, Merckx's best years were behind him. One must take such quantitative comparisons with a pinch of salt, however, because no account is taken of the standard of the races. A win is a win whether it be the criterium at Peer or the Tour de France. Yet it must also be remembered that Merckx rode to win in every race he rode. He never used to pick and choose his races. That fact gives the graph greater relevance.

TWELVE TIMES AROUND THE WORLD ON A BIKE

Not only did Merckx's eagerness manifest itself in the manner with which he always tackled races, but also in the number of races in which he actually participated. He took to the saddle for an average of 180 to 190 days of races a year. That is an incredible amount when you think about it. It means that he covered something approaching 500,000 kilometers on his bike. "I rode, on average, around 35,000 kilometers a year," says Merckx. "If you count the years from 1966 to 1977, it makes a total of 420,000 km. Add in the year I debuted, 1965, in which I didn't ride as much because of my military service, and the year of my retirement, 1978, as well as what I rode before turning pro and you

easily come to a total of 500,000 km."

That means Merckx rode the equivalent of twelve times round the world. In terms of quantity, his peak year was 1975, when he raced on no less than 210 days, mainly because he rode many six-day events that year. The tables showing a year-by-year summary of Merckx's career indicate the number of races he rode each year and the number of victories. From these, we have drawn up the graph on this page. On it is also shown the number of wins expressed as a percentage of the number of races he started.

1975

No 6th Tour Win

△ *Merckx makes Verbeeck suffer on the way to his second victory in the Tour of Flanders.*

Team	Molteni
Directeurs sportifs	Giorgio Albani (Ita), Robert Lelangue (Bel)
Teammates	Herman Beyssens, Jean-Pierre Berckmans, Joseph Bruyère, Christian De Buysschere, Ludo Delcroix, Jos De Schoenmaecker, Jos Huysmans, Edward Janssens, Marc Lievens, Frans Mintjens, Karel Rottiers, Jos Spruyt, Eddy Van Hoof, Frans Van Looy, Victor Van Schil (all Belgium).
Number of Races	151
Number of Victories	38

Major Stage Races		
Tour de France		2nd
• Points classification		2nd
• Mountain classification		2nd
• Stage victories		2
Tour of Italy		-

Major One-Day Races		
World Championship		8th
Belgian Championship		3rd
Milan-San Remo		1st
Tour of Flanders		1st
Paris-Roubaix		2nd
Liège-Bastogne-Liège		1st
Amstel Gold Race		1st
Tour of Lombardy		6th
Het Volk		6th
Ghent-Wevelgem		6th
Flèche-Wallonne		3rd
Paris-Tours		9th
Paris-Brussels		2nd

Other victories	Catalan Week, Tour of Sardinia, Montjuich Hill Climb, Super Prestige Pernod ...

"With wins in Milan-San Remo, Tour of Flanders, Liège-Bastogne-Liège and the Amstel Gold Race, you would find it hard from my spring results to conclude that I was on my way out. As a major stage-race rider, however, I did have to take a step backward. I am convinced to this day, though, that had it not been for bad luck I would have won that year's Tour. I could still make the difference count in time trials. In the first time trial over 16 kilometers, I put 30 seconds into Moser. I accept that in the mountains I would have probably lost some time, but in the end I lost that Tour to Thévenet by less than three minutes. It was the blood-thinning medication I took after being punched in the stomach on the Puy-de-Dôme that did it for me. The broken cheekbone I got before the start of the stage to Morzine didn't help either.

"Internally, however, there were unmistakable signs that the decline was setting in still further. After the Tour de Romandie, I picked up a terrible throat infection, which caused me to miss the Tour of Italy. You must also bear in mind that I was now in my 11th year as a professional. For 10 years, I had been putting my all into the sport. I must have been pretty exhausted, because later I was diagnosed as having a mononucleosis, an illness which is clearly the result of exhaustion. Although I still did have my good days, I knew that as a stage racer — where it is vital that you can recover quickly — my best days were now behind me. Mentally, too, I let myself slide somewhat. All the effort and the concentration I had been putting in for so long were beginning to take their toll."

The Bon Viveur

"A life without feasting is like a long
road without stopping places."
(Democritus)

"I have never been afraid to have
a beer or a cigarette."
(Eddy Merckx)

Merckx was a fanatical cyclist and a maniac for training: in short, he was possessed by his sport. That is the widely held view of the greatest rider of all time. It is assumed that the only reason his staggering honors list was possible is because he lived an incredibly ascetic life that a monk from the middle ages would have been proud of. Merckx did indeed apply total dedication to his profession, but there was enough room left over for relaxation, too. "I devoted a lot of time to my craft, but no more or no less than the average professional at that time," says Merckx, who came a cropper every now and then, particularly during winter.

When it came to taking their jobs seriously, he had colleagues who were a lot more fussy. If you compare the way Merckx led his life to Felice Gimondi, you could almost call the Belgian a fast liver. Gimondi was so obsessively wrapped up with his profession that he rarely allowed himself a glass of wine during the winter.

"It's true that for years now I've been pushing the boat out a bit after the season's over," said Merckx in January 1975. "At that time of year, I've never been afraid to have a cigarette or a beer."

Neither did the bon viveur Merckx spurn the chance of a tasty meal. Yet he inherited a tendency to put on weight rather easily. In the winter, it didn't take long for him to put on five kilos (10 pounds). At the start of a season Merckx weighed around 75 kilograms (165 pounds), but after a Tour, it would be down to

△ *Unlike Gimondi, Merckx was no monk, and he regularly liked to sample a drink. (Merckx here enjoys a well-earned glass of Mexican hospitality with his manager, Jean Van Buggenhout, after his successful attempt at the world hour record in 1972)*

◁ *He wasn't always uptight. In closed circles, Merckx turned out to be a bit of a joker and an impressionist.*

▷ *Merckx seen here with soigneur Michiels: "When it comes to diet I'm careful, but I'm not fanatical about it."*

72 kilograms (156 pounds). A rigorous training program during the weeks leading up to the season always brought his weight back to its racing level.

When it came to eating habits, too, Merckx was anything but fanatical. He ate what there was to eat and did not keep coming out with new diets, special grain mixtures or protein drinks. It was not he who invented carbohydrate bombs and amino-acid mixtures. In terms of innovation, he was certainly no ground breaker. Nor was he a revolutionary in areas such as preparation methods and diet or technique. He was never a trailblazer or a pioneer. In everything he did, he stuck to the tried and trusted way of doing things, for as far as that had proved its reliability. Without doubt, that was the case in the field of bike technology. He may have been the type of rider who was continually messing around with his bike, but he would never have introduced the low-profile frame, the cowhorn bar or triathlon bars. In recent years, he passed up the chance to throw himself into the ever-growing mountain bike market because he would rather continue making high-quality racing bikes. Merckx was never an experimenter or an enquiring mind to surprise the world every now and then with ridiculous ideas. The urge to innovate is something he does not have. For him, the everyday is crazy enough already.

"When I was still riding, I ate like a normal person," he says. "I only had to make sure I didn't have too much sauce or fat. I liked red meat – a bit too much, actually – but I also ate a lot of vegetables and fish. And every now and then, I drank a glass of beer or wine, without overdoing it. To this day, I don't drink beer or wine at home, unless we have company. I hate to see the sort of scene you see in Breugel paintings, but when I was a guest of honor, I was witness to them all too often. I try to eat as

healthy as possible, because I tend to put on weight too readily. It wouldn't take a great deal of effort on my part for me to top a hundred kilos (220 pounds)."

■ WHEN SMOKING WAS STILL THE NORM

Merckx is not proud of his former smoking habit. "In those days, smoking was quite normal," he says. "In 1968, during the Tour of Italy, the team doctor advised me to smoke a cigarette after my evening meal to help me relax. That seemed to help relieve the stress and I continued to smoke regularly. I never used to like going to buy them, and still don't, because it has since been made crystal clear that smoking is anything but healthy."

■ PUBLICITY PHOTOGRAPH

Merckx even appeared in advertisements for one particular brand of cigarettes, R6, something he still regrets. "The spirit of the time was different, of course," he says. "But if truth be told, being a sportsman and a smoker do not go together. Anyway, I never actually incited anyone to smoke in those ads. What I did say was: 'If you smoke, why not smoke R6 because they are less damaging than ordinary cigarettes.'

▽ *"During my career I missed out on nothing."*

"As far as I was concerned, it didn't bother me if people found out I smoked the odd cigarette. It's just, you know what it's like: People see you with a cigarette in your mouth or they see a photo of you lighting a cigarette, and the damage is done. They immediately say: 'Merckx is a smoker.' In cases like that, the public make no distinction. Anyway, I kept my 'addiction' as much of a secret as I could. I realize, though, that I was certainly not setting a good example."

This fear of being labeled as a man who did not put his all into his profession ties in, once again, with the fear of what other people might think, which had been drummed into him throughout his upbringing. You had to live up to an image that society had formed of you, and Merckx happily smoking away certainly did not fit in with that.

"Merckx did watch what he ate and drank, very much so," says former teammate, Jos Huysmans. "It's just that he wasn't fussy with it. He was rarely critical of the cooking they shoved under our noses in the hotels, even if it wasn't always haute cuisine. I hardly ever saw him drink coffee, either, because I know he was particularly wary of caffeine." "That's right. I drank mainly chicory," confirms Merckx. "My stomach won't tolerate coffee. Just like it did to my father, it tends to give me indigestion."

It is certainly not the intention here to give the impression that Merckx carved out the career we know so well mainly due to his incredible talent, and in spite of his 'debauched' life. On the contrary, one of his greatest qualities was his self-discipline and his character. That is why for the entire early season, up to the end of the Tour, everything was geared toward racing his bike, and there was no question of any sort of indulgence. "It was mainly when we were riding the criteriums that we let ourselves go a little," says Roger Swerts. "After the Limburg criteriums, for example, the whole team came around to my or to Frans Mintjens's house. The corks would pop then, that's for sure. There were never any outsiders around, as Merckx insisted that was how it should be."

IN SWERTS' ROOM

Roger Swerts was a teammate of Eddy Merckx for seven years and had a reputation as being the smoker of the team. "I always had cigarettes with me," says Swerts. "Merckx and the rest of my teammates were obviously well aware of this. Eddy himself, though, couldn't afford to be seen with a cigarette, as it would not have been good for his image. He did come to my room regularly, though, to have a smoke. He was terrified of being caught, though, and when he did smoke it was always behind closed doors."

▽ *After sinning, the poison needs to be cycled out of the system. (Training ride behind the motorcycle of Guillaume Michiels)*

Soigneur and confidant Guillaume Michiels says that Merckx regularly punished himself if he had "committed a sin". "If he had drunk a little too much, he would often train just as hard the following day," says Michiels. "He would be the first to admit that it was 'to ride the poison out of his system.'"

The happy-go-lucky, flamboyant side of Merckx's character only came to the surface once he had stopped racing. In the period of the black hole immediately after his retirement, Merckx sought comfort in cigarettes, food and drink, but he never really found it. "People were always telling me that I could really start to enjoy myself once I retired," he said, a few months after his retirement. "But they were wrong. Now I realize I wanted for nothing during my career. I was perfectly happy and had everything I needed."

Once he had sorted himself out and had found a new purpose in his life, Merckx increasingly revealed himself to be a sociable chap who could even create a certain ambiance. "I have known many people who were anti-Merckx who thought Eddy was an impenetrable cold fish," says Michiels. "When they got to know Eddy better at various occasions after his retirement, they could not believe their eyes or ears. They had never dreamed he could be such a warm, high-spirited man."

▽ *Merckx found the best way to unwind was to be on his own engaged in activities such as winter sports.*

"Eddy can sing one typical Brussels song after another," says his close friend, Paul Van Himst. "Jef Burm songs like: 'Brussels, you have stolen my heart, with your streets up and down." He would also imitate old-style French singers and even have a go at doing Louis Armstrong."

"He's become a different person entirely," says Herman Van Springel. "As a rider he was stiff, cold, and too intense. But in recent years he has become jovial, carefree and congenial. People don't know him at all, and that's because he never used to like to give much away to supporters and journalists."

"Merckx has become more human," says Johan De Muynck, "through growing older, through seeing the relative value of things and by seeing his children grow up. The God of the bike has changed into a man of flesh and blood."

The form of relaxation Merckx derived most pleasure from was not food, drink or cigarettes, but solitude. "I loved going walking or cross-country skiing during the winter months," he says. "I chose times of the year when the ski resorts wouldn't be too

'THE ANIMALS DIDN'T STAND A CHANCE'

There was a time when, for relaxation during the close season, Merckx used to go hunting. In 1971, he even stated that besides cycling it was his only hobby. In 1972, Merckx still had his hunting license, but a lack of free time meant he could no longer manage any real hunting. "I stopped going because so much gorging yourself with food and drink went on after every hunt," he says. "And also because I started having moral objections. It was not a proper battle between man and animal, as the animals never really stood a chance. Especially in the case of reared pheasants, where you had to push them out from under your feet before you shot them."

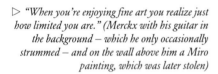 *"When you're enjoying fine art you realize just how limited you are." (Merckx with his guitar in the background – which he only occasionally strummed – and on the wall above him a Miro painting, which was later stolen)*

crowded. Going to other sporting events, too, helped blow some of the cobwebs away. Especially during the close season, I used to go and watch soccer matches."

It comes as a slight surprise to find out that Merckx is also a lover of fine art. "I am able to enjoy beautiful things like paintings," he says. "It makes you realize how limited you are. I am really hopeless when it comes to drawing or painting. Making music must be very relaxing, too, but apart from a few piano lessons I had when I was a child, I never learned to play an instrument. During my career, I could always relax on long journeys in the car by listening to popular music. In recent years, I've started enjoying soothing classical music more. I guess that's to do with my age, isn't it?"

Many Troughs, but Few Peaks

△ *A seventh victory in Milan-San Remo.*

Team	Molteni
Directeurs sportifs	Giorgio Albani (Ita), Robert Lelangue (Bel)
Teammates	Cees Bal (Neth), Jean-Pierre Berckmans, Jos Borguet, Joseph Bruyère, Ludo Delcroix, Jos De Schoenmaecker, Bernard Draux, Jos Huysmans, Edward Janssens, Alain Kaye, Marc Lievens, Frans Mintjens, Karel Rottiers, Jos Spruyt, Roger Swerts, Frans Van Looy, Victor Van Schil (all Belgium).
Number of Races	111
Number of Victories	15

Major Stage Races	
Tour de France	-
Tour of Italy	8th

Major One-Day Races	
World Championship	5th
Belgian Championship	abandoned
Milan-San Remo	1st
Tour of Flanders	17th
Paris-Roubaix	16th
Liège-Bastogne-Liège	6th
Amstel Gold Race	-
Tour of Lombardy	-
Het Volk	15th
Ghent-Wevelgem	10th
Flèche-Wallonne	4th
Paris-Tours	-
Paris-Brussels	abandoned

Other victories	Catalan Week ...

"After what had happened in 1975, I feared for the start of the 1976 season. I was soon put at ease, however. In Milan-San Remo I had another exceptional day. My seventh win in the Primavera blinded me to the truth, however. Though I won the Catalan Week, too, it was downhill all the way from then on. Sickness and minor ailments piled one on top of another and made it very clear to me that I had probably been demanding too much of my body for years. The peaks became increasingly rare and the troughs increasingly more frequent. In the Giro, I was right off form. In the high mountains especially it was clear I had lost most of the old sparkle. When injury forced me to miss the Tour de France, the world looked a darker place to me.

"My end of season form told me a great deal. In Paris-Brussels, I suddenly found myself unable to climb the Alsemberg. That was a particularly painful experience. After the criterium in Bourges at the end of September, things went even worse for me. I'd had so many back problems that I couldn't pick up an apple from the floor any more. For six long weeks I had to lie flat out, usually on a board. Over the following few weeks I seriously thought about retiring."

The Idealist

"Only he who has some kind of ideal that he
wants to turn into reality, is protected against
the poisons and sorrow of time."
(Jean Paul)

"I am always happier on a bike
than behind a desk."
(Eddy Merckx)

△ *The 'all-time best', three times World Sportsman of the Year, in the company of other greats: Paul Van Himst (l) and Pele.*

Eddy Merckx was unquestionably a cycling phenomenon. The summaries of each year, included in this book, are conclusive evidence of that. The question of whether Merckx was the greatest rider of all time is less important. Such judgments need to be based more on personal appreciation than on measurable or statistical facts. Purely on the basis of his honors list, he must indeed be regarded as the best rider of all time. For some people, Fausto Coppi gets the vote because of his special aura and the legendary manner in which he achieved his victories, which have still not been demystified by television images. Regardless of that, it is an indisputable fact that during his career, Merckx was proclaimed World Sportsman of the Year, across the boundaries of all sporting disciplines. And before we have even reached the year 2000, a number of sporting publications have already declared him to be the Sportsman of the Century.

It is beyond the aims of this book to show whether all the epithets, titles and trophies Merckx received were deserved or not. What is of greater interest to us is what sort of character structure, belief and personality was hidden behind the incredible cycling story of Eddy Merckx. Because on that level, there was clearly something going on.

◁ *Merckx: "A life without passion is empty."*
(Merckx in deep concentration before his attempt at the world hour record on October 25, 1972 in Mexico)

'A LIFE WITHOUT PASSION IS SO EMPTY'

FIDDLING ABOUT IN THE GARAGE
AT NIGHT

Claudine Merckx probably knows better than anyone else the passion for his sport that has lived within Merckx for all these years. "When I first met him, it was soon clear that his one and only dream was to become a professional cyclist," she says. "I could appreciate that and knew what impact it could have on family life. Through my father, who had been a professional cyclist himself, I knew all about the job and the sacrifices it demanded. Anyway, I never tried to spoil it for him by putting his passion for the sport into perspective for him, or by opening his eyes to the fact his was an impossible dream. If he could not race for some reason and he watched it on television, it almost made him ill. It was his greatest punishment and worst nightmare to have to miss a race.

"After winning a race he never spent very long savoring the success. On the night he had won a classic like the Tour of Flanders, he would sit there worrying about Ghent-Wevelgem or Paris-Roubaix, even though he had only won a few hours earlier.

"It is a cliché, but Eddy was and is always obsessed with bikes. I've known him get out of bed in the middle of the night on more than one occasion and go into the garage to change something on his handlebars or his saddle or gears or something like that. With Axel racing now, he's still the same. Even if he is riding well or winning, Eddy always finds some comment to make about something which was not quite right about his position. Even when Eddy bumps into a touring cyclist, he starts to chat with him about his position on the bike. It is stronger than he is."

It is our conviction that Merckx grew into the greatest cyclist of all time in spite of his background and in spite of his character. Merckx's career was so impressive that the public assumes, against its better judgment, that Merckx was born to cycle and almost effortlessly carried out the plan for which he had been cut out. It is conveniently forgotten that he had to overcome tricky obstacles on the way. One of the greatest of these was his vulnerable personality. In terms of character, Merckx was not the merciless schemer who had a sole aim that everything else had to make way for. He was easily influenced, sensitive and fragile – not exactly plus factors in the merciless world of competitive cycling. His home surroundings were not the kind to stimulate him to make his dream come true. On the contrary, his parents did all they could to talk him out of cycling. And yet Merckx still grew into a cycling phenomenon. The underlying motive behind that unparalleled career can be summed up in one word: passion. "On a physical level, nature has endowed me with a great deal," says Merckx. "You can be as passionate as you like, but it won't do any good without physical qualities. I do demand the credit for having such enormous self discipline, but the actual engine driving me was indeed that dream. That was stronger than I was myself, and I became a slave to it. Commonsense gives way to it. Having said that, though, isn't it wonderful to be able to make a career from your passion? A life without passion is so empty."

When studying people touched by greatness in all kinds of areas, the germs of success are sometimes sought in their background, in what they have experienced when they were young. Those seeking an explanation for the Merckx phenomenon by such means are left empty-handed. Merckx's childhood was unremarkable and differed hardly or not at all from what thousands of other youngsters went through in the 1940s and 50s. He did not have a fanatical relative or close family member who fashioned him with a firm hand into a confirmed cyclist; he did not have any special, intense experience that suddenly 'converted him' to the bike, and he did not display any of the extreme character traits one regularly comes across with budding champions. No, Merckx was a strictly ordinary lad from a strictly ordinary street with strictly ordinary parents and a strictly ordinary way of life. He played and fooled around the way other youngsters played and fooled around; he was sick of school in the same way other youngsters were sick of school. And he discovered the bike the way hundreds of kids discovered bikes every year and still do today.

At first sight, no specific 'deviation' in Merckx can be discerned. Sometimes at the basis of an exceptional career is a strange convergence of circumstances. In such cases, all the various elements necessary then come together in the same person in the right proportions at the same moment and they reinforce one another. The person resulting from such an exceptional reaction turns out to be a genius or ... a madman (who, according to the famous pronouncement by Arthur Schopenhauer, only lives one story higher than a genius). With Merckx, however, there is nothing to directly suggest such a well-balanced dosage. He was not blessed with the physiognomy required to make climbing easier for him. On a character level, he lacked the internal calm that aided recuperation (the worrier Merckx was a very poor sleeper). He had too kind a disposition to turn away profiteers and sweet-talkers. With a certain degree of exaggeration, one could almost claim that Merckx became Merckx the phenomenon in spite of himself.

STATE OF GRACE

Merckx did of course possess a tremendous physical capacity. That, however, is not under discussion here. What is important is what someone with such capacity does with it. In any walk of life, a vast amount of talent is lost because it is never given the chance to develop. Internal factors may be to blame in such cases. One person may have an extreme talent for a particular activity, but certain character traits (for example excessive laziness) may obstruct the expression of this innate quality. Another person may burst with ideas, but lack an instrument to give form to them (in words or pictures). To put it somewhat laconically: a person who wants to be a sculptor not only needs to have bright ideas, but he must also be able to hold a chisel. But someone who can use a chisel will not necessarily be a great sculptor as a result. For most of us, there is always either too much or too little present to lift us out of the crowd.

△ *A strictly ordinary lad from a strictly ordinary street with strictly ordinary parents. (Merckx with his first bouquet at Lettelingen on October 1, 1961, after his very first victory in the debutant category)*

External factors also may keep undiscovered qualities below the surface, or at least fail to provide sufficient a catalytic effect. A budding artist may be kept so much in check by parents that he or she neglects it completely. A young athlete may fall in love and be faced with the choice of forgoing a career or getting married. The benefits associated with gaining a qualification may be weighed against the insecurity of an artistic or sporting existence. The list goes on and on. There is always something in the way, or there is always someone or something that is not working with you enough. The situation in which everything does neatly fall into place is known as a "state of grace."

How did this apply in the case of the young Merckx? Did he have this state of grace? Was there something which set him apart from the rest? No, not really. Unless you try to point to his unbridled will-to-win when it came to cards, table tennis and soccer as being something remarkable. But most youngsters who play cards, table tennis and soccer like to win.

Perhaps Merckx's eagerness and the total abandon with which he threw himself into every physical sport and game you care to mention was exceptional. Unfortunately, it is impossible to measure to what extent.

Yet between the ages of eight and 14 there must have been some spark. The moment was probably not even recognized by the young Merckx, though he will not deny that there was 'something' when he started to think of his bike as a means of

△ *Between the ages of eight and 14 there must have been some kind of spark. "On my bike I was simply myself," says Merckx.*

competing. Suddenly, he had something with which and on which he could be himself completely. All the shackles of his upbringing fell away, the straitjacket of scruples (punishment and hell) of the Catholic faith were broken open, there was … freedom. "I was myself on my bike," is how Merckx simply puts it. In fact there is more to it than that. On his bike Merckx felt a little like God, in the same way as Michael Schumacher no longer feels involved with the worldly grind when he is sitting in the cockpit of his Formula One car; or in the way John Doe, too, feels a bit 'high' when he hits the home run that helps his neighborhood softball team win. What it is about may only be a small, very temporary victory against immortality, but it tastes so sweet and gives you such a wonderful feeling that you become addicted to the glow. Once it has gone forever, it is usually followed by a massive hangover, as Merckx was to discover on his retirement.

■ "MERCKX MUST BE OVERBURDENED"

Those people who have known Merckx as an individual use various ways to try to describe him. "His store of energy was incredibly large," says Patrick Sercu. "He seemed to be inexhaustible. Merckx always was and still is the sort of person who needs to have something at hand, he needs to be overburdened, to be under pressure. Enjoying a day in the sun or an hour on a terrace bar reading a book, are totally wasted on him. If he has nothing to do, he goes crazy."

Guillaume Michiels, for so long a confidant of Merckx, confirms this. "He had such energy," he says. "He could never sit still. He was always busy doing something. And it was nearly always connected in some way with a bike. I watched him for years in hundreds of different hotels. His waking life consisted of racing, showering, eating and, if he had no other commitments, busying himself with something to do with his job. Any moment there was nothing else he should be doing, he spent concentrating on his bike. It was pure obsession."

That fanaticism translated itself first and foremost into an almost unhealthy concern for his tool of the trade, the bicycle. "Eddy had been a pro for one year when he bought all of mechanic Jos Janssen's equipment for BF 80,000 ($2500) out of his own pocket," continues Michiels. "Besides the equipment he received from the team, he also had personal bikes and accessories, too. He always had around 500 tubular tires and 100 wheels, and he kept around 35 bikes in his workshop, 15 of which were always ready to ride. I remember us once setting off for the Giro with 17 different bikes of his. It was incredible how he occupied himself with them. He tried out everything and more and was never completely satisfied with a particular solution. In 1971, he won that memorable Liège-Bastogne-Liège, when he was caught before the end by Georges Pintens, on a bike I can only describe as a 'high chair'. That machine didn't suit him at all, but he was always wanting to test out new frame angles and saddle positions when he felt it necessary."

◁ *Merckx always had 35 bikes available, of which 15 were kept ready for immediate use.*

"It's true that I kept hundreds of tires at home in the cellar for months on end," says Merckx. "That's because they kept getting more and more expensive. The role of bike mechanic may have interested me a lot, but people greatly exaggerate it. I was asked in 1971 if it was true that I had taken a bike apart to find out how many parts it comprised. I answered that it was. I must have been mad. I did find out, though, that a bike is made up of around 1,125 separate pieces. As a matter of interest, the main reason for using the frame angles I did from 1970 on was to ease the back pain I had been feeling since my crash at Blois at the end of 1969."

FIGHTING OFF THE PAIN

Many who tried to figure out Merckx were also amazed at his ability to fight off the pain. Best qualified of all to discuss that are his direct rivals. "Merckx was able to endure suffering like no one else," claims Roger De Vlaeminck. "Even if he was absolutely shattered, he would still have a go at attacking. At least I used to assume he was shattered when I was sitting behind him, feeling like a doormat. I can talk about it because I know what it is to die on Merckx's wheel. For kilometer after kilometer, I have had to ride behind him, half dead, without him ever asking me to do any leading work. In the Tour of Belgium in 1971, Merckx had escaped with my brother Eric, who for the next 120 kilometers sat on his wheel. It was raining and it was freezing cold and Eric could barely do any lead work, but Merckx kept on pounding away and beat him in the sprint. It was barbaric what that fellow did to us. He had an iron constitution. I've known him to eat a crystal glass – everything apart from the base, of course."

"Eddy had a phenomenal constitution," says his soigneur, Guillaume Michiels. "I remember one season when he rode for 54 days in a row. He had won the Tour and was riding in criteriums day after day, at times twice a day. In between all that, we covered thousands of kilometers in his car. Remember. too, he could never sleep in the car. To be able to keep up something like that, you need to have an iron constitution."

Suffering was perfectly natural to Eddy Merckx. "His great strength lay in his ability to cross the pain threshold," says sports journalist Robert Janssens. "In order to do so, he employed a special mental mechanism. The way I see it, his way of thinking

▽ Merckx flirted with the limits of pain and pushed them back every time. (Putting his all into the climb of the Monte Carpegna during the Tour of Italy in 1974)

DIFFERENCES AND SIMILARITIES WITH ROGER DE VLAEMINCK

Roger De Vlaeminck recognizes much of himself in Merckx. "That obsessiveness about his job, that was something I had, too," he says. "Unfortunately, I had a little less talent than Eddy on every level. But that will-to-win, that always wanting to improve yourself, that was something I also had. Even now, I keep my times when I go out on a bike ride. I never once sat on the bike without hurting myself. Gimondi was the same, and Merckx more than anyone else. How lovely it would be to be young again and to be able to ride all-out."

De Vlaeminck is not bemoaning the fact that he came up against the Cannibal on numerous occasions during his career, something which probably cost him many victories. "I already had enough will-to-win of my own," he says. "But Merckx provided me with an extra incentive to win, too. I could really rely on him. I needed someone to battle against. In the beginning, my battle against Merckx made me a lot of enemies. I remember a criterium in Denderleeuw, in 1970 I think. I got the bird from virtually every person in the crowd because I had ridden against Merckx a little bit in the Tour. Take it from me, that sort of experience really hurts a young rider.

"Yet my happiest memories are of times with Merckx. I am thinking specifically of the Tour of Lombardy that I won in 1974, and my victory in Paris-Roubaix in 1975. On both those occasions, I beat Merckx, who was the reigning world champion. My final overall victory ahead of Merckx in the Tour of Switzerland in 1975 also gave me a great deal of pleasure. To beat Merckx gave a rider enormous satisfaction. I never had a complex about him. I never totally geared my race to what he would do, but I did openly go all-out against him. In the long run, that worked against me, because Merckx's rivals started to count on me to clip his wings more and more, and after that all they had to do was attack from behind my back. There were times I thought I was going to go mad because of Merckx. During the first week of the Tour in 1969, I rode a very attacking race, with the result that afterward I was on my last legs. As time went by, though, I started to use my commonsense more. I simply didn't have the same capabilities as a rider that Merckx did. He was able to control a race and then go on and win, but I couldn't do that. That was the great difference between us."

was like this: If he, who was riding alone at the front, had suffered so much, how must his rivals behind him be feeling? 'They're suffering more than me' was what he thought, and in that way he could accept the pain. He would have also found it inappropriate to have complained about that suffering. That was partly because he had an upbringing that decreed he should not trouble other people with his own problems, no matter how great or small. In his relationships with the outside world, that social screen was of vital importance."

Robert Desmet, a colleague of Janssens, also thinks that the extent to which Merckx could suffer was never made known fully. "I remember after his hour record how his

▷ *The ability to die one more time without uttering a word of complaint. (Merckx during his successful attempt at breaking the world hour record in Mexico City on October 25, 1972)*

arse was left completely exposed," says Desmet, expressively. "For three whole days afterward, he was absolutely on his knees. Yet not a single word of complaint crossed his lips."

Something brings to mind for Janssens a mental picture of Merckx during the Tour of Spain in 1973 (the only Vuelta Merckx rode – and won). "I went into his room and saw him doing something with a razor blade," says Janssens, shuddering at the thought. "He was busy cutting away an in-growing nail on his big toe with his own hands. It seemed to him to be the most natural thing in the world. My stomach turned over. It was typical of Merckx that he was not going to let anything or anyone ruin his dream. The intensity of that dream must have been enormous. It was one of the things that enabled him to fight off the after-effects of his crash in Blois, when a mere mortal would have needed months to allow displaced vertebrae to heal. Merckx simply climbed back onto his bike, when inside he was howling with pain."

▪ ONE MORE TOOTH

It is not difficult to note down frightening testimony from the mouths of Merckx's racing contemporaries. "What hasn't he subjected us to?" they cry out in chorus. Everyone who ever rode alongside him has at least one story to tell that is drenched in disbelief and pain. "As a rider, Merckx is the greatest I have ever known," testifies Jan Janssen. "He was brimming with good qualities and displayed no signs of any shortcomings worth mentioning. Let me tell you about an incident to illustrate that, one which will remain with me to the end of my days. It comes from the Tour de France in 1969, during the Pyrenean stage to Mourenx-Ville-Nouvelle. During the climb of the Tourmalet, we were all moaning to ourselves: 'why didn't our flaming mechanics set up a smaller gear on our bikes'. Suddenly, I saw Merckx messing around with his gears. For a split second, it flashed through my mind that he might be struggling, too. But within a second he had changed his gear onto a 52x17. That's bigger than the gear most people use on the flat! And it was with that gear that he rode away from us up to Tourmalet's 10-percent slope. Do you know what? It is your morale which is most badly affected by things like that. One minute you can go no further, and the next you don't want to go any further!"

What Herman Van Springel will always remember is the Tour of Piedmont in 1972. "Merckx attacked 60 kilometers before the finish," says Herman. "A small group, including Gimondi, Panizza, Bitossi and Motta, organized the chase and I was in it as Merckx's teammate. I was witness to a relentless fight of one man against the rest which lasted for 50 kilometers. The Italians fought like devils. They got to within 150 meters, but Merckx pulled away again. It continued like that. Merckx never got a lead of more than a few hundred meters, but he just wouldn't give in. I couldn't believe my eyes. With 10 kilometers to go to the finish, the spring snapped among the chasers. Yet Merckx still had enough energy left to build up his lead to more than a minute."

It would probably be possible to fill another book with the sorry tales or the perplexities of Merckx's former rivals and teammates. Their testimony, however, can be condensed into one sentence: "We do not have a word to describe it". While some add this thought to it: "What was that man made out of?"

■ A CALLING, A MISSION IN LIFE

The answer to the question of what he was made of is not simple. It seeks to probe the internal engines that drove Merckx on, through the pain, the disappointments and the injustices. What was his will-to-win based on? Why did he want to win and keep on winning? Many of our interviewees try to find an explanation by speaking of a calling in Merckx's case. "At a certain moment in his life, Merckx chose a path from which he never again wanted to stray," says sports journalist Robert Desmet. "Indeed, it may be compared with a believer who decides to become a missionary or a priest. Only with Merckx it wasn't just a question of belief, it was a life's mission. Once you have chosen something like that, you must stick to a certain way of life. Moreover, Merckx choice of cycling went against his parents' wishes. And because that was the case, he made himself even more determined to succeed."

Indeed, there was a great conflict between his calling and his nature and upbringing. But that was an obstacle Merckx managed to skirt round thanks to his boyishness. Merckx was lucky enough to cherish a dream, while most of us lose sight of ours. The dream made him immune to the tedium of the grown-up world; it provided him with a means of escape from the dullness of everyday life. That childlike nature was the great force within Merckx. The other side of the coin to that was he also displayed a certain naïvety, which he had cause to regret on more than one occasion. Without the guiding force of his innocence, however, Merckx would not have been Merckx.

LUIS OCAÑA: 'SENNA REMINDED ME OF MERCKX'

Luis Ocaña spoke with great respect about the unlimited ambition which made Merckx so great. "Eddy was a 'grinder,'" said Ocaña. "Someone who ground down everyone and everything to powder. He gave it everything he had, whatever the race — whether it was on the road or on the track, whether it was important or minor. Winning in itself was not good enough. It was keeping winning that was the watchword. I used to see some of that ability to focus in the Formula One racing driver, the late Ayrton Senna. He, too, burned with that blind, all-consuming fire, and he was also addicted to the kick you get from victory. You only find that with the true greats; winning is second nature to them. Once that has gone, there is nothing but emptiness left.

"I have always had a great deal of respect for the integrity of Merckx. The nature of his motivation speaks volumes about it. He was never out to seek recognition or glory, and he certainly didn't want to be a star. Had journalists or television not existed, then there would have been no need to invent them as far as he was concerned. He wanted to win in order to be able to satisfy himself, not to destroy his opponents. That comes from the human side of his nature. In my opinion, that is his greatest virtue. He has never thought of himself as being a cut above others, and you can't always say that about people with so much talent."

△ *The young boy within the Cannibal: He wanted to be a character in a heroic saga and wanted to match the cycling heroes who — subconsciously perhaps — haunted him. One can safely say it is a calling that he had to realize, or is a life's mission. (Merckx during Milan-San Remo in 1976)*

"His career was geared toward matching earlier cycling heroes," says journalist Joris Jacobs. "It was not idolatry, but it was love on another dimension. His ambition was as simple as it was unrealistic — he wanted to do better, he wanted to push back the barriers, starting afresh each time. He wanted to be part of a heroic saga. For that reason, he never thought about the long-term consequences. In any case, he was never confronted with a slump in fortunes or signs of weakness in his early years. And when it did eventually come, his determination to beat it became even stronger."

And Claudine Merckx who we must assume knows her husband Eddy reasonably well, refers to the young boy within him. "Eddy has always retained a sort of spontaneity that sidelines commonsense," she says. "He didn't weigh up the problem first of all, or think about the consequences of his actions."

THE BIKE AS A TOY

The bike was Merckx's toy, but whereas a child regularly changes its toys Merckx did not. "He has always had the ability to focus like a newcomer," says Johan De Muynck. "On the bike he possessed a youthful enthusiasm, which his clapped out rivals sometimes asked questions about. Like a child who suddenly discovers the joy of a playground slide, Merckx continued to "play on, "without wondering whether he would suddenly have to pay the price for his gluttony. If he had approached everything in a more rational way, his career would have lasted three or four years longer. But that would have meant that he would not have been the same Merckx."

Paul Van Himst discovered in Merckx one or two traits that point to a somewhat naïve impulsiveness. "Eddy has well-defined principles, which he can barely put into perspective," he says. "If he finds himself in a situation where one of his guiding principles is violated, he reacts fiercely. If, for example, someone in traffic acts very selfishly, he would stop his car at once and give the other driver a piece of his mind. Or he becomes furious inside if he sees a talented young cyclist make half-hearted efforts in training and in care of his equipment. He cannot understand why anyone with a gift would want to throw it away. He gets really angry about it, that waste. He reacts similarly to cases of injustice. What he finds so bad is that he is usually so powerless to do anything about it."

The problem with retiring was, first and foremost, associated with the loss of his dream. "By way of compensation for that loss, Eddy threatened to go and live with his past," says Claudine Merckx. "It would have been an easy answer, too. He was constantly having his nose rubbed in his career by the outside world. They wanted everything and then a little more, and with his kind nature, he was not able to say no often enough. 'What an imbecile I am,' he used to say. He was a prisoner of his own reputation, of his own past, and of his own image. Fortunately, he started to see in time that he would have to let his old boyish self come to the surface again. He had to start to live for himself again, to go and watch races, to ride a little himself, to help young riders and to follow Axel's progress. Anything, as long as it had something to do with competitive cycling."

Merckx realized that, too. He expresses it with the frankness so typical of him: "I am always much happier on my bike than behind my desk."

What was it that ultimately drove Merckx forward on his bike, day in day out, year after year? Where was the mental source of his extreme obsessiveness? There are a few, rather prosaic, motives that spring to mind. Merckx was at his most dangerous when he was being challenged. Scornful statements from rivals in the media, supporters spitting at him, patronizing comments from

▽ *The gaze set at infinity and always straight ahead: Where did the holy fire within Merckx come from? (Tour of Flanders 1977)*

journalists were all lashes to his being and drove him on. Injustice, too, such as the doping affair in the 1969 Giro, worked on him like a red rag to a bull. These are all external factors, however, and they can never fully explain Merckx's unremitting fervor. After all, he whose calling is not based on inner strength can say goodbye to the cloistered life.

THE FARMER, THE WORKER AND THE GROCER

Where was the seat of Merckx's fire? "His will-to-win and his unhealthy tendency to do everything to perfection were, in my opinion, inspired by a sort of notion of worthiness that was of very great importance in the environment he was brought up in," says journalist Robert Janssens. "One of the unwritten laws of that middle-class environment which shaped him was that you must prove yourself against your surroundings. Firstly, you should not be the odd man out. You must be virtuous and tenacious, and let them see you are. A farmer does not have to prove himself to his surroundings, only to nature and his family. A worker needs to prove himself to his boss and his working environment. But a grocer in one of the most wealthy of Brussels suburbs needs to prove himself to the whole of the local community. A small businessman must take great account of the neighborhood in which he lives, otherwise he would be better giving it up."

Typical of that bourgeois mentality is a fierce loyalty to these unwritten laws of that environment. You do not attack the system from which you come, certainly not in public at least. You yourself know, of course, what's wrong with it all, but the social straitjacket keeps you on the standard course. It is probably for that reason, too, that Merckx has never been really negative about the sport of cycling. He has always had a great sense of responsibility toward his chosen field, to which he felt greatly indebted. That was quite simply the essence of how one was brought up right after World War II: as a youngster, you did not ask questions, you always remained polite and considerate, you did not rebel and you never said no. It reminds one of present-day Japan, where politeness – false or not – is a pillar of the social system. The Japanese are hardly aware of the word "no". In the same way, Merckx was a product of such a sociological model, in which the notion of "respect" was dominant. Police officers, teachers and your father all represented power and wisdom. You listened to them, no matter what they said. On that level, God was the ultimate: man is an insignificant being, a pile of temporarily organized dust. That, too, made its mark on Merckx. He has always remained very humble, pretension being foreign to him. And during his career, he was always inclined to look up to somebody, and he certainly did not let any signs of contempt show for his fiercest rivals. That is why he was able to accept an authoritarian figure like Jean Van Buggenhout, his manager, even though there were times when he called Merckx everything under the sun. But he had a kind of fundamental respect for Van Buggenhout, the gray-haired God, the father figure who commanded great respect in the sport and who always knew what needed to be done."

◁ *Happiness for Merckx was on his bike and not behind his desk.*

BEING HAPPY

Merckx's fear of other people's opinions of him, which had been spoon-fed into him, continually gave him a hard time. "What would people have thought of me if I had ridden at the back of the bunch during a criterium, let alone abandon," he says. Or: "After winning a race, the first thing I always thought about was the race coming up, because people expected me to perform well in that one, too." To fulfill expectations: that is how the well brought-up grocer's son from Sint-Pieters-Woluwe was moulded. Merckx still cannot understand the "you can kiss my arse" attitude that Bernard Hinault or Laurent Fignon seemed to have, or the "I'll do what I like" attitude of Greg LeMond.

Those riders are partly a product of a shift in mentality that Merckx was never attuned to. They were from the generation after Merckx, which at the end of the '60s threatened the existing model of society: anything that reeked of authority was knocked off its pedestal, imagination came to power, everyone was born naked and should take pleasure in dying the same way. That movement, characterized by student revolts, flower power and an utterly unbridgeable generation gap, escaped Merckx completely. From the moment he turned professional in 1965 – even earlier in fact, from the moment he had made his choice to go with the bike – social reality and everything that went on within it meant nothing to him. Merckx was barely interested in what was going on in the madhouse that was called the world. And the social revolution of the '60s pretty much passed him by. Imagination ruled, and what was he supposed to do about that? His generation had been brought up with subjugated imaginations, as anyone who had too much imagination said and did things that did not fit in with the society model that had taken root. You could not say Merckx ever had to worry about having a surfeit of imagination. He can hardly be referred to as a creative person. He may have been obsessed with his equipment, but really new ideas like aero bars and the disc wheel were not launched by him. He tried out everything, but it was all within the existing concept of how a bicycle was supposed to look. Merckx pushed back the barriers within his sport, but he did not mark out any new paths. He did what had been done before, only he did it better, more frequently and more tenaciously. Merckx was no genius: he lacked the sparkle, the sudden seemingly insane insight or the brilliance for entirely new trains of thought. Merckx was no rebel, no innovator: he hung on too grimly to the threads of his middle-class upbringing. Merckx was, however, an idealist: he wanted to enter a world that was not human, which was intended for comic strip heroes, for the gods of mythology. To do that, he constantly needed to keep pushing back the barriers. As his career progressed, it meant he was increasingly living on borrowed time. And because he really is of this earth, it was something that from 1975 onward he was to discover more and more. The fall (like that of Icarus) came sooner than he expected.

For 10 full years, however, he had flown. "It was only later that I realized how happy I had been," says Merckx.

▽ *The star leaves the hustle and bustle, behind and can only now grasp the intensity of the moment. "Only afterward did I realize how lucky I was," Merckx now says.*

1977-1978

The Barrel is Empty

△ *The suffering gets worse and worse. (Merckx during his last Tour)*

◆ 1977

Team	Fiat
Directeurs sportifs	Raphäel Geminiani (Fra), Robert Lelangue (Bel)
Teammates	Cees Bal (Neth), Robert Bouloux, Jean-Luc Molineris (Fra), Joseph Bruyère, Etienne De Beule, Ludo Delcroix, Jos De Schoenmaecker, Bernard Draux, Jos Huysmans, Edward Janssens, Jacques Martin (all Bel), Karel Rottiers, Roger Swerts, Patrick Sercu (all Bel).
Number of Races	119
Number of Victories	17
Major Stage Races	Tour de France 6th
	Tour of Italy -
Major One-Day Races	World Championship 33rd
	Belgian Championship 9th
	Milan-San Remo -
	Tour of Flanders abandoned
	Paris-Roubaix 11th
	Liège-Bastogne-Liège 6th
	Amstel Gold Race 9th
	Tour of Lombardy -
	Het Volk 5th
	Ghent-Wevelgem -
	Flèche-Wallonne abandoned
	Paris-Tours -
	Paris-Brussels -

◆ 1978

Team	C & A
Directeurs sportifs	Jos Huysmans (Bel), Rudi Altig (Ger)
Teammates	Joseph Bruyère, Etienne De Beule, Jos De Schoenmaecker, Ren Dillen, Eduoard Janssens, Marcel Laurens, Ludo Loos, René Martens, Jacques Martin (all Bel), Robert Mintkiewicz (Fra), Walter Planckaert, Willy Planckaert, Eddy Schepers, Guido Van Calster Etienne Van der Helst, Frank Van Impe, Lucien Van Impe (all Bel).
Number of Races	5
Number of Victories	-

"After six years with Molteni, I moved to Fiat. It gave me extra motivation, and in the beginning things looked very promising, with overall victory in the Tour of the Mediterranean. But then I had to pull out of Paris-Nice through illness. My body seemed to be able to offer less and less resistance to all the minor complaints. I also made the mistake of trying to do too much about it, with the result that I became increasingly susceptible to injuries and illness. In the Tour de France, it started getting better again. Together with some of my teammates, however, I was struck down with food poisoning.

"In 1977, it had become fairly clear that I was not a robot but a human after all. For years I had been racing day in day out, summer and winter. With hindsight, I can say it was no more than was to be expected, I got what was coming to me.

"After the trouble I had finding a sponsor during that winter, I started the 1978 season with the intention of taking part in the Tour one last time and then retiring. However, I began the season making an unforgivable mistake. The sponsorship problem had taken a heavy toll on me mentally and was only solved at the eleventh hour. Once everything had been sorted out with C&A it would have been better if I had not worried too much about the season's start. A training camp in the mountains would have done me a lot more good, but I wanted to taste competition again right away and I was to live to regret it. Mentally, particularly, I was exhausted. Everything was too much for me. I also had to put up with all sorts of minor complaints, both real and imaginary.

"On April 19, I drove with my soigneur, Pierrot Dewit, to the Circuit of the Waasland race starting at Kemzeke. I said to him: 'This is going to be my last race.' As it happened, it went quite well, and I came sixth. 'You see,' said Pierrot afterward. 'You can still do it.' 'No I can't,' I answered. 'The barrel's empty.' I continued to train listlessly for a few more weeks, but after a final run-out on May 17, I decided to call it a day. The following day I announced my retirement in public. I'd had enough."

Results of major races

Race	1965	'66	'67	'68	'69	'70	'71	'72	'73	'74	'75	'76	'77	'78
World Championship	29	12	1	8	0	29	1	4	4	1	8	5	33	–
Belgian Championship	2	15	0	0	0	1	5	2	2	–	3	0	9	–
Milan-San Remo	–	1	1	0	1	8	1	1	–	–	1	1	–	–
Tour of Flanders	–	–	3	9	1	3	76	7	3	4	1	17	0	–
Paris-Roubaix	–	15	8	1	2	1	5	7	1	4	2	16	11	–
Liège-Bastogne-Liège	–	8	2	0	1	3	1	1	1	–	1	6	6	–
Amstel Gold Race	–	–	–	–	3	8	–	1	–	–	1	–	9	–
Tour of Lombardy	–	2	7	3	–	4	1	1	0	2	6	–	–	–
Het Volk	–	3	–	–	12	7	1	3	1	6	6	15	5	–
Ghent-Wevelgem	–	9	1	9	–	1	14	3	1	2	6	10	–	–
Flèche-Wallonne	0	–	1	–	5	1	–	1	2	–	3	4	0	–
Paris-Brussels	–	20	–	–	–	–	–	–	1	–	2	0	–	–
Paris-Tours	–	20	–	8	–	–	–	116	6	0	9	–	–	–
Scheldt G.P.	10	–	–	–	–	–	–	1	9	–	–	0	–	–
Championship of Zürich	–	–	–	–	4	–	–	–	–	–	2	7	4	–
Henninger Turm	–	–	7	–	–	8	1	2	–	2	7	7	–	–
Tour de France	–	–	–	–	1	1	1	1	–	1	2	–	6	–
Tour of Italy	–	–	9	1	0	1	–	1	1	1	–	8	–	–
Tour of Switzerland	–	–	–	–	–	–	–	–	–	1	2	–	12	–
Tour of Spain	–	–	–	–	–	–	–	–	–	1	–	–	–	–
Tour of Belgium	–	11	–	0	–	1	1	–	0	–	–	23	–	–
Dauphiné Libéré F	–	–	–	–	–	–	1	–	–	–	10	–	8	–
G.P. de Fourmies F	–	–	–	–	–	–	–	–	1	–	–	–	–	–
Midi-Libre F	–	11	–	–	–	–	1	–	–	–	–	–	–	–
Paris-Nice F	–	4	10	0	1	1	1	2	3	3	2	–	5	–
4 Days of Dunkirk F	–	–	–	–	–	–	–	–	–	4	–	–	–	–
Tour de Morbihan F	–	1	–	–	–	–	–	–	–	–	–	–	–	–
Mediterranean Tour F	–	–	–	–	–	–	–	–	–	–	23	–	1	–
Catalan Week Sp	–	–	–	–	–	–	–	–	–	2	1	1	–	–
Tour of Catalonia Sp	–	–	–	1	–	–	–	–	2	–	–	–	–	–
Tour of Levante Sp	–	–	–	–	1	–	–	–	–	–	–	–	–	–
Tour of Majorca Sp	–	–	–	–	0	–	–	–	–	–	–	–	–	–
Tour of Sardinia I	–	–	28	1	–	2	1	33	1	4	1	8	–	–
Tirreno-Adriatico I	–	–	–	–	–	–	–	–	–	–	–	2	–	–
Tour de Romandie Sw	–	–	–	1	–	–	–	–	–	–	14	3	7	–
Paris-Luxembourg Lux	14	–	6	7	1	–	–	–	–	–	–	–	–	–
A travers la Belgique	–	4	–	–	–	–	–	–	–	–	–	–	–	–
Championship of Flanders	–	1	–	–	–	–	–	2	19	0	–	15	–	–
Cir/Flemish Provinces	–	–	–	–	10	–	–	–	–	–	–	–	–	–
Circuit of the Leiedal	–	–	–	–	–	–	–	–	–	–	–	1	–	–
Flèche Brabançonne	–	–	–	8	–	–	2	1	–	0	18	2	–	–
G.P. Cerami-Wasmuel	–	1	–	–	–	–	–	–	–	–	–	–	–	–
End of Season-Putte	–	–	1	–	–	–	–	2	–	–	–	–	–	–
E 3 GP-Harelbeke	–	–	8	–	–	–	3	2	14	–	0	–	–	–
G.P. Union–Dortmund G	–	–	4	–	–	1	3	1	3	9	5	–	–	–
Coppa Agostoni I	–	2	–	–	–	1	–	–	33	5	5	–	–	–
Trofeo Laigueglia I	–	–	–	–	2	–	4	2	1	1	–	–	–	–
G.P. des Nations F	–	3	–	–	–	–	–	–	1	–	–	–	–	–
G.P. Lugano F	–	4	–	1	–	–	–	–	–	–	–	–	–	–
Baracchi Trophy I	–	1	1	–	3	–	–	1	–	3	–	–	–	–
Montjuich Hill Climb Sp	–	1	–	–	–	1	1	1	–	1	1	–	–	–
A travers Lausanne Sw	–	–	2	1	–	1	2	1	1	4	2	–	–	–
Criterium des As F	–	–	1	–	–	1	–	–	3	1	4	2	–	–
Châteaulin F	–	1	–	–	1	–	–	3	–	6	1	3	–	–

Review of races

DEBUTANTS

1961

• 17.7 Laken, 6 • 23.7 Korbeek-Lo, fell - abandoned • 30.7 Blanden, abandoned • 13.8 St-Genesius-Rode, 17 • 20.8 Geldenaken, 7 • 24.9 Meensel-Kiezegem, abandoned • 27.8 Humbeek, punctured - abandoned • 2.9 Etterbeek, 3 • 10.9 Waterloo, 3 • 17.9 Wavre, 11 • 24.9 St-Joris-Winge, 11 • 1.10 Lettelingen, 1 • 9.10 Kortrijk-Dutsel, l8

DEBUTANTS

1962

• 11.3 Haacht, 1 • 18.3 Halle, 1 • 25.3 Wilsele, abandoned • 31.3 Beersel, 1 • 8.4 Roux, 1 • 14.4 Evere, 6 • 21.4 Edingen, 7 • 23.4 Nieuwrode, 3 • 29.4 Haacht, 1 • 1.5 Halle, 1 • 6.5 Anderlecht, 1 • 8.5 Court St-Etienne, punctured - abandoned • 13.5 Haasrode, 8 • 20.5 Schaffen, 1 • 27.5 Gelrode, 1 • 3.6 Rosières, 5 • 10.6 Linden,1 • 11.6 St-Genesius-Rode, 12 • 14.6 Forchies, 2• 17.6 St-Laureins-Berchem, 1• 20.6 Bergen,1 • 24.6 St-Genesius-Rode, 1 • 26.6 Hofstade (Prov. Team Champs.), 2 • 1.7 Huldenberg, 4 • 2.7 St-Pieters-Woluwe, 1 • 8.7 Drieslinter, 7 • 15.7 Libramont, Belgian Championship, 1 • 19.7 Evere, 2 • 22.7 Aspelare, 1 • 26.7 Kwaremont, punctured - abandoned • 28.7 Hever, 1 • 29.7 Hamme, abandoned • 1.8 St-Gillis, punctured - abandoned • 2.8 Veurne, 11 • 5.8 Achter-Olen, 2 • 12.8 Vilvoorde, punctured - abandoned • 13.8 Limette, 1 • 15.8 Kester, abandoned • 16.8 Huldenberg, 1 • 19.8 La Glaize, 1 • 22.8 Torhout, abandoned • 23.8 Meensel-Kiezegem, 2 • 25.8 Heppem, 3 • 26.8 Kontich, abandoned • 29.8 Alsemberg, 3 • 1.9 Pamel, 2 • 3.9 O-L-V-Lombeek,1 • 8.9 Vilvoorde, 1 • 9.9 Virginal, 2 • 11.9 Kapellen, 10 • 15.9 Schepdaal, 1 • 17.9 Schepdaal, 4 (cat. 1) • 23.9 Geldenaken, abandoned • 24.9 Wavre, 1• 2.l0 Gooik, 2

AMATEURS

1963

• 9.3 Circuit of the Flemish Provinces, fell - abandoned • 17.3 St-Genesius-Rode, 4• 24.3 Brussels-O.L.V-Tielt, fell - abandoned • 30.3 G.P. Bodson-Laken, abandoned • 3.4 Flèche Brabançonne, finished in main bunch • 7.4 Edingen, 4 • 11.4 Genappe, 1 • 14.4 Ophasselt-Hekelgem, 3 • 15.4 Wervik, 7 • 21.4 Riimenam, 3 • 25.4 Oudergem, 3 • 27.4 Duisburg, 1 • 28.4 Vorst, 1 • 29.4 Duisburg, 2 (cat. 1) • 1.5 La Hulpe, 1 • 5.5 Dworp, 1 • 11.5 Brussels-Liedekerke, 6 • 13.5 Baasrode, 1 • 18.5 Halle, 1 • 19.5 St-Genesius Rode, 2 • Tour of Limburg, 1 (25.5 Hasselt- Dilsen, 5 / Bilzal [time trial], 2 / 26.5 Bilzen - Lummen, 5 / Lummen [time trial], 1 / 27.5 Lummen--Hasselt, 3 / 8.6 Brussels-Saintes, 1 / 10.6 Strombeek-Bever, 1) • 13.6 Geldenaken, 4 • 14.6 Ottignies, punctured - abandoned • 15.6 Strombeek-Bever, 1 • 21.6 Isle of Man, 16 • 23.6 Schakkebroek, 2 • 25.6 Huizingen, 1 • 29.6 Kessel-Lo, 1 • 2.7 Opdorp, abandoned • 2.7 Heusden, 10 • 6.7 Desteldonk, punctured - abandoned • 8.7 Jezus-Eik, 22 • 10.7 Kontich, 3 • 13.7 Wemmel, 5 • 15.7 Ronse, 9 • 16.7 St-Lambrechts-Woluwe, 6 • 18.7 Evere, 3 • 20.7 Kortriik, 12 • 22.7 Mons, abandoned • 23.7 Bornem, punctured - abandoned • 24.7 Mons [team time trial] Brussels team, 11 • 25.7 Viane, 7 • 28.7 Vloesberg, abandoned • 5.8 Strombeek-Bever, 1 • 7.8 Alsemberg, 2 • 15.8 O-L-V-Tielt, 4 • 17.8 Vilvoorde, 8 • 20.8 St-Kwintens-Lennik, 3 • 22.8 Laken, 1 • 24.8 Anderlecht, 1 • 25.8 Kortenaken, abandoned • 27.8 Merksem, abandoned • 29.8 Tienen, 2 • 31.8 Etterbeek, 1 • 1.9 Anderlecht, 1 • 2.9 Grimbergen, 1 • 7.9 Brussels-Lasne, 1 • 8.9 Ganshoren, abandoned • 10.9 Sint-Katelijne-Waver, 1 • 12.9 Tienen, 1 • 14.9 Laken, 1 • 15.9 Evere, 1 • 17.9 Nieuwerkerken, 1 • 21.9 Dresden, 1 • 22.9 Sebnitz, 1 • 1.10 St-Lievens-Houtem, 13 • 3.10 Tielt, 11 • 6.10 Tienen, 4

AMATEURS

1964

• 1.3 Brussels-Opwijk, 1 • 7.3 Circuit of the Flemish Provinces, abandoned • 14.3 Harelbeke, 2 • 15.3 St-Genesius-Rode, 1 • 21.3 Ukkel, abandoned • 22.3 Ghent-Wevelgem, 4 • 26.3 Genappe, 1 • 28.3 Diegem, punctured - abandoned • 29.3 Ophasselt-Hekelgem, 1 • 11.4 Aalst, 1 • 12.4 Wijnendale, punctured - abandoned • 16.4 Oudergem, abandoned • 18.4 Edegem, punctured - abandoned • 19.4 Haasrode, 1 • 20.4 St-Martens-Lierde, 3 . 25.4 Steenokkerzeel, 1 • 26.4 Vorst [omnium], 1 • 28.4 Mariakerke, 6 • 1.5 Tollembeek, 3 • 2.5 Halle-Boeienhoven, fell - abandoned • 15.5 Mons, 6 • 17.5 Oud Turnhout, 4 • 19.5 Oostrozebeke, 1 • 23.5 Brussels-Saintes, punctured - abandoned • 24.5 St-Genesius-Rode, 2 • 25.5 Strombeek-Bever, 1 • 28.5 Assent, 2 • 30.5 Strombeek-Bever, 9 • 1.6 Dilbeek, abandoned • 7.6 Hekelgem, 1 • 11.6 Geldenaken, 1 • 14.6 Aartselaar, 9 • 21.6 Asse, 3 • 23.6 Ottignies, 1 • 28.6 St-Genesius-Rode, punctured 6 • 1.7 Enghien, 3 • 4.7 Beringen, 13 • 6.7 Jezus-Eik,

punctured twice - abandoned • 9.7 Tienen, broken frame - abandoned • 11.7 Vilvoorde, abandoned • 12.7 Laken, abandoned • 14.7 Kwatrecht, 7 • 16.7 Woluwe, fell - abandoned • 19.7 Schatten, 3 • 21.7 Bornem, 4 • 23.7 Evere, 7 • 26.7 Pulle, abandoned • 29.7 Menen, punctured twice - abandoned • 30.7 Kerksken, 1 • 1.8 Aalst, 1 • 2.8 Gelrode, 11 • 6.8 Middelkerke, 1 • 9.8 Antwerp, 3 • 13.8 Lebbeke, 4 • 15.8 Oostrozebeke, 1• 17.8 Oud-Genappe, 1 • 20.8 Jauche, 1 • 23.8 St-Laureins-Berchem, 2 • 26.8 Evere, 1 • 29.8 Eeklo, 11 • 1.9 Merchtem, 46 • 5.9 Sallanches, World Championship, 1 • 9.9 Overboelare, 2 • 10.9 Oudegem, 2 • 13.9 Ganshoren, 1 • 16.9 Retie, 3 • 18.9 Braine-le-Comte, 1 • 20.9 Berlin, 2 •. 22.9 Nieuwerkerken, 1 • 26.9 Laken, 1 • 29.9 Jemappe s / Sambre, - • 28.10 Tokyo, Olympic Games, 12

AMATEURS

1965

• 28.3 Oetingen, 1 • 11.4 Wijnendale, 1 • 14.4 Ophasselt,1 • 19.4 Liedekerke, 8 • 24.4 Enschede-Munster, 1

PROFESSIONAL

1965

• 29.4 Flèche Wallonne, abandoned • 3.5 Beverlo, 5 • 8.5 Leuven, 2 • 9.5 Auxerre, 3 • 11.5 Vilvoorde, 1 • 15.5 Vorst, 26 • 18.5 Templeuve, 8 • 23.5 Meulebeke, abandoned • 25.5 Werchter, 2 • 29.5 Oudenaarde, 3 • 2.6 St-Amandsberg, abandoned • 3.6 Ostend, 10 • 6.6 Walshoutem, 27 • 10.6 Tervuren, abandoned • 12.6 Aalst, 2 • 14.6 Strombeek, 6 • 16.6 Brussels-Ingooigem, abandoned • 17.6 Wondelgem, 3 • 19.6 Erembodegem, 10 • 22.6 Isle of Man, 2 • 27.6 Torhout, 1 • 30.6 Wavre, abandoned • 3.7 Itterbeek, 1 • 5.7 Denderleeuw, 10 • 8.7 Wezembeek-Oppem, 1 • 11.7 Kessel-Lo, 1 • 13.7 St-Niklaas, abandoned • 15.7 Ronse, 1 • 17.7 Aalst, 17 • 19.7 Denderleeuw, abandoned • 20.7 Rijmenam, 14 • 21.7 Zolder, 25 • 22.7 De Panne, 11 • 24.7 Nederbrakel, 1 • 25.7 Pommeroeul, 7 • 26.7 Auvelais, 5 • 27.7 Schoten, 10 • 28.7 Vorselaar, 4 • 29.7 Mol, fell - abandoned • 1.8 Vilvoorde, Belgian Championship, 2 • 2.8 Bierges, 4 • 3.8 Zwevegem, abandoned • 5.8 Hechtel, 7 • 6.8 Merelbeke, abandoned • 8.8 Tessenderlo, abandoned • 8.8 Assent, 14 • 14.8 Wezet, 1 • 15.8 Moorslede, punctured twice • 17.8 Lokeren, 3 • 18.8 St-Lambrechts-Woluwe, 13 • 21.8 Liedekerke, 11 • 22.8 Londerzeel, 2 • 23.8 Zingem, 13 • 24.8 Eeklo, 2 • Paris-Luxembourg, 14 (27.8 Paris - Amiens, 21 / 28.8 Amiens - Jambes, 2 / 29.8 Jambes - Charleville, 3 / 30.8 Charleville - Luxembourg, 15) • 5.9 San Sebastian, World Championship, 29 • 6.9 Leuven, 11 • 7.9 Brasschaat, 17 • 9.9 Buggenhout, abandoned • 10.9 Braine-le-Comte, 6 • 11.9 Putte, abandoned • 14.9 Waarschoot, abandoned • 16.9 Koolskamp, 12 • 19.9 St-Jansteen, 1 • 22.9 Ath, 6 • 26.9 G.P. Parisien [team time trial], 2

1966

• 5.3 Circuit Het Volk, 3 • Paris-Nice, 4 (8.3 Montereau - Auxerre, 3 / 9.3 Avallon - Montereau, 9 / Montereau-Mâcon, 9 / 10.3 Mâcon - St-Etienne, 17 / 11.3 St-Etienne - Bagnols, 8 / 12.3 Bagnols - Marseille, 9 / 13.3 Bastia -Bastia, 5 / Bastia - Ile Rousse [time trial], 4 / 14.3 Ile Rousse - Ajaccio, 6 / 15.3 Antibes - Nice, 5) • 20.3 Milan-San Remo, 4 • 23.3 Ghent-Wevelgem, 9 • 26.3 Harelbeke-Antwerp-Harelbeke, abandoned • 3.4 Waregem, 1 / declassified • 6.4 Wasmuel G.P. Cerami, 1 • 9.4 Tour of Flanders, fell - abandoned • 10.4 Alken, abandoned • Tour of Belgium, 11 (11.4 Brussels - Namur, 10 / Namur Citadel [time trial], 11 / 12.4 Namur - Wellin, 10 finished in main bunch / Wellin [team time trial], 3 / 13.4 Wellin-Ostend, 20, finished in main bunch / 14.4 Ostend - Bosvoorde, 17) • 17.4 Paris-Roubaix, 14 • 24.4 Paris-Brussels, 20 • 29.4 Flèche Wallonne, fell - abandoned • 2.5 Liège-Bastogne-Liège, 8 • 8.5 St-Brieuc, 2 • 17.5 Belsele-Waas, 22 • 19.5 Tour of Frankfurt, 23 • 23.5 Vorst-Meulebeke, 1 • 29.5 La Tredion, 23 • 30.5 Ploudalmezeau, 1 • 2.6 Helchteren, 1 • 6.6 Maubeuge, 1 • 12.6 La Levade, 3 • Midi Libre, 11 (13.6 Nimes - Montpellier, 37 / 14.6 Montpellier - Millau, 1 / 15.6 Millau - Carcassonne, 7 / 16.6 Carcassonne - Bézières, 6) •30.6 Heusden, abandoned • 3.7 Bavegem, abandoned • 4.7 Denderleeuw, 1 • 12.7 Tessenderlo, abandoned • 13.7 Temse, abandoned • 15.7 St-Pieters-Woluwe, 3 • 16.7 Aalst, 2 • 18.7 Denderleeuw, 4 • 19.7 De Panne, punctured - abandoned • 20.7 Rijmenam, 3 • 21.7 Zolder, abandoned • 22.7 Oudenaarde, 11 • 23.7 Rumbeke, 3 • 24.7 Visé, 8 • 25.7 Auvelais, 6 • 27.7 Emelgem, 16 • 29.7 Ronse, 19 • 31.7 Waregem, Belgian Championship, 5 • 1.8 Herentals, 3 • 3.8 Mol, 13 • 4.8 Drongen, 7 • 6.8 Rummen, 1 • 8.8 Berlare, punctured - abandoned • 9.8 Zwevegem, 4 • Tour de Morbihan, 1 (11.8 Lorient - Auray, 3 / 12.8 Auray - Gourin. 5 / 13.8 Gourin - Hennebont, 1 / 14.8 Hennebont - Le Caeilly, 1) • 18.8 Heusden, punctured - abandoned • 20.8 Moorslede, 2 • 21.8 Londerzeel, 9 • 22.8 Zingem, 15 • 23.8 Eeklo, 6 • 28.8 Nurburgring, World Championship, 12 • 31.8 Overijse, 1 • 4.9 Briande, 5 • 5.9

Châteaulin, 1 • 6.9 **Brasschaat**, 7 • 7.9 **La Louvière**, 6 • 9.9 **Braine-le-Comte**, 3 • 10.9 **Paris**, Criterium des As, 6 • 11.9 **Laval** [team criterium], 2 • 12.9 **Bannalec**, 2 • 15.9 **Koolskamp**, Championship of Flanders, 1 • 19.9 **Viane**, 1 • 20.9 **Bonheiden**, 4 • 25.9 **Grand Prix des Nations**, 3 • 29.9 **Berlare**, abandoned • 3.10 **Oostrozebeke**, 3 • 4.10 **Templeuve**, 1 • 6.10 **Puteaux**, 1 • 9.10 **Paris-Tours**, 20 • 12.10 **Montjuich**, 1 • 16.l0 **G.P. Lugano**, 4 • 19.10 **Coppa Agostoni**, 2 • 22.10 **Tour of Lombardy**, 2 • 30.10 **Bergamo**, abandoned • 4.11 **Baracchi Trophy**, 1

1967

• 26.1 **Alghero**, 56, sick • **Tour of Sardinia**, 28 (27.2 Ozieri - Nuoro, 29 / 28.2 Orgosola - Monte di Torregrande, 21 / 1.3 Oristano - Cagliari, 56 / 2.3 Cagliari - La Caletta, 5 / 3.3 Siniscola - Sassari, 1 / 4.3 Sassari - Sassari, 1 / 5.3 Sassari - Cagliari, 1) • **Paris-Nice**, 10 (8.3 Athis Mons - Châteaurenard, 32 / 9.3 Toucy - Château-Chinon, 1 / 10.3 Lucy - St-Etienne, 10 / 11.3 St-Etienne - Bollène, 26 / 12.3 Bollène - Marignane, 10 / 13.3 Marignane - Hyères, 1 / 14.3 Hyères - Antibes, 8 / 15.3 Antibes - Nice [time trial], 4) • 18.3 **Milan-San Remo**, 1 • 19.3 **Ospedaletti**, 2 • 25.3 **Harelbeke-Antwerp-Harelbeke**, 8 • 26.3 **Camors**, 1 • 27.3 **St-Claud**, 14 • 29.3 **Ghent-Wevelgem**, 1 • 2.4 **Tour of Flanders**, 3 • 9.4 **Paris-Roubaix**, 8 • 11.4 **G.P. Salvarani**, 1 • 15.4 **Amstel Gold Race**, 16 • 16.4 **Henninger Turm Frankfurt**, 7 • 25.4 **Templeuve**, 1 • 28.4 **Flèche Wallonne**, 1 • 1.5 **Liège-Bastogne-Liège**, 2 • 4.5 **Nandrin**, 1 • 6.5 **Hockenheim** [dernys], 2 • 7.5 **St-Brieuc**, 2 • 13.5 **Brussels-Bever**, abandoned • 15.5 **Simpelveld**, 1 • 16.5 **Lommel**, abandoned • **Tour of Italy**, 9 (20.5 Treviglio - Alessandria, 5 / 21.5 Alessandria -La Spezia, 4 / 22.5 La Spezia - Prato, 8 / 23.5 Florence - Chianciano Terme, 15 / 24.5 Rome - Naples, 11 / 25.5 Palermo, 5 / 26.5 Catania - Etna, 6 / 27.5 Reggio di Calabria - Cosenza, 8 / 28.5 Cosenza - Tarante, 20 / 29.5 Bari - Potenza, 10 / 30.5 Potenza - Salerno, 4 / 31.5 Caserta - Block Haus, 1 / 1.6 Chieti - Riccione, 20 / 2.6 Riccione - Lido degli Estensi, 1 / 3.6 Lido degli Estensi - Mantova, 53 / 4.6 Mantova - Verona [time trial], 23 / 5.6 Verona - Vicenza, 11 / 7.6 Vicenza - Udine, 4 / 8.6 Udine - Tre Cime di Lavardo, 2, stage cancelled / 9.6 Cortina d'Ampezzo - Trento, 6 - punctured 4 times / 10.6 Trento -Tirano, 53 -sick / 11.6 Tirano - Madonna del Ghisallo, 11 / Madonna del Ghisallo - Milan, 4) • 21.6 **De Panne**, abandoned • 22.6 **Tienen**, 30 • 25.6 **G.P. Dortmund**, 4 • 1.7 **Rotselaar**, 4 • 8.7 **Yerzeke**, 3 • 15.7 **Enter**, 1 • 16.7 **La Clayette**, 1 • 24.7 **Aalst**, 3 • 25.7 **Ronse**, finished in main bunch • 26.7 **St-Lambrechts-Woluwe**, 2 • 27.7 **De Panne**, 1 • 28.7 **Eine**, 15 • 30.7 **Mettet**, Belgian Championship, fell - abandoned • 7.8 **Ohain**, 9 • 8.8 **Mol**, abandoned • 10.8 **Hasselt**, 11 • 11.8 **Gentbrugge**, 7 • 12.8 **Bilzen**, 5 • 13.8 **St-Lenaarts**, 1 • 14.8 **Lokeren**, 3 • 15.8 **Dworp**,1 • 16.8 **Turnhout**, abandoned • 17.8 **Heusden**, 15 • 20.8 **Moorslede**, 7 • 21.8 **Zingem**, 12 • 23.8 **Hensies**, 2 • 24.8 **Liedekerke**, 1 • 26.8 **Londerzeel**, 6 • **Bertrix Two Days**, 5 (27.8 Ohain - Bertrix, 2 / 28.8 Bertrix - Bertrix, 6) • 29.8 **Schoten** (Sels Plate), 18 • 3.9 **Heerlen**, World Championship, 1 • 4.9 **Leuven**, fell - abandoned • 5.9 **Brasschaat**, fell - abandoned • 6.9 **Avelgem**, 6 • 8.9 **Valdagno**, 7 • 9.9 **Châteaugiron**, 3 • 10.9 **Charlieu**, 2 • 11.9 **Armentières**, 1 • 12.9 **Anzin**, 1 • **Paris-Luxembourg**, 6 (15.9 Nogent - Châlons-s / Marne, 7 / 16.9 Châlons-s/Marne - Nancy, 3 / 17.9 Nancy - Luxembourg, 1) • 18.9 **Viane**, abandoned • **Mariakerke** (evening), abandoned • 19.9 **Suzzara**, 2 • 22.9 **Braine-le-Comte**, 4 • 24.9 **Scorze**, 2 • 30.9 **Dieren**, 2 • 2.10 **Oostrozebeke**, 14 • 17.10 **Putte-Kappellen**, 1 • 21.10 **Tour of Lombardy**, 7 • 22.10 **Daumesnil**, Criterium des As, 1 • 28.l0 **A Travers Lausanne**, 2 • 1.11 **Bergamo**, 3 • 4.11 **Baracchi Trophy** (with Ferdinand Bracke), 1

1968

• 18.2 **Cannes**, 5 • 21.2 **Monaco**, abandoned • **Tour of Sardinia**, 1 (24.2 Rome - Civitavecchia, 1 / 25.2 Porto Torres - Alghero, 7, finished in main bunch / 26.2 Itriri - Oristano, 14, finished in main bunch / 27.2 Oristano - Cagliari, 51, fell and finished in main bunch / 28.2 Quartu San Elena - Arbatax, finished in main bunch / 28.2 Arbatax - Nuoro, 1 / 29.2 Nuoro - Olbia, 8, finished in main bunch / 1.3 Olbia - Sassari, 8 / 3.3 Sassari - Cagliari, 3) • **Paris-Nice**, abandoned-knee injury (7.3 Athis Mons - Paray [prologue], 2 / 8.3 Ris Orangis - Blois, 9, fell / 9.3 Blois - Nevers, 3 / 10.3 St-Etienne - Marcigny, 7 / 11.3 Marcigny - Charlieu [team time trial], 1 / Charlieu - St-Etienne, 15 / 12.3 St-Etienne - Bollène, abandoned - knee injury) • 17.3 **Romano-Lombardo**, 1 • 19.3 **Milan-San Remo**, 31 • 23.3 **Harelbeke-Antwerp-Harelbeke**, 17 • **Catalan Week**, abandoned [preparation for Tour of Flanders] (26.3 Barcelona - Gerona, 2 / 27.3 Figueras - Sadabell, 2 / 28.3 Tarrasa - Manresa [time trial], 1 / 28.3 Manresa - Lerida, 3) • 30.3 **Tour of Flanders**, 9 • **Tour of Belgium** (2.4 Brussels - Bertrix, 14, eye injury / 3.4 Bertrix - Verviers, 1 / 4.4 Spa - Genk, abandoned) • 7.4 **Paris-Roubaix**, 1 • 13.4 **Alken**, abandoned • 14.4 **Flèche Brabançonne**, 8 • 16.4 **Ghent-Wevelgem**, 9, stomach ache • 30.4 **Geleen**, 23 • 1.5 **Henninger Turm**, abandoned • 5.5 **G.P. Zurich**, 12, finished in main bunch • **Tour de Romandie**, 1 (9.5 Geneva [team time trial], 4 / Geneva - Boncourt, 1 / 10.5 Boncourt - Bulle, 5 / 11.5 Bulle - Sierre, 4 / 11.5 Sierre - Super Crans [time trial], 2 / 12.5 Crans - Geneva, 18 / 13.5 Scandiano team circuit, 2) • **Tour of Italy**, 1 (20.5 Campione [prologue] / 21.5 Campione - Novara, 1 / 22.5 Novara - St-Vincent, 2 / 23.5 St-Vincent - Alba, 13 / 24.5 Alba - San Remo, 33 / 25.5 San Remo - Circuito Romolo et Remo, 2 / 26.5 San Remo - Alessandria, 8 / 27.5 Alessandria - Piacenza, 100 / 28.5 San Giorgio - Brescia, 1 / 29.5 Brescia - Lago di Caldonazzo, 1 / 30.5 Trente - Monte Grappa, 2 / 31.5 Bassano del Grappa - Trieste, 29 / 1.6 Goriza - Tre Cime di Lavaredo, 1 / 2.6 Cortina d'Ampezzo - Vittorio Veneto, 23 / 3.6 Vittorio Veneto - Marina Romea, 67 / 4.6 Ravenna - Imola, 85 / 6.6 Cesenatico - San Marino [time trial], 2 / 7.6 San Marino - Foligno, 42 / 8.6 Foligno - Abbadia San Salvatore, 9 / 9.6 Abbadia San Salvatore - Rome, 60 / 10.6 Rome - Rocca di Cambio, 14 / 11.6 Rocca di Cambio - Block Haus, 7 / 12.6 Chieti - Naples, 30) • 13.6 **Castelfranco**, 2 • 14.6 **Figliné Valdarno**, 2 • 17.6 **Cinisello**, 1 • 18.6 **Magenta**, 3 • 21.6 **Salsomaggiore**, 1 • 23.6 **Castrocaro**, 2 • 28.6 **Pomponsco**, 2 • 29.6 **St.Adrea Bagni**, 3 • 11.7 **Melle**, abandoned • 14.7 **La Clayette**, 1 • 16.7 **Bornem**, 1 • 20.7 **Zedelgem**, 6 • 21.7 **Castiglione**, 4 / 22.7 **Aalst**, 2 • 23.7 **Ronse**, 3 • 24.7 **St-Lambrechts-Woluwe**, 1 • 25.7 **De Panne**, 1 • 26.7 **Eine**, 3 • 28.7 **Mettet**, Belgian Championship, 11 • 31.7 **Bilze**, 6 • 1.8 **Vielsalm**, 5 • 2.8 **Drongen**, 5 • 3.8 **Rijmenam**, punctured - abandoned • 4.8 **St-Lenaarts**, 15 • 5.8 **Auvelais**, 4 • 6.8 **Ohain**, 1 • 7.8 **Hasselt**, 3 • 10.8 **Varèse**, 1 • 11.8 **Alsemberg**, 1 • 12.8 **Lokeren**, 27 • 13.8 **Cirie**, 3 • 15.8 **Dworp**, 2 • 15.8 **Denderleeuw**, 11 • 16.8 **St.Niklaas**, 4 • 17.8 **Malderen**, 1 • 18.8 **Moorslede**, 4 • 19.8 **Zingem**, 4 • 20.8 **Heultje**, - • **Paris-Luxembourg**, 7 (22.8 Compiègne - Maubeuge, 4 / 23.8 Maubeuge - Liège, 7 / 24.8 Barchon - Maastricht [team time trial], 1 / Maastricht - Cologne, 23 / 25.8 Cologne - Luxembourg, 29) • 27.8 **Merksem**, Sels Plate, 6 • 1.9 **Imola**, World Championship, 8 • 4.9 **Assebroek**, 4 • **Tour of Catalonia**, 1 (8.9 Tona -Villafortuny, 16 / 9.9 Villafortuny - Tarrega, 1 / 10.9 Tarrega - Viella, 9 / 11.9 Valencia de Aneu - Tremp, 2 / 12.9 Tremp - Vich, 18, finished in main bunch / 13.9 Vich - Figueras, 5 / Figueras - Rosas [time trial], 1 / 14.9 Rosas - Caldetas, 8, finished in main bunch / 15.9 Caldets - Barcelona, 10, finished in main bunch) •17.9 **Suzzara**, 7 • 18.9 **Larciano**, 4 • 20.9 **Tieve di Soligo**, 1 • 21.9 **Tour of Venezia**, 18 • 22.9 **Scorze**, 3 • 24.9 **Pesaro**, 3 • 6.10 **Paris-Tours**, 8 • 10.10 **Coppa Agostoni**, abandoned • 12.10 **Tour of Lombardy**, 3 • 15.10 **Putte-Kapellen**, 5 • 20.10 Lugano (GP Cynar), 1 • 27.10 **A Travers Lausanne**, 1

1969

• 15.2 **Trofeo Laigueglia**, 2 • 17.2 **Aix-en-Provence**, 1 • 1.3 **Circuit Het Volk**, 12 • **Tour of Levante**, 1 (3.3 Elche - Elche, 2 / 4.3 Elche - Benidorm, 2 / 5.3 Benidorm - Cullera, 1 / 6.3 Cullera - Bunol, 1 / 7.3 Valencia - Benicasim, 1 / 8.3 Benicasim - Villa Real, 5 / 9.3 Villa Real, 3) • **Paris-Nice**, 1 (10.3 Villebon-sur-Yvette [time trial], 2 / Villebon - Joigny, 3 / 11.3 Joigny - Le Creusot, 1 / 12.3 Paray-le-Monial - St-Etienne, 3 / St-Etienne [time trial], 1 / 13.3 St-Etienne - Bollène, 33 / 14.3 Tavel [team time trial], 2 / Cavaillon - Hyères, 6 / 15.3 Hyères - Draguignan, 13, in main bunch / 16.3 Draguignan - Nice, 16, in main bunch / Col d'Eze [time trial], 1) • 19.3 **Milan-San Remo**, 1 • 22.3 **Harelbeke E3 GP**, 7 • 23.3 **Flèche Brabançonne**, abandoned - knee injury • 26.3 **Knokke**, 13 • 30.3 **Tour of Flanders**, 1 • **Tour of Majorca**, abandoned (31.3 Palma - Palma, in main bunch / 1.4 Palma - Benisalem, in main bunch / Benisalem - Palma, 1 / 2.4 El Arenal - El Arenal, abandoned- stomach ache) • 9.4 **Diksmuide**, 32 • 13.4 **Paris-Roubaix**, 2 • 18.4 **Amstel Gold Race**, 3 • 20.4 **Flèche Wallonne**, 5 • 22.4 **Liège-Bastogne-Liège**, 1 • 26.4 **Scandrano**, - • 27.4 **Circuit of the Flemish Provinces**, 10 • 1.5 **Garancières-en-Beauce**, 3 • 4.5 **Championship of Zürich**, 4 • 7.5 **Yvetot** [omnium], 1 • 10.5 **La Trimouille**, 1 • 11.5 **Vorst-Meulebeke** [dernys], 1 • **Tour of Italy**, disqualified (16.5 Circ. Lago di Garda - Brescia, in main bunch / 17.5 Brescia - Mirandola, 9 / 18.5 Mirandola - Montecatini, 1 / 19.S Montecatini [time trial], 1 / 20.5 Montecatini - Follonica, 15 / 21.5 Follonica - Viterbo, 18 / 22.5 Viterbo - Terracia, 1 / 23.5 Terracia - Naples, 16 / 24.5 Naples - Potenza, 12 / 25.5 Potenza - Campitello Matese, 7 / 26.5 Campobasso - Scanno, 8 / 27.5 Scanno - Silvi Marina, 6 / 28.5 Silvi Marina - Senigallia, in main bunch / 29.5 Senigallia - San Marino, 15 / 30.5 Cesenatico - San Marino [time trial], 1 / 1.6 Parma - Savona, disqualified) • 18.6 **Caen**, 2 • 19.6 **Brugge St-Andries**, in main bunch • 20.6 **Mettet**, Belgian Championshlp, 31 • 23.6 **Ottignies**, 1 • 24.6 **Machelen**, abandoned • **Tour de France**, 1 (28.6 Roubaix [prologue], 2 / 29.6 Roubaix - Woluwe, 5 / St-Pieters-Woluwe [team time trial], 1 / 30.6 St-Pieters-Woluwe - Maastricht, 15 / 1.7 Maastricht - Charleville-Méz., 15 / 2.7 Charleville-Méz. - Nancy, 39 / 3.7 Nancy - Mulhouse, 4 / 4.7 Mulhouse - Belfort (Ballon d'Alsace), 1 / 5.7 Belfort - Divonne-les-Bains, 28 / 6.7 Divonne-les-Bains [time trial], 1 / Divonne - Thonon, 29 / 7.7 Thonon - Chamonix, 2 / 8.7 Chamonix - Briançon, 2 / 9.7 Briançon - Digne, 1 / 10.7 Digne - Aubagne, 3 / 11.7 Aubagne - La Grande Motte, 32 / 12.7 La Grande Motte - Revel, 31 / 13.7 Revel [time trial], 1 / 14.7 Castelnaudry - Luchon, 4 / 15.7 Luchon - Mourenx, 1 / 16.7 Mourenx - Bordeaux. 56 / 17.7 Libourne - Brive, 34 / 18.7 Brive - Clermont-Ferrand, 2 / 19.7 Clermont-Ferrand - Montargis, 62 / 20.7 Montargis - Créteil, 54 / Créteil - Paris [time trial], 1) • 21.7 **Aalst**, 1 • 22.7 **Ronse**, 2 • 23.7 **St-Lambrechts-Woluwe**, 1 • 24.7 **De Panne**, 2 • 25.7 **Eine**, 26 • 26.7 **Denderleeuw**, 34 • **Rijmenam**, 2 • 27.7 **Vincennes**, 1 • 28.7 **Seignelay** (Auxerre), 4 • 29.7 **Guerlesquin**, 1 • 1.8 **Brette-les-Pins**, 4 • 2.8 Remiremont, 1 • 3.8 **Commentry**, 3 • 4.8 **Château-Chinon**, 1 • **Paris-Luxembourg**, 1 (5.8 Paris - Reims, 4 / 6.8 Rethel - Luxembourg, 1) • 10.8 **Zolder**, World Championship, abandoned • 11.8 **Lokeren**, 2 • 12.8 **Heusden**, 33 • 13.8 **Turnhout**, 3 • 13.8 **Honselersdijk**, 2 • 15.8 **Londerzeel**, 1 • 17.8 **Saussignac**, 1 • 17.8 **Moorslede**, 1 • 18.8 **Tienen**, 13, in main bunch • 19.8 **Bilzen**, 3 • 20.8 Auvelais, 1 • 21.8 **Schaarbeek**, 1 • 22.8 **Sint-Niklaas**, 20, in main bunch • 23.8 **Assebroek**, 4 • 24.8 **St-Lenaerts**, 5 • 25.8 **Bussières**, abandoned • 26.8 **Villeneuve-s / Lot**, 2 • 30.8 **Poperinge**, 21 • 3.9 **Alès**, 1 • 4.9 **Hyon**, 5 • 5.9 **Namur**, 10 • 7.9 **Châteaugiron**, 3 • 8.9 **Châteaulin**, 1 • 17.9 **Merelbeke**, abandoned • 21.9 **Schaarbeek**, 1 • 29.9 **St-Genesius-Rode**, abandoned • 2.10 **Baracchi Trophy** (with D. Boifava), 3 • 4.10 **Heultje**, 24 • 6.10 **Oostrozebeke**, 2 • 11.10 **Soumagne**, 2 • 12.10 **A Travers Lausanne**, 6 • 14.10 **Putte-**

Kapellen, abandoned • 18.10 **Venegono**, 5 • 19.10 **Scorze**, 1 • 26.10 **Romano**, 5

1970

• **Tour of Sardinia**, 2 (22.2 Rome - Civittavecchia, 4 / 23.2 Lanusel - Cagliari, 1 / 24.2 Cagliari - Oristano, 21, in main bunch / 25.2 Oristano - Alghero, 6 / 26.2 Portotours - Sassari [time trial], 1 / Sassari - Ollia, 42 / 27.2 Ollia - Monte Ortobene, 3) • 29.2 **Circuit Het Volk**, 7 • 7.3 **Sanary**, 1 • **Paris-Nice**, 1 (8.3 [team time trial], 6 / 9.3 Dourdan - Joigny, 52 / 10.3 Joigny - Autun, 7 / 11.3 Autun - St-Etienne, 1 / 12.3 St-Etienne - Bollène, 37 / 13.3 Bollène - Plan de Cuques, 16 / 14.3 Plan de Cuques - Hyères, 2 / 15.3 Hyères - St-Maxime, 12 / St-Maxime - Seillains, 1 / 16.3 Seillans - Nice, 6 / La Turbie [time trial], 1) • 19.3 **Milan-San Remo**, 8 • 29.3 **Montaglio**, 2 • 30.3 **Col San Martino**, 1 • 1.4 **Ghent-Wevelgem**, 1 • 5.4 **Tour of Flanders**, 3 • **Tour of Belgium**, 1 (6.4 Spa [in heats], 6 / 7.4 Spa - Virton, 3 / Virton [time trial], 1 / 8.4 Virton - Jambes, 3 / 9.4 Jambes - Heist a/Zee, 3 / Heist a/Zee [time trial], 1 / 10.4 Heist - St-Lambrechts-Woluwe, 15) • 12.4 **Paris-Roubaix**, 1 • 17.4 **Liège-Bastogne-Liège**, 3 • 19.3 **Flèche Wallonne**, 1 • 25.4 **Amstel Gold Race**, 8 • 26.4 **Polymultiplié**, 5 • 1.5 **Henniger Turm Frankfurt**, 8 • 2.5 **La Bastide d'Armagnac**, 6 • 7.5 **Nandrin**, 4 • 9.5 **Lorient**, 1 • 16.5 **Paderno d'Adda**, 4 • **Tour of Italy**, 1 (18.5 San Pellegrino - Biandronno, 32 / 19.5 Biandronno - St-Vincent, 1 / 20.5 St-Vincent - Aosta, 3 / 21.5 Aosta - Lodi, 43 / 22.5 Lodi - Lingonia, 5 / 23.5 Lingonia - Malescine, 19 / 24.5 Malescine - Brentonico, 1 / 25.5 Rovereto - Bassano del Grappa, 1 / 26.5 Bassano del Grappa - Treviso [time trial], 1 / 28.5 Terracina- Rivisondoli, 5 / 29.5 Rivisondoli, 7 / 30.5 Francavilla al Mare - Loretto, 4 / 31.5 Lorerto - Faenza, 57 / 1.6 Faenza - Sasciana Terme, 5 / 2.6 Sasciana - Mirandola, 54 / 3.6 Mirandola - Lido di Jesolo, 34 / 4.6 Lido di Jesolo - Arta Terme, 13 / 5.6 Arta Terme - Marmolada, 4 / 6.6 Rocca Pietore - Dobbiaco, 4 / 7.6 Dobbiaco - Bolzano, 5) • 8.6 **Cittadella**, 2 • 9.6 **Villafranca**, 1 • 10.6 **Caen**, 1 • 14.6 **Evergem**, 3 • 21.6 **Yvoir**, Belgian Championship, 1 • **Tour de France**, 1 (26.6 Limoges [prologue], 1 / 27.6 Limoges - La Rochelle, 3 / 28.6 La Rochelle - Angers, 24 / 29.6 Angers [team time trial], 1 / Angers - Reims, 65 / 30.6 Reims - Lisieux, 5 / 1.7 Lisieux - Rouen, 7 / Rouen - Amiens, 7 / 2.7 Amiens - Valenciennes, 7 / 3.7 Valenciennes - Vorst, 1 / Vorst [time trial], 2 / 4.7 Ciney - Felssberg, 6 / 5.7 Saarlouis - Mulhouse, 65 / 6.7 Belfort - Divonne-les-Bains, 1 / 7.7 Divonne-les-Bains [time trial], 1 / Divonne-les-Bains - Thonon-les-Bains, 33 / 8.7 Thonon - Crenoble, 1 / 9.7 Grenoble - Gap, 4 / 10.7 Gap - Ventoux, 1 / 11.7 Carpentras - Montpellier, 38 / 12.7 Montpellier - Toulouse, 18 / 13.7 Toulouse - St-Gaudens, 11 / 14.7 St-Gaudens - La Mongie, 4 / 15.7 Bagnères de Bigorie - Mourenux, 44 / 16.7 Mourenux - Bordeaux, 37 / 16.7 Bordeaux [time trial], 1 / 17.7 Ruffex - Tours, 39 / 18.7 Tours - Versailles, 13 / 19.7 Versailles - Paris [time trial], 1) • 20.7 **Aalst**, 4 • 21.7 **Ronse**, 1 • 22.7 **St-Pieters-Woluwe**, 1 • 23.7 **De Panne**, 10 • 25.7 **Rijmenam**, 27 • 27.7 **Seignelay**, 1 • 28.7 **Callae**, 4 • 2.8 **Vailly**, 1 • 3.8 **Château-Chinon**, 2 • 4.8 **Ussel**, 4 • 7.8 **St-Cyprien**, 1 • 8.8 **Saussignac**, 3 • 9.8 **Moorslede**, abandoned • 11.8 **Heusden**, 7 • 16.8 **Leicester, World Championship**, 29 • 17.8 **Lokeren**, 4 • 18.8 **Bilzen**, 1 • 18.8 **Honselersdijk**, 1 • 19.8 **Schaarbeek**, - • 20.8 **Hyon**, abandoned • 21.8 **Sint-Niklaas**, 1 • 22.8 **Montbasillac**, 5 • 23.8 **Felletin**, 2 • 24.8 **Bussières**, 1 • 25.8 **Quillian**, 5 • 26.8 **Varrilhes**, 1 • 28.8 **Tienen**, 10 • 29.8 **Poperinge**, 2 • 30.8 **G.P. Dortmund**, 1 • 3.9 **Milan** [omnium with JP Monseré], 1 • 4.9 **Martinengo**, 2 • 6.9 **Varèse**, 2 • 7.9 **Châteaulin**, 3 • 8.9 **Berlaar**, 3 • 12.9 **Châteaugiron**, 1 • 13.9 **Puy-de-Dôme**, 2 • 17.9 **Koolskamp**, Championship of Flanders, 7 • 20.9 **Giro di Lazio**, 6 • 21.9 **Laciano**, 4 • 24.9 **Montjuich** [time trial], 1 • 3.10 **Tour of Emilia**, 7 • 4.10 **Daumesnil**, Criterium des As, 1 • 6.10 **Coppa Agostoni**, 1 • 10.10 **Tour of Lombardy**, 4 • 11.10 **Lausanne**, 1 • 17.10 **Varèse**, 6 • 18.10 **Scorzé**, 4

1971

• 21.2 **Trofeo Laigueglia**, 4 • 24.2 **Monaco GP**, 2 • **Tour of Sardinia**, 1 (27.2 Potenza - Salerno, 1 / 28.2 Cagliari - Oristano, 11, in main bunch / 1.3 Oristano - Macomer, 1 / Macomer - Capo Falcone, in main bunch / 2.3 Sassari - Porto Torrès [time trial], 2 / Sassari - Olbia, in main bunch / 3.3 Olbia - Nuoro [time trial], 1) • **Paris-Nice**, 1 (10.3 Dourdan [prologue], 1 / 11.3 Dourdan - Troyes, 2 / 12.3 Châblis - Autun, 8 / Autun [time trial], 1 / 13.3 Autun - St-Etienne, 10 / 14.3 St-Etienne - Bollène, 6 / 15.3 Bollène - St-Rémy-de-Provence, 8 in main bunch / 16.3 St-Rémy-de-Provence - Draguignan, 3 / 17.3 Draguignan - Nice, 12 in main bunch / Col d'Eze, 1) • 19.3 **Milan-San Remo**, 1 • 21.3 **Flèche Brabançonne**, 2 • 25.3 **Circuit Het Volk**, 1 • 27.3 **Harelbeke E3 Race**, 3 • 31.3 **Ghent-Wevelgem**, 14 • 4.3 **Tour of Flanders**, 74 • **Tour of Belgium**, 1 (11.4 Heist [time trial], 1 / 12.4 Heist - Hyon-Ciply, 1 / 13.4 Hyon - Mont Rigi, 3 / 14.4 Spa - Herbeumont, 1 / 15.4 Herbeumont - Oudergem, 19) • 18.4 **Paris-Roubaix**, 5 • 25.4 **Liège-Bastogne-Liège**, 1 • 1.5 **Henniger Turm Frankfurt**, 1 • 2.5 **Chignolo Po**, 16 • 9.5 **Henon**, 3 • 10.5 **L'Armel**, sick - in main bunch • 12.5 **Legnano**, 7 • 15.5 **Le Creusot**, 1 • 16.5 **Paderna**, cancelled • **Dauphiné Libéré**, 1 (18.5 Avignon [team time trial], 1 / 19.5 Orange - Tournon, in main bunch / Tournon - St-Etienne, 1 / 20.5 St.Etienne - Grenoble, 19 / 21.5 Grenoble - Annecy, 2 / 22.5 Annecy - Mâcon, in main bunch / 23.5 Mâcon - Le Creusot, in main bunch / Le Creusot - Montcelu-les-Mines [time trial], 1) • 30.5 **Bourg-en-Bresse**, 3 • 1.6 **La Souterraine**, 1 • **Midi Libre**, 1 (3.6 Carcasonne - Béziers, 1 / 4.6 Béziers - Millau, 1 / 5.6 Milhu - Alès, 7 in main bunch / 6.6 Alès - Montpellier, 16, in main bunch) • 13.6 **Evergem**, punctured - abandoned • 16.6 **Camaiore GP**, 1 • 20.6 **Martelange**, Belgian Championship, 5 • 23.6 **Berg-Kampenhout**, in main bunch • **Tour de France**, 1 (26.6 Mulhouse prologue, 1 / 27.6 Mulhouse - Basle, 16 / Basle - Freiburg, 11 / Freiburg - Mulhouse, 15 / 28.6 Mulhouse - Strasbourg, 1 / 29.6 Strasbourg - Nancy, 64 / 30.6 Nancy - Marche-en-Famenne, 9 / 1.7 Dinant - Roubaix, 10 / 2.7 Roubaix - Amiens, 15 / Amiens - Le Touquet, 25 / 4.7 Rungis - Nevers, 23 / 5.7 Nevers - Puy-de-Dôme, 4 / 6.7 Clermont-Ferrand - St-Etienne, 14 / 7.7 St-Etienne - Grenoble, 7 / 8.7 Grenoble - Orcières-Merlette, 3 / 10.7 Orcières-Merlette - Marseille, 2 / 11.7 Albi [time trial], 1 / 12.7 Revel - Luchon, 2 / 13.7 Luchon - SuperBagnères, 4 / 14.7 Luchon - Gourette, 2 / Gourette - Pau, 4 / 15.7 Mont-de-Marsan - Bordeaux, 1 / 16.7 Bordeaux - Poitiers, 37 / 17.7 Blois - Versailles, 83 / 18.7 Versailles - Vincennes [time trial], 1) • 19.7 **Aalst**, 1 • 21.7 **Ronse**, 34 • **Ronse** [time trial], 1 • 21.7 **Rocourt**, 2 • 22.7 **De Panne**, 1 • 23.7 **St-Lambrechts-Woluwe**,14 • 24.7 **Rijmenam**, 6 • 25.7 **Vincennes**, 1 • 1.8 **Moorslede**, 2 • 2.8 **Badia-Settimo**, 1 • 3.8 **Cirie**, 2 • 5.8 **Grado**, 2 • 6.8 **Ghedi**, 1 • 8.8 **St-Lenaerts**, 1 • 10.8 **Bellariva-Rimini**, 2 • 13.8 **Sint-Niklaas**, 9 • 14.8 **Bilzen**, 1 • 15.8 **Hyon**, 7 • 16.8 **Zingem**, 9 • 20.8 **Modigliana**, 2 • 22.8 **Colonella - Colonnella**, 1 • 28.8 **Poperinge**, 1 • 29.8 **St-Pieters-Leeuw**, 3 • 1.9 **Geraardsbergen**, 1 • 5.9 **Mendrisio**, 1 • 7.9 **Lendinara**, 2 • 8.9 **Voghera**, 1 • 9.9 **Villafranca**, 1 • 11.9 **Beek**, 1 • 12.9 **Dortmund GP**, 3 • 13.9 **Longwy**, 2 • 16.9 **Koolskamp**, Championship of Flanders, 8 • 20.9 **Viane**, 1 • 24.9 **Montjuich**, 1 • 26.9 **Baden-Baden** (with H. Vanspringel), 1 • 28.9 **Larciano**, Aces Criterium, in main bunch • 29.9 **Bilbao**, 1 • 30.9 **Guernica-Sollube**, 4 • 4.10 **Tour of Emilia**, 5 • 5.10 **Coppa Agostoni**, 36 • 9.10 **Tour of Lombardy**, 1 • 10.10 **A Travers Lausanne**, 2 • 12.10 **Putte-Kapellen**, 4 • 16.10 **Calvisano**, 5 • 17.10 **Cordenons**, 1 • 23.10 **Casalecchio di Reno**, 3 • 24.10 **San Maria Infante**, 5

1972

• 20.2 **Trofeo Laigueglia**, 2 • **Tour of Sardinia**, 37 (27.2 Rome - Civitavccchia, in main bunch / 28.2 Cagliari - San Antioco, 7 / San Antioco - Cagliari, 7 / 29.2 Oristano - Nuoro, in main bunch / 1.3 Nuoro - Porto Torrès, 45 / 2.3 Sassari - Santa Teresa di Galura, 5) • 4.3 **Circuit Het Volk**, 1 • **Paris-Nice**, 2 (9.3 Dourdan [prologue], 1 / 10.3 Dourdan - Vierzon, 4 / 11.3 Vierzon - Autun, 1 / 12.3 Autun - St-Etienne, 15, in main bunch / 13.3 St-Etienne - Valence, 20, in main bunch / Valence [team time trial], 4 / 14.3 Valence - Manosque, 1 / 15.3 Manosque - Le Castellet, 4 / 16.3 Hyères - Nice, 8, in main bunch / Col d'Eze [time trial], 2) • 18.3 **Milan-San Remo**, 1 • 19.3 **Pontoglio**, 2 • 20.3 **Petite-Foret** [omnium], 2 • 20.3 **Valenciennes**, 2 • 25.3 **Harelbeke E3 GP**, 2 • 26.3 **Flèche Brabançonne**, 1 • 2.4 **Gavardo**, 7 • 3.4 **San Martino**, 2 • 9.4 **Tour of Flanders**, 7 • 12.4 **Ghent-Wevelgem**, 3 • 16.4 **Paris-Roubaix**, 7 • 20.4 **Liège-Bastogne-Liège**, 1 • 23.4 **Flèche Wallonne**, 1 • 1.5 **Henninger Turm Frankfurt**, 2 • 6.5 **Momignies**, 1 • 11.5 **Nandrin**, 8 • 16.5 **Mirandola**, 5 • **Tour of Italy**, 1 (21.5 Venice - Ravenna, 12 / 22.5 Ravenna - Fermo, 4 / 23.5 Porto San Giorgio - Francavilla, 2 / 24.5 Francavilla - Block Haus, 5 / Block Haus - Foggia, 35 / 25.5 Foggia - Montesano, 4 / 26.5 Montesano Terme - Cosenza, 19 / 27.5 Cosenza - Catanzaro, 2 / 28.5 Catanzaro - Reggio di Calabria, 28 / 29.5 Messina - Circ. Peloritani, 8 / 31.5 Rome - Monte Argentario, 7 / 1.6 Monte Argentario - Forte dei Marmi, 14 / 2.6 Forte dei Marmi [time trial], 1 / 3.6 Forte del Marmi - Savona, 26 / 4.6 Savona - Bardonecchia - Jafferau, 1 / 6.6 Circ. Parabiago, 34 / 7.6 Parabiago - Livigno, 1 / 9.6 Livigno - Stelvio, 3 / 9.6 Solda - Asiago, 30 / 10.6 Asiago - Arco, 17 / Circuit. Arco [time trial], 1 / 11.6 Arco - Milan, 10) • 12.6 **Castelfranco - Veneto**, 1 • 13.6 **Busto Arsizio**, 2 • 14.6 **Mantua**, 1• 15.6 **Monsummano**, 2 • 16.6 **Rimini** (with R. Swerts), 1 • 16.6 **Poggio a Caiano**, 2 • 20.6 **Zomergem**, 1 • 21.6 **Boulogne**, 1 • 25.6 **Bornem**, Belgian Championship, 2 • 27.6 **Peer**, fell - abandoned • 28.6 **Wavre**, 2 • **Tour de France**, 1 (1.7 Angers [prologue], 1 / 2.7 Angers - Saint-Brieuc, 6 / 3.7 Saint-Brieuc - La Baule, 37 / 4.7 Pornichet - Saint-Jean-de-Monts, 30 / Merlin- Plage [team time trial], 1 / 5.7 Merlin-Plage - Royan, 7 / 6.7 Royan - Bordeaux, 22 / Bordeaux [time trial], 1 / 7.7 Bordeaux - Bayonne, 9 / 9.7 Bayonne - Pau, 5 / 10.7 Pau - Luchon, 1 / 11.7 Luchon - Colomiers, 55 / 12.7 Castres - La Grande-Motte, 29 / 13.7 Carnon-Plage - Mont-Ventoux, 2 / 14.7 Carpentras - Orcières-Merlette, 3 / 16.7 Orcières-Merlette - Briançon, 1 / 17.7 Briançon - Valloire, 1 / Valloire - Aix-les-Bains, 2 / 18.7 Aix-les-Bains - Le Revard, 2 / 19.7 Aix-les-Bains - Pontarlier, 57 / 20.7 Pontarlier - Ballon d'Alsace, 4 / 21.7 Vesoul - Auxerre, 35 / 22.7 Auxerre - Versailles, 48 / 23.7 Versailles [time trial], 1 / Versailles - Vincennes, 48) • 24.7 **Aalst**, 4 • 25.7 **Ronse**, 1 • 26.7 **St-Lambrechts-Woluwe**, 1 • 27.7 **De Panne**, abandoned • 28.7 **Londerzeel**, 8, in main bunch • 29.7 **Rijmenam**, 6 • 30.7 **Rocourt track**, 2 • 31.7 **Heusden**, 12 • 1.8 **Schoten**, Scheldt GP, 1 • 6.8 **Gap**, World Championship, 4 • 7.8 **Château-Chinon**, 4 • 9.8 **Bilzen**, 4 • 11.8 **Tienen**, 1 • 12.8 **Drongen**, 26 • 13.8 **G.P. Dortmund**, 1 • 14.8 **Quiberon**, 1 • 15.8 **Moorslede**, 11 • 25.8 **Heusden** (Limb.), 4 • 27.8 **St-Lenaerts**, 4 • 28.8 **Brustem**, 1 • 31.8 **Rummen**, 1 • 1.9 **Hyon-Ciply**, 2 • 2.9 **Zingem**, 1 • 3.9 **Plelan-le-Petit**, 1 • 4.9 **Châteaulin**, 3 • 7.9 **Volgera**, 1 • 9.9 **Tour of Piedmont**, 1 • 10.9 **Mendrisio**, 1 • 14.9 **Koolskamp**, Championship of Flanders, 2 • 15.9 **Ougrée**, 1 • 16.9 **Mont-sur-Marchienne**, 10 • 19.9 **Maldegem**, 1 • 22.9 **Beernem**, 1 • 24.9 **Montjuich**, 1 • 25.9 **St-Laureins**, 2 • 29.9 **Ayneux- Fléron**, 1 • 1.10 **Paris-Tours**, in main bunch • 4.10 **Bologna**, 1 • 7.10 **Tour of Lombardy**, 1 • 8.10 **Sallanches**, 1 • 8.10 **Lausanne**, 1: RR 1 / TT 1 • 11.10 **Baracchi Trophy** (with R. Swerts), 1 • 17.10 **Putte-Kapellen**, 2 • 25.10 **Mexico**, World Hour Record

1973

• 18.2 **Trofeo Laiguеglia**, 1 • **Tour of Sardinia**, 1 (24.2 Florence - Livorno, in main bunch / 25.2 Porto Torrés - Alghero, 2 / 26.2 Macomer - San Antioco, 3 / 27.2 Campu

Omu [time trial], 1 / Cagliari - Lanusei, 2 / 28.2 Lanusei - Nuoro, 3 / 1.3 Nuoro - Olbia, 6 / Olbia - Sassari, 6, in main bunch) • 3.3 **Circuit Het Volk**, 1 • 7.3 **Milan-Turin**, 4 • **Paris-Nice**, 3 (11.3 Ponthierry [prologue], 1 / 12.3 Auxerre - Saulieu, 4 / Saulieu - Châlon-s/ Saône, in main bunch / 13.3 Châlon-s /Saône - St.Etienne, 15, in main bunch / 14.3 Tournon - Valence, in main bunch / Valence [team time trial], 5 / 15.3 Viviers - Manosque, 2 / 16.3 Manosque - Draguignan, 4 / 17.3 Frejus - Nice, 8, in main bunch / La Turbie [time trial], 7) • 24.3 **Harelbeke E3 GP**, 14 • **Catalan Week**, 2 (26.3 Malgrat de Mar - Berga, 6 / 27.3 Guardiola - Andorra, 10 / 28.3 Seo de Urgel - Tossa Bontbui, 11 / 29.3 Montserrat - Castelldefels, 4 / 30.3 Molins de Rey - Vallvidrera, 2 / Sabadell Hospitales, 10, in main bunch) • 1.4 **Tour of Flanders**, 3 • 3.4 **Ghent-Wevelgem**, 1 • 7.4 **Amstel Gold Race**, 1 • **Tour of Belgium**, abandoned (8.4 Ostend [team time trial], 4 / 9.4 Ostend - Zottegem, 3 / 10.4 Zottegem - Dampremy, 2 / 11.4 Dampremy - Dinant, 5 / 12.4 Dinant - Genk, abandoned) • 15.4 **Paris-Roubaix**, 1 • 19.4 **Flèche Wallonne**, 2 • 22.4 **Liège-Bastogne-Liège**, 1 • **Tour of Spain**, 1 (26.4 Calpe [prologue], 1 / 27.4 Calpe - Murcia, 22 / 28.4 Murcia - Albacete, 8 / 29.4 Albacete - Alcazar de S.Juan, 21 / 30.4 Alcazar de S.Juan - Cuenca, 3 / 1.5 Cuenca - Turuel, 2 / 2.5 Turuel Puebla de Farnas, 5 / Puebla de F. [team time trial], 1 / 3.5 Playa de Farnais - Castellon, in main bunch / 4.5 Castellon - Calafell, 1 / 5.5 Calafell - Barcelona, 9 / 6.5 Barcelona - Ampuriabrava, 1 / 7.5 Ampuriabrava - Manresa, 2 / 8.5 Manresa - Zaragoza, 9 / 9.5 Mallen - Irache, 2 / 10.5 Irache - Bilbao, in main bunch / 11.5 Bilbao Torrelavega, in main bunch / Torrelavega [time trial], 1 / 12.5 Torrelavega - Miranda de Ebro, 1 / 13.5 Miranda de Ebro - Tolosa, 47 / Hernani - San Sebastian [time trial], 1) • **Tour of Italy**, 1 (18.5 Verviers [prologue with R. Swerts], 1 / 19.5 Verviers - Cologne, 1 / 20.5 Cologne - Luxembourg, 3 / 21.5 Luxembourg - Strasbourg, in main bunch / 22.5 Geneva - Aosta, 1 / 24.5 St-Vincent-Aosta - Milan, 10 / 25.5 Milan - Iseo de Lago, 6 / 26.5 Iseo de Lago - Lido delle Nazioni, 9 / 27.5 Lido delle Nazioni - Monte Carpegna, 1 / 28.5 Carpegna - Alba Adriatica, in main bunch / 29.5 Alba Adriatica - Lanciano, 1 / 30.5 Lanciano - Benevento, 3 / 31.5 Benevento - Fiuggi Terme, 14 / 1.6 Fiuggi Terme - Bolsena, in main bunch / 2.6 Bolsena - Florence, in main bunch / 3.6 Florence - Forte dei Marmi, 6 / 4.6 Forte dei Marmi [time trial], 3 / 6.6 Forte dei Marmi - Verona, 32 / 7.6 Verona - Andalo, 1 / 8.6 Andalo - Auronzo di Cadore, 4 / 9.6 Auronzo - Trieste, 99) • 10.6 **Castelfranco - Veneto**, 3 • 12.6 **Monsummano**, 1 • 13.6 **Lainate**, 2 • 17.6 **Evergem**, 1 • 20.6 **Camaiore**, 15 • 21.6 **Maggiore**, 1 • 22.6 **Peer**, in main bunch • 24.6 **Soumagne**, Belgian Championship, 2 • 26.6 **Zomergem**, 6 • 28.6 **Cittadella**, 2 • 29.6 **Monte San Pietrangeli**, 2 • 30.6 **San Michel Angliani**, 2 • 1.7 **Pavullo**, 1 • 4.7 **Ulvenhout**, 3 • 8.7 **Nandrin**, 1 • 21.7 **Ostend**, [summer track omnium], 1 • 22.7 **Merchtem**, Championship of Brabant, 1 • 23.7 **Aalst**, 3 • 24.7 **Ronse**, 4 • 25.7 **St-Lambrechts-Woluwe**, 1 • 26.7 **De Panne**, 1 • 27.7 **Londerzeel**, 1 • 28.7 **Rijmenam**, sick - abandoned • 31.7 **Schoten**, 9 • 1.8 **Bilzen**, 5 • 2.8 **Amsterdam**, [summer track pursuit], 1 • 3.8 **Tienen**, 22 • 4.8 **Brustem**, 2 • 5.8 **Moorslede**, 1 • 10.8 **Sint-Niklaas**, 6 • 12.8 **G.P. Dortmund**, 3 • 13.8 **Wilrijk**, 1 • 14.8 **Heusden**, 6 • 15.8 **St-Lenaerts**, 1 • 17.8 **Montecampione**, 1: RR 1 / TT 1 • 19.8 **Cronostaffetta**, 1 • 20.8 **Misano** [time trial], 1 • 21.8 **Merano**, 2 • 24.9 **Heusden** (Limburg), 1 • 25.8 **Poperinge**, 3 • 26.8 **St-Pieters-Leeuw**, punctured - abandoned • 29.8 **Geraardsbergen**, 13 • 2.9 **Montjuich**, World Championship, 4 • 4.9 **Brasschaat**, 5 • 7.9 **Valkenburg**, 6 • 9.9 **Mendrisio**, 1 • 10.9 **Roccastrada**, 1 • 11.9 **Larciano**, 2 • 13.9 **Koolskamp**, Championship of Flanders, 19 • 14.9 **Ernegem**, in main bunch • 15.9 **Tilburg**, Aces Criterium, 3 • 22.9 **Two Day G.P. Fourmies**, 1 • 23.9 **G.P. Fourmies**, 1 • 26.9 **Paris-Brussels**, 1 • 27.9 **Liège**, 1 • 30.9 **Paris-Tours**, 6 • 1.10 **Jeumont**, 1 • 6.10 **Landenprijs**, 1 • 7.10 **Lausanne**, 1 • 7.10 **Diesenhofen**, 1 • 8.10 **Oostrozebeke**, punctured - abandoned • 13.10 **Tour of Lombardy**, disqualified • 15.10 **Eeklo**, 6

1974

• 13.1 **Castelldefels**, [cyclo-cross], 3 • 9.2 **Viarregio**, 3 • 10.2 **Follonica**, 2 • 18.2 **Nice**, abandoned • 20.2 **Trofeo Laiguеglia**, 1 • **Tour of Sardinia**, 4 (23.2 Arezzo - Viterbo, 45 / 24.2 San Antioco, 3 / 25.2 Cagliari - Bosa, 5 / 26.2 Thiesi - Alghero, 32 / 27.2 Porto Torrés - Nuoro, 2 • 28.2 Sassari - Cagliari, 15) • 2.3 **Circuit Het Volk**, 6 • **Paris - Nice**, 3 (9.3 Ponthierry [prologue], 1 / 10.3 Ponthierry-Orléans, 1 / 11.3 Sully-sur-Loire - Château-Chinon, 9 / 12.3 Paray-le-Monial - St-Etienne, 7 / 13.3 St-Etienne - Orange, 26 / 14.3 Orange - Bandol, 1 / 15.3 Carqueiranne - Mont Faron, 6 / Toulon - Draguignan, in main bunch / 16.3 Seillans - Nice, 10 / Col d'Eze [time trial], 4) • 24.3 **Flèche Brabançonne**, abandoned • **Catalan Week**, 2 (25.3 Hospitalet de Llobregat - Berga, 4 / 26.3 Ripoll - Malgrat de Mar, 17 / 27.3 Gerona - Castelldefels, 8 / 28.3 Vilafranca - Lerida, 25 / Corbins - Balaguer [time trial], 2 / 29.3 Fontdepou - Envalira, 4) • 31.3 **Tour of Flanders**, 4 • 2.4 **Ghent-Wevelgem**, 2 - 7.4 **Paris-Roubaix**, 4 • 25.4 **Imola**, Coppa Placci, 3 • 27.4 **Tavarnelle**, 1 • 28.4 **Calenzano**, 2 • 1.5 **Henninger Turm Frankfurt**, 5 • 4.5 **Momignies**, 1 • **Dunkirk Five Days**, 4 (8.5 Dunkirk - Lille, 3 / 9.5 Lille - St-Quentin, 8 / 10.5 St-Quentin - Valenciennes, 13 / St-Amand-les-Eaux, 2 / 11.5 Valenciennes - Dunkirk, 30 / 12.5 Dunkirk - Kassel, 4) • **Tour of Italy**, 1 (16.5 Rome (Vatican) - Formia, 72 / 17.5 Formia - Pompei, 4 / 18.5 Pompei - Sorrente, 11 / 20.5 Sorrente - Sapri, 69 / 21.5 Sapri - Taranto, 11 / 22.5 Taranto - Foggia, 21 / 23.5 Foggia - Chieti, 4 / 24.5 Chieti - Macerata, 27 / 25.5 Macerata - Carpegna, 2 / 26.5 Carpegna - Modena, 38 / 27.5 Modena - II Ciocco, 2 / II Ciocco - Forte dei Marmi, 71 / 28.5 Forte dei Marmi [time trial], 1 / 30.5 Forte dei Marmi - Pietra Ligure, 44 / 31.5 Pietra Ligure - San Remo, 12 / 1.6 San Remo - Valenza, 36 / 2.6 Valenza - Mendrisio (Mte Generoso), 15 / 3.6 Como - Iseo, 12 / 4.6 Iseo - Sella Valsugana, 2 / 5.6 Borgo Valsugana - Pordenone, 31 / 6.6 Pordenone - Tre Cime di Lavaredo, 4 / 7.6 Misurina - Bassano del Grappa, 1 / 8.6 Bassano - Milan, 12 / 9.6 Epilogue, 20) • **Tour of Switzerland**, 1 (12.6 Gippingen [prologue], 1 / 13.6 Zurzach - Diessenhofen, 3 / 14.6 Diessenhofen - Eschenbach, 1 / 15.6 Eschenbach - Lenzerheide, 2 / Lenzerheide - Tgantieni [time trial], 5 / Lenzerheide - Tgantieni, 2 / 16.6 Lenzerheide - Valbella - Bellinzona, 3 / 17.6 Bellinzona - Naters / Blatten, 3 / 18.6 Naters - Lausanne, 2 / 19.6 Lausanne - Grenchen, 3 / 20.6 Grenchen - Fislisbach, 5 / 21.6 Fislisbach - Olten, 9 / Olten - Olten, 1) • **Tour de France**, 1 927.6 Brest [prologue], 1 / 28.6 Brest - St. Paul-de-Léon, 6 / 29.6 Plymouth [circuit race], 15 / 30.6 Morlaix - St-Malo, 26 / 1.7 St-Malo - Caen, 20 / 2.7 Caen - Dieppe, 21 / 3.7 Dieppe - Harelbeke, 18 / Harelbeke [team time trial], 1 / 4.7 Mons - Châlons-s/Marne, 1 / 5.7 Châlons-s /Marne - Chaumont, 7 / Chaumont - Besançon, 4 / 6.7 Besançon - Gaillard, 1 / 7.7 Gaillard - Aix-les-Bains, 1 / 9.7 Aix-les-Bains - Serre-Chevalier, 2 / 10.7 Savines-le-Lac - Orange, 11 / 11.7 Avignon - Montpellier, 31 / 12.7 Lodève - Colomiers, 27 / 14.7 Colomiers - Seo de Urgel, 1 / 15.7 Seo de Urgel - Saint-Lary-Soulan, 5 / 16.7 Saint-Lary-Soulan - Tourmalet, 7 / 17.7 Bagnères-de-Bigorre - Pau, 16 / 18.7 Pau - Bordeaux, 7 / Bordeaux [time trial], 1 / 19.7 Saint-Gilles-Croix de Vie - Nantes, 7 / 20.7 Vouvray - Orléans, 1 / Orléans [time trial], 2 / 21.7 Orléans - Paris, 1) • 22.7 **Aalst**, abandoned • 23.7 **Ronse**, 6 • 25.7 **De Panne**, 6 • 26.7 **Londerzeel**, 1 • 27.7 **Verviers**, 3 • 28.7 **Moorslede**, 1 • 1.8 **Poilzere**, abandoned • 2.8 **Tienen**, 4 • 3.8 **Rijmenam**, 1 • 4.8 **St-Lenaerts**, 2 • 7.8 **Molenbeek**, 3 • 9.8 **Sint-Niklaas**, 7 • 10.8 **Heusden** (Limburg), 1 • 11.8 **St-Pieters-Leeuw**, 5 • 13.8 **Heusden**, 11 • 14.8 **Vielsalm**, 5 • 15.8 **Seraing**, 2 • 16.8 **Ninove**, 1 • 17.8 **Peer**, 8 • 18.8 **G.P. Dortmund**, 9 • 19.8 **Eeklo**, 2 • 25.8 **Montreal**, World Championship, 1 • 27.8 **Cannes**, 2 • 29.8 **Rummen**, 22 • 31.8 **Poperinge**, 1 • 1.9 **Nogaro**, Aces Criterium, 1 / 2.9 **Châteaulin**, 6 • 3.9 **Brasschaat**, 11 • 6.9 **Valkenburg**, 5 • 7.9 **Deinze**, 5 • 8.9 **Malderen**, 1 • 12.9 **Koolskamp**, Championship of Flanders, abandoned • 14.9 **Geneva** [omnium], 1 • 15.9 **Jeumont**, 2 • 17.9 **Luxembourg** [omnium], 1 • 18.9 **Retie**, 26 • 29.9 **Tours - Versailles**, abandoned • 3.10 **Knokke**, 1 • 4.10 **Duffel**, 3 • 5.10 **Hendrik-Ido-Ambacht**, 1 • 7.10 **Oostrozebeke**, 4 • 9.10 **Coppa Agostoni**, 5 • 12.10 **Tour of Lo**

1975

• 2.2 **G.P. Aix-en-Provence**, 9 • 18.1 **Wetzikon**, [cyclo-cross], 4 • **Mediterranean Tour**, 23 (15.2 Port-de-Bouc [team time trial], 2 / Port-de-Bouc - Les Martigues, 15, in main bunch / 16.2 La Crau d'Hyères, 13, in main bunch / La Crau d'Hyères [time trial], 16 / 17.2 Le Lavandou - Fréjus, 6, in main bunch / 18.2 Grimaud - Menton, 11, in main bunch / 19.2 Beausoleil - Antibes, 31) • **Tour of Sardinia**, 1 (22.2 Rome - Lago di Bracciano, 20 / 23.2 Alghero, 1 / 24.2 Sassari - San Teresa di Gallura, 16 / 25.2 Palau - Nuoro, 3 / 26.2 Nuoro - Monte Spada [time trial], 2 / Monte Spada - Oristano, 11) • 27.2 **Sassari-Cagliari**, 1 • 1.3 **Circuit Het Volk**, 6 • **Paris-Nice**, 2 (9.3 Fontenay-sous-Bois [time trial], 1 / 10.3 Evry - Saint-Doulchard, 7 / 11.3 La Guerche - Beaune, 25, in main bunch / 12.3 Cuisery - St-Etienne, 17 / 13.3 St-Etienne - Orange, 20 / 14.3 Orange - St-Rémy-de-Provence, 1 / 15.3 Mont Faron [time trial], 4 / Toulon - Draguignan, 3 / 16.3 Seillans - Nice, in main bunch / Col d'Eze [time trial], 5) • 19.3 **Milan-San Remo**, 1 • 22.3 **Harelbeke E3 GP**, abandoned • 23.3 **Flèche Brabançonne**, 18 • 29.3 **Amstel Gold Race**, 1 • **Catalan Week**, 1 (31.3 Hospitalet - Valls, 4 / 1.4 Valls - Les Escaldes, 2 / 2.4 Organa - Gironella, 2 / Caserras - N.Sen.Queralt [time trial], 1 / 3.4 Berga - San Bartolomé del Grau, 3 / 4.4 Roda de Ter - Malgrat de Mar, 3) • 6.4 **Tour of Flanders**, 1 • 9.4 **Ghent-Wevelgem**, 6 • 13.4 **Paris-Roubaix**, 2 • 15.4 **Liège-Ligny**, 2 • 17.4 **Flèche Wallonne**, 3 • 20.4 **Liège-Bastogne-Liège**, 1 • 26.4 **Geneva** [omnium], 1 • 27.4 **Poigny**, 1 • 30.4 **Geleen**, 4 • 1.5 **Henninger Turm Frankfurt**, 7 • 2.5 **Zürich** [omnium], 1 • 3.5 **Saint-Cloud**, 3 • 4.5 **Championship of Zürich**, 2 • **Tour de Romandie**, 14 (6.5 Geneva [team time trial], 19 / 7.5 Geneva - Ste-Croix, 1 / 8.5 Ste-Croix - Porrentruy, 3 / 9.5 Porrentruy - Gruyères, 2 / 10.5 Bulle - Verbier, 15 / 11.5 Verbier - Grand-Lancy, 2 / Lancy [time trial], 1) • 13.5 **Copenhagen**, 1 • 24.5 **St-Amands**, in main bunch • 26.5 **Ronse**, 4 • 31.5 **Woerden**, 1 • **Dauphiné Libéré**, 10 (2.6 Annecy [team time trial], 5 / 3.6 Annecy - Mâcon, in main bunch / 4.6 Mâcon - Le Creusot, in main bunch / Le Creusot - Monceau-les-Mines, in main bunch / 5.6 Monceau-les-Mines - St-Etienne, in main bunch / 6.6 St-Etienne - Valence, in main bunch / 7.6 Romans - Grenoble, 17 / 8.6 Grenoble - Briançon, 4 / 9.6 Veynes - Avignon, in main bunch / Avignon [time trial], 10) • **Tour of Switzerland**, 2 (11.6 Baden - Baldegg [prologue], 7 / 12.6 Baden - Frick, 4 / 13.6 Frick - Oftringen, 9 / 14.6 Oftringen - Mürten, 39 / 15.6 Mürten - Tösch, 4 / 16.6 Tösch - Lugano, 7 / 17.6 Lugano - Silvaplana, 3 / 18.6 Silvaplana - Laax, 6 / 19.6 Laax - Frauenfeld, 1 / 20.6 Frauenfeld - Affoltern, 2 / Affoltern [time trial], 2) • 21.6 **Mettet**, Belgian Championship, 3 • 24.6 **Zomergem**, 7 • **Tour de France**, 2 (26.6 Charleroi [prologue], 2 / 27.6 Charleroi - Molenbeek, 2 / Molenbeek - Roubaix, 7 / 28.6 Roubaix - Amiens, in main bunch / 29.6 Amiens - Versailles, 6 / 30.6 Versailles - Le Mans, in main bunch / 1.7 Sablé-s/Sarthe - Merlin-Plage, 3 / 2.7 Merlin-Plage [time trial], 1 / 3.7 St-Gilles-Croix de Vie - Angoulême, 4 / 4.7 Angoulême - Bordeaux, 53 / 5.7 Langon - Fleurance, 4 / Fleurance - Auch [time trial], 1 / 7.7 Auch - Pau, 8 / 8.7 Pau - Saint-Lary-Soulan, 4 / 9.7 Tarbes - Albi, 48 / 10.7 Albi - Super-Lioran, 2 / 11.7 Aurillac - Puy-de-Dôme, 3 / 13.7 Nice - Pra-Loup, 5 / 14.7 Barcelonnette - Serre Chevalier, 2 / 15.7 Valloire - Morzine - Avoriaz, 3 / 16.7 Morzine - Chatel [time trial], 3 / 17.7 Thonon-les-Bains - Châlon.s/Saône, 6 / 18.7 Pouilly-en-Auxois - Melun, 57 / 19.7 Melun - Senlis, 40 / 20.7 Paris (Champs Elysées), 16) • 21.7 **Aalst**, 27 • 22.7 **Ronse**, 1 • 23.7 **Woluwe**, 2 • 24.7 **De Panne**, 8 • 25.7 **Londerzeel**, 12 • 26.7 **Bilzen**, 11 • 27.7 **Maria-Aalter**, abandoned • 29.7 **Callac**, 1 • 1.8 **Tienen**, 2 • 2.8 **Rijmenam**, 1 • 3.8 **Moorslede**, 7 • 4.8 **Château-Chinon**, 1 • 5.8 **Peer**, 5 • 6.8 **Linne**, 8 • 7.8 **Ostend** [summer track meeting], 3 • 9.8 **Heusden** (Limburg), 1 • 10.8 **Nandrin**, 5 • 11.8 **Wilrijk**, 1 • 12.8

Heusden, 4 • 13.8 **Plancoët**, 1 • 14.8 **Quiberon**, 4 • 15.8 **Geraardsbergen**, 7 • 17.8
G.P. Dortmund, 5 • 19.8 **Eeklo**, 1 • 19.9 **Heverlee**, 6 • 22.8 **Oostduinkerke**, 1 • 24.8
St-Pieters-Leeuw, 20 • 25.8 **Ninove**, 10 • 27.8 **Overijse**, 1 • 3l.8 **Yvoir**, World
Championship, 8 • 1.9 **Merchtem**, 6 • 4.9 **Rummen**, in main bunch • 5.9 **Valkenburg**,
1 • 6.9 **Deinze**, 16 • 7.9 **Belfort**, Aces Criterium, 4 • 8.9 **Châteaulin**, 1 • 9.9 **Brasschaat**,
4 • 10.9 **Hendrik-Ido-Ambacht**, 6 • 12.9 **Beveren-Waas**, abandoned • 14.9 **Paris-
Brussels**, 2 • 17.9 **Retie**, 1 • 19.9 **Stuttgart - Böblingen**, 1 • 21.9 **Leuven**, 3 • 22.9
Viane, in main bunch • 24.9 **Montjuich**, 1 (with L. Van Impe): RR 14 / TT 1 • 28.9
Tours - Versailles, 9 • 1.10 **Knokke**, 28 • 1.10 **Berlare**, abandoned • 4.10 **Weert**, 3 •
8.10 **Coppa Agostoni**, 5 • 11.10 **Tour of Lombardy**, 6 • 12.10 **A Travers Lausanne**,
2: RR 16 / TT 3 • 13.10 **Boom**, abandoned • 14.10 **Châteauroux**, 1

1976

• **Tour of Sardinia**, 8 (26.2 Cassino - Sora, 29 / 27.2 Sora - Avezzano, 2 / Avezzano
- Toia - Vanica, 43 / 28.2 Cagliari - Oristano, 44 / 29.2 Oristano - Nuoro, 1 / 1.3 Nuoro
- Sassari, 19 • 2.3 Sassari-Cagliari, 17) • 6.3 **Circuit Het Volk**, 15 • **Tirreno Adriatico**,
2 (12.3 Santamanella - Fiuggi, 4 / 13.3 Ferrentino - Monte Livata, 1 / 14.3 Subiaco -
Tortoreto Lido, 2 / 15.3 Tortoreto - Civitanova Marche, 40 / 16.3 S. Benedetto del
Tronto, 59, in main bunch / S. Benedetto del Tronto, [time trial], 1) • 19.3 **Milan-
San Remo**, 1 • 21.3 **Flèche Brabançonne**, 2 • **Catalan Week**, 1 (22.3 Olot - Torello
[prologue], 1 / 23.3 Torello - Andorra, 2 / 24.3 Organa - Martorell, 2 / 25.3
Martorell - Hospitalet de Llobregat, 2 / Hospitalet [time trial], 1 / 26.3 Hospitalet -
Sante Eulalia de Ronsana, 9) • **Tour of Belgium**, 23 (28.3 Meerbeke - Meerbeke, 29
/ Meerbeke - Ronse, 25, in main bunch / 29.3 Drongen - Mol, in main bunch / 30.3
Mol - Kelmis, 39 / 31.3 Kelmis - Mons, in main bunch / 1.4 Mons - Molenbeek, 16
/ Molenbeek - Molenbeek, 18) • 4.4 **Tour of Flanders**, 17 • 6.4 **Ghent-Wevelgem**,
10 • 11.4 **Paris-Roubaix**, 16 • 15.4 **Flèche Wallonne**, 4 • 18.4 **Liège-Bastogne-
Liège**, 6 • 21.4 **Charleroi-Ligny**, 7 • 25.4 **Bavikhove**, 1 • 28.4 **Vincennes** [track], 1 •
1.5 **Henninger Turm Frankfurt**, 7 • 2.5 **Championship of Zürich**, 7 • **Tour de
Romandie**, 3 (4.5 Geneva [prologue], - / 5.5 Geneva - Vevey, 10 / 6.5 Vevey -
Leysin, 4 / 7.5 Leysin - Bassecourt, 6 / 8.5 Coufaivre - Chaumont Neuchatel, 9 / 9.5
Neuchatel - Fribourg, 7 / Fribourg [time trial], 2) • 12.5 **De Panne**, 1 • 14.5
Evergem, 1 • 15.5 **Berlin**, 1 • **Tour of Italy**, 8 (21.5 Giro Catania, 25 / Catania -
Siracusa, 72 / 22.5 Siracusa - Caltanisetta, 8 / 23.5 Caltanisetta - Palermo, 25 / 24.5
Cefalu - Messina, 7 / 25.5 Reggio Calabria - Cosenza, 3 / 26.5 Cosenza - Matera, 15
/ 27.5 Ostuni [time trial], 7 / 28.5 Selva di Fasano - Lago Laceno, 2 / 29.5 Bagnoli
Irpino - Roccaraso, 5 / 30.5 Roccaraso - Terni, 72 / 31.5 Terni - Gabicce Mare, 5 /
1.6 Gabicce Mare - Porretta Terma, 20 / 2.6 Porretta Terma - II Ciocco, 15 / 3.6 II
Ciocco - Varazze, 37 / 5.6 Varazze - Ozegna, 67 / 6.6 Castellamonte - Arosio, 6 / 7.6
Arasio - Verona, 14 / 8.6 Verona - Longarone, 21 / 9.6 Longarone - Torri del Vaiolet,
10 / 10.6 Vigo di Fassa - Terme di Comano, 23 / 11.6 Terme di Comano - Bergamo,
2 / 12.6 Arcore - Arcore [time trial], 4 / Giro di Milano, 7) • 3.7 **Mendrisio**, 2 • 5.7
Humbeek, abandoned • 7.7 **Ulvenhout**, in main bunch • 10.7 **Kalmthout**, abandoned
• 22.7 **Ninove**, abandoned • 23.7 **Londerzeel**, in main bunch • 24.7 **Bilzen**, 13 • 25.7
Maria-Aalter, 25 • 28.7 **Welkenraedt**, 11 • 29.7 **Peer**, 14, in main bunch • 30.7 **Tienen**,
1 • 1.8 **Moorslede**, 5 • 2.8 **Château-Chinon**, 1 • 4.8 **Linne**, 21 • 6.8 **Sint-Niklaas**, 6
• 7.8 **St-Brieuc**, 5 • 8.8 **Quiberon**, 1 • 9.8 **Bain-de-Bretagne**, 3 • 11.8 **Valkenswaard**,
2 • 12.8 **Echt**, 5 • 13.8 **Oostduinkerke**, 14, in main bunch • 14.8 **Assebroek**, 1 • 15.8
Nandrin, 6 • 17.8 **Zottegem**, 2 • 19.8 **Eindonk**, 6 • 21.8 **Varèse**, 6 • 22.8
Geraardsbergen, TT 6 / RR 15 • 25.8 **Overijse**, 13 • 28.8 **Tour of Lazio**, 3 • 29.8 **St-
Pieters-Leeuw**, 11 • 31.8 **Giro delle Marche**, in main bunch • 5.9 **Ostuni**, World
Championship, 5 • 5.9 **Châteaulin**, 3 • 7.9 **Brasschaat**, 1 • 8.9 **St-Agatha-Berchem**,
6 • 9.9 **St-Vith**, 3 • 10.9 **Valkenburg**, 2 • 11.9 **Deinze**, 2 • 13.9 **Châteauroux**, 2 • 15.9
Retie, 10 • 17.9 **Marseille** [omnium], 1 • 22.9 **Paris-Brussels**, abandoned • 23.9
Stekene, 7 • 24.9 **Bourges**, 1

1977

• 13.2 **G.P. Aix-en-Provence**, 1 • **Mediterranean Tour**, 1 (19.2 Port-de-Bouc [team
time trial], 2 / Port-de-Bouc - Marseille, 12 / 20.2 La Penne - Hyères, 5 / Mont Faron
[time trial], 4 / 21.2 Hyeres - Nice, 43 / 22.2 Cavalaire - Grasse, 3 / 23.2 Menton -
Antibes, 10, in main bunch) • **Tour of Sardinia**, 20 (26.2 Rome - Pomezzia, 1 / 27.2
Cagliari, 31, in main bunch / 28.2 Cagliari - Nuoro, 10 / 1.3 Nuoro - Porto Torres,
36) • 5.3 **Circuit Het Volk**, 5 • **Paris-Nice**, abandoned (10.3 Aulnay-sous-Bois
[prologue], 4 / 11.3 Provence - Auxerre, 13 / Noyers - Nuits-St-Georges, 4, in main
bunch / 12.3 St-Trivier-sur-Moignans - St-Etienne, 30 / 13.3 St-Etienne - Romans,
24 / 14.3 Vaison-la-Romaine - Digne, 1 / 15.3 Digne - Plan-de-Campagne, 93 / Plan-
de-Campagne - Le Castellet, 19 / 16.3 Le Lavandou - Draguignan, l3 / Côte d'Ampus
[time trial], 15 / 17.3 Draguignan - Nice, abandoned) • 19.3 **Milan-San Remo**, in
main bunch • **Catalan Week**, 5 (21.3 Montserrat Expres [team time trial], 2 / Montserrar
Expres - Montblanc, 3 / 22.3 Montblanc - Andorra, 3 / 23.3 Puigcerda - San
Hipolito de Voltrega, 4 / 24.3 San Hipolito de Voltrega - Sta Eulalia de Ronsana, 3 /
25.3 Sta Eulalia de Ronsana - Gironella, 10 / Santuari de Querait [time trial], 5) • 3.4
Tour of Flanders, abandoned • 7.4 **Flèche Wallonne**, disqualified • 9.4 **Amstel Gold
Race**, 9 • 10.4 **Camors**, 1 • 11.4 **St-Claud**, 1 • 17.4 **Paris-Roubaix**, 11 • 20.4 **Wenen**,
[track omnium - with P. Sercu], 1 • 21.4 **Oostkamp**, 3 • 24.4 **Liège-Bastogne-Liège**,
6 • 8.5 **Championship of Zürich**, 4 • **Tour de Romandie**, 7 (10.5 Fribourg [prologue],

5 / 11.5 Fribourg - Courtélette, 63 / 12.5 Delsberg - Le Locle, 12 / 13.5 Le Locle -
Bulle, in main bunch / 14.5 Bulle - Savigny, 10 / Savigny [time trial], 9 / 15.5 Lausanne
- Geneva, 5) • 19.5 **Nandrin**, 1 • 21.5 **Boxmeer**, 1 • 22.5 **Poigny**, 2 • 25.5 **Châteauroux**,
2 • 28.5 **Berlin**, 1 • **Dauphiné Libéré**, 8 (30.5 Avignon [prologue], 4 / 31.5 Orange -
St-Etienne, 2 / 1.6 St-Etienne - Montceau-les-Mines, 11 / 2.6 Montceau-les-Mines -
Mâcon, 59 / 3.6 Mâcon - Vienne, 45 / Vienne - Valence, 25 / 4.6 Valence - Grenoble,
16 / 5.6 Grenoble - Annecy, 13 / 6.6 Annecy - Thonon-les-Bains, in main bunch /
Thonon-les-Bains [time trial], 7) • 10.6 **Copenhagen**, 3 • 11.6 **London**, 3 • 12.6
Vincennes, [summer track omnium - with P. Sercu], 1 • **Tour of Switzerland**, 12
(15.6 Baden - Baldegg [prologue], 18 / 16.6 Baden - Widnau, 5 / 17.6 Widnau - Möhlin,
63 / 18.6 Möhlin - Olten, 32 / Olten - Allerheiligenberg [time trial], 14 / 19.6 Olten
- Meiringen, 4 / 20.6 Spiez - Fiesch, 4 / 21.6 Fiesch - Bellinzona, 1 / 22.6 Bellinzona
- Bürglen, 12 / 23.6 Bürglen - Flumserberg, 15 / 24.6 Flumserberg - Effretikon, 6 /
Effretikon [time trial], 12) • 26.6 **Yvoir**, Belgian Championship, 9 • **Tour de France**,
6 (30.6 Fleurance [time trial], 3 / 1.7 Fleurance - Auch, 8 / 2.7 Auch - Pau, 3 / 3.7
Oloron-Ste-Marie - Vittoria, 71 / 4.7 Vitoria - Seignosse-le-Penon, 18 / 5.7 Mourenx
- Bordeaux, 75 / Bordeaux [time trial], 2 / 7.7 Bordeaux - Limoges, 30 / 8.7 Jaunay-
Clan - Angers, 63 / Angers [team time trial], 1 / 9.7 Angers - Lorient, 37 / 10.7 Lorient
- Rennes, 30 / 11.7 Bagnoles-de-l'Orne - Rouen, 55 / 12.7 Rouen - Roubaix, 38 /
13.7 Roubaix - Charleroi, 16 / 15.7 Freiburg im Breisgau, 23 / Altkirch - Besançon,
30 / 16.7 Besançon - Thonon-les-Bains, 7 / 17.7 Thonon-les-Bains - Morzine, 9 /
Morzine - Avoriaz [time trial], 10 / 18.7 Morzine - Chamonix, 13 / 19.7 Chamonix
- Alpe d'Huez, 20 / 20.7 Rossignol-Voiron - St-Etienne, 3 / 21.7 St-Trivier - Dijon,
31 / 22.7 Dijon - Dijon [time trial], 6 / 23.7 Montereau - Versailles, 47 / 24.7 Paris
Champs Elysées [time trial], 4 / Paris Champs Elysées, 5) • 25.7 **Caen** (with P. Sercu),
2 • 26.7 **Ronse**, 3 • 27.7 **Alsemberg**, 1 • 2.8 **Neuchatel-en-Bray**, 1 • 4.8 **Nice**, 1 • 5.8
Tienen, 2 • 7.8 **Bain-de-Bretagne**, 1 • 8.8 **Maël-Pestivien**, 2 • 9.8 **Lannion**, 1 • 10.8
Oostduinkerke, 12 • 11.8 **Vienna**, [track omnium], 2 • 12.8 **Sint-Niklaas**, 9 • 13.8
Assebroek, 24 • 14.8 **Heindonk-Willebroek**, 6 • 15.8 **Dilsen**, 2 • 19.8 **Dendermonde**,
7 • 20.8 **Kaprijke**, 3 • 21.8 **Moorslede**, 7 • 25.8 **Athus**, 1 • 26.8 **Merchtem**, 4 • 27.8
Herselt, 3 • 28.8 **St-Pieters-Leeuw**, 5 • 4.9 **San Cristobal**, World Championship, 33
• 14.9 **Retie**, 1 • l5.9 **Koolskamp**, Championship of Flanders, 35 • 17.9 **Kluisbergen**,
1 • 18.9 **Isbergues**, 2 • 21.9 **Paris-Brussels**, fell - abandoned • 25.9 **Tours-Versailles**,
38 • 27.9 **O-L-V-Waver**, in main bunch

1978

• 19.2 **Montouroux**, abandoned • 26.2 **Haut Var**, 5 • 4.3 **Circuit Het Volk**, abandoned
• 11.3 **Wilsele**, abandoned • 19.3 **Kemzeke**, 12

Major track victories

1964	Belgian Madison Championship (amateur - with P. Sercu)
1965	Ghent Six Days (with P. Sercu)
	Belgian Madison Championship (amateur - with P. Sercu)
1966	Belgian Madison Championship (with P. Sercu)
1967	Ghent Six Days (with P. Sercu)
1968	Charleroi Six Days (with F. Bracke)
	Belgian Madison Championship (with P. Sercu)
1970	European Madison Championship (with P. Sercu)
1971	Milan Six Days (with J. Stevens)
1973	Dortmund Six Days (with P. Sercu)
	Grenoble Six Days (with P. Sercu)
1974	Antwerp Six Days (with P. Sercu)
	Belgian Madison Championship (with P. Sercu)
1975	Ghent Six Days (with P. Sercu)
	Grenoble Six Days (with P. Sercu)
	Antwerp Six Days (with P. Sercu)
	Belgian Madison Championship (with P. Sercu)
	European Omnium Championship
1976	Antwerp Six Days (with P. Sercu)
	Rotterdam Six Days (with P. Sercu)
	Belgian Madison Championship (with P. Sercu)
1977	Ghent Six Days (with P. Sercu)
	Berlin Six Days (with P. Sercu)
	Maastricht Six Days (with P. Sercu)
	Münich Six Days (with P. Serru)
	Zurich Six Days (with P. Sercu)
1978	European Madison Championship (with P. Sercu)

Index of Names

Photograph acknowledgements

Het Nieuwsblad	9, 11, 12, 13, 14, 20, 22, 29, 35, 36, 46,top, 50 (x2), 52, 56 bottom, 59, 64, 68, 69, 71, 75, 90, 91, 94, 95, 97 top, 100, 110, 115, 119, 123, 124, 125 (x3), 126, 128, 131, 137, 144, 147, 152, 153, 161, 165 bottom, 181, 185, 190
Presse-Sports	8, 16, 77, 163, 164, 166
Het Laatste Nieuws	10, 24-25, 31, 32, 34, 37, 40, 44, 46 bottom, 47, 53, 56 top, 58, 63, 92, 99, 102, 113, 122, 127, 130, 133, 135, 139, 141, 143, 148, 154, 167, 168, 171, 177, 179, 180, 182, 186, 187, 194, 197, 201
Heleven Family Archive	18, 21, 23, 26, 39, 48, 54, 62, 66, 70, 101, 103, 105, 106, 107, 108, 109, 114, 121, 129, 146, 151, 155, 156, 158, 159, 160, 165 top, 175, 178, 183 (x2), 184, 189, 191, 192, 193, 196
Publi Foto	38
Eddy Stichnoth Archive	41, 174
Associated Press	19, 112
U.P.I.	97 bottom, 116, 136, 150, 169
Media Press Agency	200
Belga	30, 74, 96
Yvan De Saedeleer	collage on pages 72-73, 76 (x2)
Merckx's mother's archive	all photos in chapter VII (pages 78-89), 140
Maurice Terryn	67, 142
Marc Barbieux	173
Paul Coerten	170, 199
Front page photo	Werek

Graph on page 176: Source, Velo-Gotha

Collage on page 72-73 from Eddy Stichnoth's collection

Thanks

With thanks to Eddy Merckx, Claudine Merckx-Acou, Jenny Pittomvils (Merckx's mother), Axel Merckx, Johan De Muynck, Robert Desmet, Roger De Vlaeminck, André D'Hont, Felice Gimondi, Walter Godefroot, Jos Huysmans, Jan Janssen, Robert Janssens, Joris Jacobs, Freddy Maertens, Guillaume Michiels, Luis Ocaña, Roger Pingeon, Patrick Sercu, Roger Swerts, Bernard Thévenet, Martin Van den Bossche, Paul Van Himst, Rik Van Looy, Herman Vanspringel, Frans Verbeeck, Marc Barbieux, Yvan De Saedeleer, Cecile and Maurice Heleven and children, Fons Marin, Eddy Stichnoth, Bernard Vanhoutte, Joël Godaert, Kris Ruymbeke, Matthias Lannoo, Ludo Vandenabeele, Rob Discart, Georges Belien, Marc Van der Perre, Chantal De Saveur, Ignace Van Nevel, Mr. and Mrs. Paul Godaert, Bedicte Godaert, Jos Braes, Pascale for the coffee and biscuits.

Bibliography

'Velo-Gotha'
(René Jacobs, Hector Mahau, Harry Van Den Bremt, René Pirotte 1984,
published by Persen van België)

'Velo'
(René Jacobs, Robert Desmet, Hector Mahau - 1966-67-68-69-70-71-72-73-74-75-76-77-78-79)

'De Ronde van Vlaanderen'
(Rik Vanwalleghem - 1991, Pinguin Productions)

'Eddy Merckx I. Van Libramont tot Heerlen'
(Louis Clicteur, Lucien Berghmans - 1967, published by DeSchorpioen)

'Eddy Merckx II. Van regenboog tot gele trui'
(Louis Clicteur, Lucien Berghmans - 1970, published by DeSchorpioen)

'Heldenlevens'
(Martin Ros - 1987, published by Agathon)

'Het zweet der goden'
(Benjo Masso - 1990, published by De Arbeiderspers)

'Toen Merckx er nog was'
(André Blancke - 1979, published by Het Volk)

'La fabuleuse histoire du cyclisme'
(Pierre Chany - 1975, Paris)

'La fabuleuse histoire du Tour de France'
(Pierre Chany - 1983, Paris)

'La fabuleuse histoire des grandes classiques et des championnats du monde'
(Pierre Chany - 1979, Paris)

'Da Coppi a Merckx'
(Nello Bertellini - 1977, Milan)

'L'Equipée Belle'
(Jacques Goddet - 1991, Ed. Lafont/Stock)

'Niet van horen zeggen'
(Freddy Maertens - Manu Adriaens - 1988)

'Eddy Merckx. Mijn Levensverhaal'
(Robert Janssens - 1989, Pelckmans/Helios)

'Vreugde en Verdriet in de Tour' (Robert Janssens - 1985, published by Helios)

'Eddy Merckx. La roue de la Fortune'
(Joël Godaert - 1989, Ed. Gamma)

'Tour de France, hemel en hel op een stukje leer'
(Jean Nelissen - 1973, Brussels/Amsterdam)

'De Vedetten van de weg'
(Jean Nelissen - 1972, Baren)

'Mon escalade'
(Bernard Thévenet - 1974, Paris)

'Alles uit de kast'
(Frans Van Schoonderwalt - 1988, Hapert)

References, records: Het Nieuwsblad- de Gentenaar archive, Eddy Merckx archive

Original Publication Information

An initiative of Bo Decramer, Geert Vandenbon
and Rik Vanwalleghem in collaboration with Eddy
Merckx and with the cooperation of Lannoo
Publishing, The Flemish Publishing Company (Het
Nieuwsbald-De Gentenaar) and ASLK-CGER.

Adapted for the French version by Joël Godaert.

A publication by Pinguin Productions, Ghent

Layout, illustrations and graphic production:
Krisgrafiek, Elversele

Pinguin Productions bvba
Derbystraat 87
9051 Ghent, Belgium
Tel. 09-221-8785
Fax. 09-220-0650

D/1993-5715-003
ISBN 90-73322-05-7

October 1993